MORE PRAISE FOR *THE WAY OF CONFLICT*

"*The Way of Conflict* is an immensely liberating, accessible, and practical book. By synthesizing ancient wisdom traditions with useful concepts and tools from her own extensive experience as a mediator, Dr. Combs transforms that much-dreaded aspect of human dynamics — conflict — into a powerful source of personal growth. She equips her readers with the knowledge and understanding necessary to become more creative and constructive in dealing with the inevitable everyday problems of interpersonal and organizational relations."

— Bill George, author of *Authentic Leadership* and former chairman and CEO of Medtronic

"Deidre Combs's *The Way of Conflict* is a deeply healing and important guide to navigating the often rough waters of conflict with mindfulness, openness, grace, and above all, hope. By offering readers the perspective that conflict can be a creative opportunity — and including tools for exploring those opportunities — Combs has given us a resource that is not only immediately practical but also profoundly inspiring."

— Maggie Oman Shannon, author of *The Way We Pray* and *One God, Shared Hope*

"An invigorating and thoughtful book that manages to capture and foster one's spiritual growth as it works on giving practical solutions to conflicts. I just found my new guide as I work in wars and witness the worst and most beautiful aspects of humanity."

— Zainab Salbi, founder of Women for Women, an international relief organization for women in war-torn countries

"In the heated, conflicted moments of living we all may wish for that gentle state known as equilibrium, but it turns out that in biology when you reach equilibrium you are dead. Show me an organization or individual without conflict, and I will show you one that does not care. And without that most essential passionate concern, they might as well be dead. Deidre Combs helps us to understand why this

is so, and how we may effectively release the energy of our conflicts for productive results. Given the state of our world, this book could not have arrived at a better time."
— Harrison Owen, creator of Open Space Technology and author of *The Practice of Peace*

"*The Way of Conflict* offers a comprehensive vision and powerful tools for embracing change and conflict within our organizations. This book is a must-read for all leaders who wish to be revered for both their insight and their understanding when dealing with difficult situations."
— Carmen McSpadden, director of Montana State University Leadership Institute and past president of the Montana School Boards Association

The
WAY *of*
CONFLICT

The
WAY of
CONFLICT

*Elemental Wisdom for Resolving Disputes
and Transcending Differences*

DEIDRE COMBS
FOREWORD BY MATTHEW FOX

New World Library
Novato, California

New World Library
14 Pamaron Way
Novato, CA 94949

Library of Congress Cataloging-in-Publication Data
Combs, Deidre, 1962–
    The way of conflict : elemental wisdom for resolving disputes and transcending
differences / Deidre Combs ; foreword by Matthew Fox.
        p.   cm.
    Includes bibliographical references and index.
    ISBN 1-57731-449-2 (pbk. : alk. paper)
    1. Interpersonal conflict. 2. Interpersonal relations. I. Title.
    BF637.I48C62 2004
    303.6'9—dc22   2004002040

First printing, May 2004
ISBN 1-57731-449-2
Printed in Canada on acid-free, recycled paper
Distributed to the trade by Publishers Group West

10   9   8   7   6   5   4   3   2   1

To my sisters and parents, with love and appreciation

CONTENTS

PART 4: IMPROVE YOUR CONDITIONING

The problem is not that there are problems.
The problem is expecting otherwise and thinking that
having problems is a problem.

— Theodore Rubin

Conflict As Blessing

Man is made by his belief.
As he believes, so he is.

— Bhagavad Gita

This book, entitled *The Way of Conflict*, might just as well have been called *The Tao of Conflict* or *The Zen of Conflict*. For in it the author does a bold and special thing: instead of seeing conflict as a problem to be solved, she sees it as an opportunity to be seized, an occasion to be taken advantage of, even a chance for a mystical experience, one of awe and wonder and possibility. Clearly Deidre Combs is on special terrain when she makes these daring assertions, terrain that challenges all of us to move beyond self-pity and reptilian action-reaction responses to something much deeper, to our authentic interaction as true human beings. Combs challenges us to take the occasion of conflict, the blessing of conflict, one might say, to its deepest spiritual conclusion: that conflict can be a spiritual path, a yoga, an opportunity for growth and deepening, indeed, an occasion for creativity and compassion to rise like never before.

All this is to say that this book is profoundly well timed. Do any of us living in the world today live without conflict? Do we interact in families and communities where there is no conflict? Do we live in cultures that are not in conflict with other cultures? Obviously not. Whether we are monks, professors, accountants, parents, or politicians, we all experience conflict. For where there are humans, there is conflict.

Yet there is also creativity yearning to be set loose, forgiveness begging to assert itself, the capacity to reach deep inside to the depths of Nothingness from which all true new beginnings spring. This is the wisdom offered to us in this book, whose author brings more than twenty years of experience helping people in businesses and other forums to resolve conflict. In the course of her learning (isn't all our work a learning, a continuing education process?) she has gained a mature awareness that behind all conflict lies real potential for magnificent opportunities for growth and healing. But of course we are tempted to 1) live in denial that conflict exists, or 2) live in fear, so we dare not do anything about it, or 3) live in cynicism and the belief that we cannot improve things.

This book puts the lie to denial, fear, and cynicism. As such it is liberating and releases us from tired solutions and insipid nonsolutions to conflict. Just as Martin Luther King Jr. and Mahatma Gandhi found creative ways to respond to injustice by awakening conflict and steering it to social justice instead of toward more violence, so this book shows us the deeper meaning of conflict, and deeper ways out of injustice. Like King and Gandhi, therefore, it is practical; it is about changing us in order to change the world. And like King and Gandhi, it is demanding. For the hardest thing to change is usually us. This book, like any spiritual practice, requires both self-criticism and self-knowledge of its readers. Combs truly infiltrates the world of conflict resolution, a world that needs to burgeon swiftly if humankind is to survive. She brings ancient practices and insights from the world's spiritual traditions and applies them in both personal and social settings to bring about peaceful resolutions to conflict. And she demonstrates the immense practicality of spiritual practice — how truly applicable to everyday problems of discord and disagreement spiritual wisdom can be.

The author sees conflict as a vehicle for traveling to new and better worlds. It serves as "the portal, or the wormhole, as it is called in physics, to take us there." Taking the enemy whole is important to Combs. *The Way of Conflict* is about finding win-win and not I-win-and-you-lose solutions. It is about loving or holding our adversaries instead of reducing them to parts or objects. It all seems to concern largeness and cosmology, the study of the whole. Of course since we live in a culture that has taught for centuries that our souls are puny, stuck in our bodies trying to escape instead of being "capable of the universe," as Thomas Aquinas put it in the thirteenth century, then we have trouble imagining large solutions that can embrace differences. In other words, we are stuck in conflict.

Very early in the universe's existence conflict and tension emerged. And they provided both stimulus and creative advancement. Creative tension or chaos is built into all the systems of the universe, according to today's scientific understanding. Here we undergo chaos and darkness and confusion and unraveling and not being in control. The author's advice is not to run from these disturbances but rather to mine them for their wisdom. Out of the depths of darkness come the deepest renewal and rebirth.

Fear itself is no excuse. Of course darkness conjures up fear. But what do we do with that fear? Do we let it run our lives, our politics, our way of seeing the world? Do we allow it to trigger a fight-or-flight reaction? The author cites Marie Curie: "Nothing in life is to be feared. It is only to be understood." The darkness is our teacher, for in the darkness we can taste true wisdom. Enemies are also our teachers. We need not fear our enemies, for we ought to learn from them and even praise them for the strength and insight they solicit from us. Hatred interferes with the development of happiness and compassion; it is a distraction.

Combs believes in creativity and co-creation. She believes that we can recycle conflict into resolutions that bring peace to all parties. "Controlling fire allowed us to create civilization," she writes. "To move through conflict and through life, we must create balance between love and power." Isn't all creativity a bringing together of love and power? Finding a creative outlet for our love? Are we living as creatively as possible? Or would we rather wallow in our victimhood and our projections of blame and hatred, thereby reinforcing our pain? Creativity can move us beyond being and making others into victims. Or we can go deeper into stuckness and the cynicism that goes with it.

The author feels that the opposite of "being stuck" is not being right or being wrong: it is the process of evolving. All conflict is an invitation to evolve. "Stuck, we will try to rescue others instead of evolving." Rescuing others, even when our intentions are good, can be an obstacle to growth and evolution. A deep part of evolution is the release of creativity that inevitably comes when we dare to travel to our "growing edges." For our "growing edge is the point that our ever-evolving self is moving toward next."

I see this book as a grand invitation to our species at this critical point in our history to join the forces of evolution and to expand our powers by moving beyond stalemate and win-lose, reptilian-brain consciousness to win-win experiences. It serves our species' profound need to move into its next stage of evolution, that of finding peace where there seems only to be conflict. That of making peace instead of cultivating unrest. May this book and its message flourish, and may all the readers who drink from its well of practical wisdom be refreshed.

Matthew Fox, 2003
University of Creation Spirituality/Naropa
Oakland, California

Conflict As Contest

There once lived a young man and his father in a tiny Chinese village. They had little more than a roof over their heads and a sturdy mare. The young man loved to ride this mare each morning, drinking in the horse's speed and loving the feel of the wind in his hair. However, early one day the mare suddenly reared, for no reason at all, and rode off into the woods to the north, throwing the young man and breaking his leg. When the villagers heard of this event, they said, "We are so sorry, what a terrible thing to have happened. Your horse is gone and your son lame. This is a great misfortune." The father, who was wise in the ways of the Tao, simply replied, "Maybe so, maybe not."

A few weeks later, the mare returned from the north with a fine steed at her side. The villagers cheered, "What great fortune. How lucky you are." The father calmly replied, "Maybe so, maybe not." This fine steed had come from a band of nomads to the north. When they went searching for the horse, and whatever else they could find, they came upon the young man's village and decided to invade. All able-bodied young men took up arms and fought against the invaders, and as a result, nine out of ten men died. The son could not join in the fighting due to his broken leg, so both the boy and his father survived.

BLESSING OR BANE?

My three sisters and I grew up fighting. We battled over everything and nothing, scratching each other, wounding each other both verbally and physically. In the summer, insults, shrieks, and obscenities floated out our inner-city windows. The neighbors must have said, "What a pity those children cannot get along."

Maybe so, maybe not.

Now when we gather as adults, with children and husbands in tow, my siblings and I try to be polite and to skirt delicate issues in the name of harmony. "How lucky you have such peaceful holidays," my friends have remarked.

Maybe so, maybe not.

More than a decade ago I was facilitating a large, contentious software user's conference for a Fortune 10 company. As the executives tried to break the news that the company might discontinue a critical product, vendors were shifting nervously and angry customers were walking out. I was at my wit's end. I thought, "This meeting and I are both miserable failures."

Maybe so, maybe not.

That meeting threw me, a bit like the young man off the mare, into a fantastic journey to uncover the true nature of conflict. As clients rose to leave in frustration, I stumbled on what I would later learn were two basic multicultural conflict skills. First, in desperation, I pretended to be one of the angry customers and began asking tough questions of the corporate executives — the questions I believed the clients wanted to ask. Then, for lack of a better idea, I reiterated each response using terminology I thought the customers would understand. To my surprise, the room's climate changed immediately. The furious customers sat down, and the group re-engaged to talk candidly about developing solutions. Hours later, the diverse groups all committed to a common, and now strengthened, partnership. I had had a glimpse of a philosophy and of skills that would transform my work and my life.

Up to that point conflict had baffled and bothered me. Between my childhood and my job, I figured I had had more than a standard daily allowance. I had experienced, to my mind, too many confrontations,

Be kind; everyone you meet is fighting a hard battle.

— John Watson

both covert and direct, with fellow employees. I was secretly embarrassed by a number of tense battles suffered by a nonprofit board of directors I served on. There were uncomfortable-even-to-remember disputes with friends left over from college.

I avoided conflict. But that didn't seem to work. I had tried ignoring painful exchanges, placating or intimidating others into silence to make conflict go away. Not one of these approaches was successful. I felt I lived at conflict's mercy. As a result of that conference, I realized that one person with even a few simple skills could quickly transform fifty people into a cohesive solution-focused team. I realized I wasn't at the mercy of conflict's whims and that within each dispute hides great opportunity. I wondered, "Are there other strategies I might use to manage conflict and reap its benefits? Can I fully participate in every dispute without injuring or being injured?"

On a quest to answer my own questions, I looked for skills in communities that have coexisted and worked through internal disputes for thousands of years, including the Tibetan, Basque, and Native American traditions. I searched the common wisdom of our major religions. Buddhism, Judaism, Christianity, Sufism, and Hinduism all talked about conflict. I read text after text on quantum physics and systems theory, trying to understand what healthy systems, like functional human communities, do when faced with chaos or conflict. I investigated martial arts philosophies like Aikido. I studied modern mediation techniques to find additional tips on keeping disputants at the table and away from the courts.

I initially found that discord is widely perceived as a character flaw or even a curse. I was not alone in my fear of and confusion surrounding conflict. During my years of research, I became a certified mediator, which gave me another perspective on conflict. I now act as a neutral third party in resolving business, family, and court disputes and as I mediate, I am not surprised when participants thank me as though I had been willing to take out their garbage or wash their dirty laundry. When I am teaching the strategies contained in this book and ask at the beginning of workshops what words people associate with conflict, I expect to hear *bad, miserable,* and *embarrassing.*

Through my search, however, I also discovered what the Taoist father in the story understood: that conflict is neither bane nor blessing. It is simply a fundamental element of our lives. It is part of existence. And, as with the world's other natural elements, it possesses an inherent power that we can harness. Misunderstood, this energy can cause wanton destruction. Managed, it can provide great opportunity and benefit.

Using air or wind, another fundamental element, as an example, while it is true that a strong gust can topple homes, a gentle breeze can also cool us on a hot day and bring music through a wind chime. And as we have discovered more of wind's characteristics, we have learned to avert destruction and capture its energy to sail boats across the sea, to grind our food, to generate power, and to fly. We have learned when to board up windows and when to bring out our delicate kites. As with air, the better you understand conflict the more you can harness its potential.

Or to use the common metaphor of conflict as fire, one might say that my sisters and I were playing with a great box of matches given to us at birth. Without understanding conflict's potential, we set rooms ablaze and singed many people close to us. Fortunately, it also fired the clay from which we molded our relationships into fine, solid containers. After such a strong dose of conflict as kids, we still directly confront one another as adults, despite our holiday manners. I trust our fiery exchanges and believe my siblings to be my strongest advocates and teachers.

Conflict is not just angry people yelling at or hurting one another. This limited picture keeps us from understanding confrontation as a fundamental element of the universe. Conflict appears any time two or more parties disagree, and it disappears when they agree. In the natural world, the water in a river pushes against rock. The water is diverted and the rock is smoothed. This battle continues until the stream shifts or the rock is worn away. Human conflict encompasses not only interpersonal disputes but also internal contests among beliefs, aging, and illness. Any challenge or problem can be defined as a conflict that holds opportunity. The skills and strategies contained in this book can be applied to any difficulty, be it internal, interpersonal, or metaphysical.

The scientific and cultural sources I studied all contained a similar philosophy of conflict resolution, which I have synthesized into a step-by-step process. I have applied this common approach in organizations, through mediation, and to my own conflicts. As a result, I have seen creative, lasting resolutions materialize where none could be initially imagined. This process has naturally strengthened relationships and energized groups engaged in all types of disputes. I consistently witness honest, deep conversations between estranged family members, friends, and business partners that awe the participants. This philosophy has brought possibility and promise to the most hopeless challenges.

As a mediator, teacher, and consultant, I have observed that *staying with conflict until resolution* significantly improves each participant's emotional welfare. When conflict is resolved in a manner amenable to all parties, at a minimum stress dissipates and everyone relaxes. On exit surveys that I have distributed in more than sixty mediations, the people involved overwhelmingly expressed satisfaction in a process that allowed them to co-create a solution.

I want to emphasize that sticking with conflict does not mean that you should ever stay in a relationship in which any type of violence is involved. However, after a decade of personal practice, I have found that recognizing and addressing conflict by taking small steps toward resolution always improves relationships and personal well-being. Conflict is a vehicle for transformation, and you can "ride it" so both you and your opponents can win. Will you find "winning" anything close to what you imagined?

Maybe so, maybe not.

> *The game isn't over*
> *till it's over.*
>
> —Yogi Berra

WINNING THE GAME

When mapping competition between nations or markets, economists often use the words *conflict* and *game* interchangeably. For thousands of years human beings have created every imaginable variety of game. As a species we are drawn to the energy and creativity hidden in games and, thus, conflict. We intuitively know the positive potential of opposing forces meeting and engaging. It is no surprise that the Super Bowl draws the highest worldwide television viewing audience each year.

The object of every game is to win. One way to play is to say that if I win you must lose. We enjoy turning some conflicts, like sports, into win-lose games with a single victor by predetermining the "winner" as whoever earns the most points or completes the course in the least time.

In athletic contests this is often fun, but in the rest of our lives, this win-lose approach to conflict has its shortcomings. At an extreme, it enables us to state that others are wrong or evil and must not only be defeated but also destroyed. On a societal scale we have often played conflict as a win-lose game, wiping out civilizations, religions, and ecosystems in an effort to triumph at all costs. We are now realizing that this method hurts us more than it solves problems. When *you* are crushed, *I* always ultimately lose. When I destroy an eco-system, I have fewer places to live. Without my competitor, I am no longer driven to innovate and create, and I cannot benefit from her unique perspectives and potential support. Over time win-lose play seems to always become a lose-lose game.

The basic oneness of the universe is not only the central characteristic of the mystical experience, but is also one of the most important revelations of modern physics.

— Fritjof Capra

Thankfully, we have another approach to winning. In 1981 William Ury and Roger Fisher introduced the concept of the "win-win solution" in their influential book *Getting to Yes: Negotiating Agreement without Giving In.* They argued that every problem holds a solution that allows everyone to win. In other words, we can always reach a solution that leaves everyone satisfied and content. Win-win solutions incorporate all parties' needs and perspectives; they support and strengthen relationships. This is not compromise, but the practice of collaboration.

Spiritual traditions have also long advocated the win-win approach. Buddhist and Hindu teachings say that we should always seek a reality in which disagreements dissolve and opposing parties are unified. This vision of harmony resides in the Christian verse "That all of them may be one, Father, just as you are in me, and I am in you.... May they be brought to complete unity (John 17:21). Taoism's yin/yang symbol depicts the collaborative viewpoint that marries the perceived opposites of black and white. To paraphrase the Koran, Islam teaches that to kill one person is to kill all humankind; to help one person is to help all humankind.

Win-win solutions make good business sense. In the early 1990s, through hundreds of interviews with top academics, management consultants, and CEOs, James Collins and Jerry Porras derived a list of the twenty-five most visionary U.S. corporations. The average founding date for these companies was 1902. In their book *Built to Last,* Collins and Porras show that a main characteristic of these successful organizations is that they do not succumb to the view that only one principle or party may win, which they call "the tyranny of the *'or.'* " Instead, the authors explain that these companies embrace the "genius of the *'and;* win-win.' " They understand the power in finding a solution in which all perspectives can win, even those of their competitors. These companies do not compromise their values or choose between ones that appear to be opposite. These market leaders find ways to be productive *and* to be good to their workers, to be profitable *and* to be kind to the environment. They know how to evolve their products to provide the best that both they *and* their competitors offer. As a result, according to Collins and Porras, these twenty-five organizations and their employees continue to thrive decade after decade.

Win-win solutions are readily available. The only catch is that to find them we must be willing to play the game to the end. In myths, spiritual teachings, and scientific quantum theory, conflict is depicted as a process with four key stages:

- the appearance of conflict,
- the absence of hope,
- the occurrence of creativity,
- and the emergence of stability.

Finding the dynamic win-win solution necessitates sticking with the process through all four quarters of the game.

Every conflict is like an iceberg; what we initially see or understand is only a portion of what is happening. Our initial positions provide clues about the conflict; however, they are only part of the story. Often multiple conflicts are embedded within one another. Through this four-staged process we uncover underlying needs and concerns to find a solution that can leave everyone feeling satisfied. The results are often surprising and always invigorating.

For example, one court mediation I conducted involved a man I'll

In short, a highly visionary company doesn't want to blend yin and yang into a gray, indistinguishable circle...it aims to be distinctly yin and yang — both at the same time, all the time.

— James Collins and Jerry Porras

call Robert, who had been asked by a customer, Sam, a few months earlier to repaint his car. The dispute started when Sam, unhappy with the result, refused to pay. Robert sued Sam for $800 and began our mediation session by describing why he should be paid. He explained his assumptions resulting from Sam's request for the paint job. Sam then responded with all the reasons why the paint job was not only inferior but also incorrect: Robert had used low-quality paint, for example, and had painted the pinstripes the wrong color. They took turns trying to convince each other of the merits of their positions. Phase one, conflict appears.

The dispute then moved to chaos as the discussion became heated and neither would bend. Emotions intensified until, at one point, it looked as though they might come to blows. Eventually, upset and despondent, Robert and Sam both stopped talking. Typical of the second, chaotic phase of conflict, they seemed to give up hope for any solution.

After about five minutes of stone silence, Sam said, "I'll call Bill." Robert then said, "I'd be happy to testify for you at the other trial." I had no idea who Bill was or anything about the "other trial," but it didn't matter. This was the third phase of conflict, where evolution or creativity occurs. "I'm willing to pay $500 for the paint job," Sam replied. "Can I pay you in installments?" Robert was more than willing to cooperate.

Finally, as their relationship returned to the fourth phase, or stability, they chatted happily as I drew up the settlement papers. The room was filled with a sense of peace and optimism as they shook hands heartily with promises to call the following week. They had clearly found a solution that no one could have imagined at the outset. They had ridden conflict's wave to its end. Both left feeling completely satisfied and relaxed.

Conflict becomes a win-lose game if we do not realize that all four stages of the process must be completed. Instead of playing through, we might attempt to run away or destroy the other parties before reaching stability. By becoming fixed on our initial positions, we can stop the process as we push the opponents away and refuse to engage. Yet, the battle endures until together we return to stability. Some

Understanding shatters old knowledge to make room for the new that accords with reality.

— Thich Nhat Hanh

conflicts can thus continue for months or lifetimes. What might appear as multiple skirmishes is often one prolonged conflict. We see this in the Middle East and in seven hundred years of violence within the former Yugoslavia.

Many people misunderstand the win-win concept since it has been co-opted by those who wish to manipulate others into believing that their initial positions are the best solutions. Too often I have heard a slick salesman say, "Oh, this is a real win-win," and have thought, "Maybe for you, but not for me." Win-win solutions can never be envisioned alone at the outset. In my experience a true win-win solution is developed when we search for an answer that gathers and incorporates everyone's needs and beliefs.

This philosophy can be applied not only interpersonally, but also at the community and international levels. English Prime Minister Tony Blair acknowledges the necessity for this mind-set when he states, "The idea that if one side wins something in Northern Ireland, the other loses, that's gone. The essence of what we have agreed is a choice: we are all winners or all losers. It is mutually assured benefit or mutually assured destruction."

It is impossible to find a win-win solution if we believe that our initial positions are the only possible solutions. For example, if Robert had decided that the only way their conflict would be resolved was if Sam paid him $800, he would be using a win-lose approach. Instead, he was willing to investigate other options and to work to understand Sam's underlying requirements and wishes. By deciding that there can only be one possible outcome to a problem, we prolong conflict and sever relationships as we battle it out to see who gets to survive. This reaction makes sense when we are in immediate physical danger and our initial position is to stay alive. Yet most conflicts in our daily lives are not life and death and call for a collaborative approach.

I want to note that this philosophy teaches that *true* win-win solutions *include loss.* Paradoxical as it might sound, the path to stability requires that we let go of how we think things *should* be to move to an understanding of how things *can* be. Sam had to give up his initial position of not paying for the paint job to find a lasting solution. In

"With so much water in her personality," Mother said, "probably she will be able to smell a fire before it has begun."

— Arthur Golden,
Memoirs of a Geisha

the case of domestic unrest, for everyone to win, the marriage might need to dissolve. At a minimum, we must each relinquish the belief that our proposed answer is the only way to resolve the dispute. We must be willing to explore other options.

The Way of Conflict will teach you how to find creative, mutually beneficial solutions. This method yields positive results even if your opponent assumes a winner-takes-all approach. You may pass through unknown territory as you move beyond old beliefs. You will be rewarded, however, with a new perspective, stronger relationships, and an exciting solution.

WHAT WE WILL LEARN

The Way of Conflict offers multicultural guidance on how to confidently overcome conflict and find lasting win-win solutions. The format follows wisdom from the three-thousand-year-old Chinese classic on conflict *The Art of War*:

> *And so it is said—*
> *Know the other and know oneself,*
> *Then victory is not in danger.*
> *Know earth and know heaven,*
> *Then victory can be complete.*

In part 1 we will begin by learning more about ourselves and the other players to ensure that "victory is not in danger." We will employ the elements of Earth, Water, Fire, and Air to describe four basic conflict styles. I chose to use this elemental metaphor for three reasons: 1) It is the one common personality typing system found across all major cultures, 2) We need all four elements to survive; we cannot say that it is better to be an "Air" person versus an "Earth," and 3) It connects us to the natural world, a rich source of information and insight on how to address conflict. This personality typing system not only helps to determine each participant's innate strengths and weaknesses, but it also uncovers how best to respond to keep everyone in the game.

The four elements can also be used to describe the components or nature of a situation. We will employ this metaphor to illustrate four main personality types and also to understand more fully the key phases of conflict.

Following *The Art of War,* we will discover how "victory can be complete" by investigating in part 2 the "heaven," or the natural rules of engagement, finally moving on in part 3 to practical, "earthy" conflict strategies and skills. Although a mediator can act as a referee to keep everyone safe through conflict's four stages, I have designed the rules and techniques so that anyone can engage in conflict and win without professional intervention.

The key to staying in conflict is to stay out of fear. Fear signals the fight-or-flight reflex, which stops our learning and our progress toward a win-win solution. The focus of this book is to reduce fear so that you can continue to work with the conflict until it is complete. We feel safer if we know where we are, armed with the knowledge of what might be ahead and how we might handle it.

We each have unique and valuable perspectives on resolving the complex issues found in our homes, organizations, and ecosystems. I hope to provide you with the skills and encouragement you will need to completely face all of today's challenges and to play *until resolution.* When a difficult relative comes to visit, I hope you'll perceive the waiting opportunity. When your employees begin to bicker, you'll be able to take that energy in new and exciting directions. And when the town council makes a poor decision or international battles heat up and all seems lost, my wish for you is that you contribute to finding a creative solution that brings us all lasting calm. We need you.

> *The most intense conflicts if overcome, leave behind a sense of security and calm that is not easily disturbed. It is just these intense conflicts and their conflagration which are needed to produce valuable and lasting results.*
>
> — C. G. Jung

The
WAY *of*
CONFLICT

PART 1

THE PARTICIPANTS

Man . . . has the self as his only friend,
or as his only enemy.
— Bhagavad Gita

The situation recounted in this story could happen down the street or in your office. Four friends form a construction company, Diamond Construction, by renting a small office and hiring a secretary. The company grows. It grows and grows until the founders manage almost a hundred employees. The friends are very successful until the building industry declines and the bills begin to mount. The four friends grow nervous and meet one morning to save their enterprise.

The first friend, Tom, or "Blaze," as everyone called him, is the company's creative CEO. In good times, the founders often gathered at Blaze's house, where he would entertain them with eclectic meals and outrageous ideas. But this morning in a stark conference room, Blaze's natural charm is not apparent. "We are going broke, and we employ too many people. This is unacceptable," he rages. "Why did Human Resources let this happen?"

The second friend, Gene, Vice President of Human Resources, does not respond. "Blaze approved all the hires," Gene thinks. "What is the use in bringing that up?" Gene felt sick over the current situation. He had personally interviewed each employee, and he knew that layoffs would be catastrophic for many. During the past weeks, Gene had rallied the troops, spending hours listening to their concerns. Meanwhile, he could not sleep at night and wanted to quit.

Edina, Blaze's wife and another founder, quietly takes notes. She trusted her husband's grand vision for the company and had meticulously looked after the details. Edina had ordered computers, tracked inventory, and negotiated real estate leases. This morning she told herself, "I don't see a problem. Blaze has pulled us out of worse situations than this."

As the CFO, the fourth compatriot, Amy, could adeptly develop schedules, budgets, and business strategies. Amy responds quickly to Blaze's outburst: "It's simple, really. We need to cut expenses by 40 percent within the next ninety days. We should immediately lay off our ten remote employees and fifteen latest hires. We must curtail all extraneous spending and remove at least five additional employees, thirty in all." Amy, disgusted by Gene's morose nature and constant backstabbing and Edina's lack of initiative, impatiently finishes, "We can solve this today if everyone will choose to participate."

Gene finally speaks, "Amy, these are people's lives, not numbers you are throwing around," while he thinks to himself, "What a heartless battle-ax."

"Could we consider a few alternatives over the next few weeks?" Edina asks. "Is there a way to cut expenses without firing employees?"

"We don't have a week, can't you see that? It's our names on the bank loan, and we have puttered away too much time already," Blaze responds, banging his fist on the table.

And the discussion continued.

CHAPTER 1

Discovering Your Elemental Nature

He who knows others is clever;
he who knows himself is enlightened.

— Lao-tzu

Blaze, Gene, Edina, and Amy probably feel familiar to you. We work with them, live with them, and at different times we appreciate what each has to offer. For example, we will seek out a Blaze when we need enthusiasm or vision poured into a project. Edina's loyal support is welcomed when we want diligent care for the details. A Gene is just the ticket when we need a sympathetic ear, and an Amy creates clear organization and structure when needed. Together, the four friends create a balanced organization.

We might also recognize the unique stress-related attributes that the friends display. Everyone has a distinct battle style. For example, you may quietly look for cover or passionately drive a point home. You might instantly articulate the "perfect" solution or hold back an opinion and methodically pose questions. Depending on the dispute and your default method, you too might resort to the outbursts, sulking, insensitivity, or inertia described above.

This chapter explores individual default conflict approaches. Knowing not only your own but also your opponent's unique playing style can be a powerful conflict tool. I used to work with a man I'll call Saul. Quiet by nature, he was respected for his fine attention to detail and his methodical approach to problems. Saul would say he is a simple man with simple needs; he loved to play with his kids and watch football. When conflict struck, Saul stopped in his tracks. He'd ask questions, analyze options, and wait. Cross him, and he'd hold a grudge for what seemed like eons. In comparison, a fellow co-worker, Jeannie, was busy most of the time. She was like a bird, flitting from project to project, eating sporadically in between. In conflict, Jeannie looked for fast resolution and would talk a mile a minute trying to accomplish this goal. In contrast to Saul, who saw and remembered every detail, she would simply not notice that she might have offended someone and forgot about previous outbursts.

To develop a creative solution to conflict with Saul, I had to be willing to slow down and look at the situation in detail. However, to work with Jeannie, I was best served by talking quickly and not taking her lack of sensitivity personally. "Know the other and know oneself, then victory is not in danger," says *The Art of War.* By understanding their elemental personalities and monitoring my own fiery disposition, I was able to select an appropriate approach with each to find a winning solution.

Although identifying unique personality types might appear to be a fairly recent leadership innovation and woman's magazine phenomenon, it is actually a universal tool that has been used among indigenous and religious traditions for thousands of years. A common cross-cultural method uses the natural elements (Earth, Water, Fire, and Air) to distinguish at least four main personality types. For example, determining that you are an Air or Water person will help you to define how you are best treated in most Chinese healing disciplines, Indian Ayurvedic medicine, and Native American shamanism. Buddhist and Hindu initiates choose spiritual practices based on their elemental proclivity. Taoism assigns the elements to the roles of mother, father, son, and daughter to explain each archetype. For example, the *I Ching,* the Taoist *Book of Changes,* associates the father with air and sky and the mother with earth.

Everybody is all right really.

— Winnie the Pooh

When you are connected with a natural element, you exhibit traits similar to that element. For example, people who contain more Earth exhibit personality traits that are inherent in rocks, mountains, or soil. These folks move more slowly and are observant of their physical environment. Often strong and grounded, an Earth person can be compared to a glacier at times. Whereas an Air person will blow in and out of a room in conflict, an Earth person may follow the famous refrain in Maya Angelou's poem, "Our Grandmothers": *I shall not, I shall not be moved.*

There are many explanations of how we become connected to an element. Chinese and African teachings say that your birthday or year of birth determines your elemental personality. In the Sufi mystical tradition, it is where you were conceived that drives who you become. Some Western psychologists explain that we lead with a particular element because when we were children it was reinforced by our family or community.

Although the natural elements typing system is not commonly used in mainstream Western culture, it is hidden in our language. In a 2002 interview with *Washington Post* reporter Bob Woodward, President George W. Bush unknowingly revealed himself as a classic Fire personality: "Sometimes that's the way I am — fiery," he said, adding, "I can be an impatient person." He alluded to his "instincts" or his "instinctive" reactions a dozen times during this interview. "I will seize the opportunity to achieve big goals," Bush said. "There is nothing bigger than to achieve world peace.... The vision thing matters. That's another lesson I learned." Not only does Western culture use elemental language to describe our base personality types, but it is also found in the educational models of "learning styles" or "multiple intelligences." We refer to physical (Earth), emotional (Water), spiritual or creative (Fire), and mental (Air) intelligence. The educational system has embraced this approach by identifying and accommodating these different types. We acknowledge our Water students by fostering emotional intelligence in the classroom. We include kinesthetic or movement exercises to clarify theories for our more physical Earth-based pupils.

Sobonfu Somé, a spiritual leader and author from the African

*You are unique.
Just like everyone else.*

— Anonymous

*And so the general who knows
the military is the people's
fate star,
the ruler of the state's
security and danger.*

— Sun Tzu,
Art of War

Dagara tribe of Burkina Faso, reminds us that although we are naturally born with one or two elements predominant, *the healthy person nurtures all the elements within her or him.* In Western terms, we are all physical, emotional, spiritual, and mental beings. We need to create internal balance by fostering all four elements. Using the metaphor of war, there is not one right or wrong way to fight; rather, the more flexible and robust your army, the more sure will be your victory.

Regardless of how our conflict style is derived, think of the four elemental approaches as different tools in your toolbox. If we unconsciously reach into that box for our favorite implement without considering which would be best for a particular job, our choice might yield mixed results. Often we are surprised that our habitual yelling or intimidation isn't able to fix every situation. Sometimes it might, but other situations call for waiting and listening.

While you read this chapter, pretend that you are a general surveying your troops before battle. What resources are available to you, and when and where are they best used? Where are your weak points, and how do you guard against attack? What camaraderie, or esprit de corps, exists among the troops? When we understand our own strengths, weaknesses, and personalities in conflict we can implement our best strategy of attack and stay engaged until the solution that serves all the players emerges.

I designed the following self-assessment test to help you identify your elemental conflict style. Personality tests often try to define the indefinable. We are each complex, ever-changing beings. This test should not box you in but instead lend you insight into your innate gifts and help you to identify additional skills that you might wish to foster.

ELEMENTAL CONFLICT STYLES

Answer the six questions below by ranking your responses horizontally from 1 to 4. Assign the highest value to your most common response. Then total your responses vertically. You may wish to complete this quiz with your professional environment in mind first, then retake it with personal relationships in mind.

THE WAY OF CONFLICT STYLE INVENTORY

WHEN CONFLICT STRIKES, DO YOU:			
Slow down, assess the situation, and ask questions?	Want to disappear or smooth things over?	Get energized and see this as a symptom of something bigger?	Quickly try to develop a logical approach to addressing the problem?
___	___	___	___

WHEN PRESSED, DO YOU WISH OTHERS WOULD:			
Stop running around and making rash decisions?	Stop yelling and being so cruel?	Engage; see the bigger picture and what's at stake?	Stop being overly sensitive and dramatic?
___	___	___	___

WHEN THINGS REALLY HEAT UP, ARE YOU:			
Likely to hang back and wait in hopes the problem will go away on its own?	Acutely aware of others' strong emotions, such as anger or despair?	Overwhelmed by all the competing and pressing demands?	Thinking often about what should be done; your brain can't let it go?
___	___	___	___

WHEN POTENTIAL SOLUTIONS ARE DISCUSSED, DO YOU:			
Need ample time and information to fully understand them?	Sense that something isn't right, but you might have a hard time expressing it?	Sometimes exaggerate the gravity of the situation to make a point?	Quickly search for faulty assumptions or structures in the argument?
___	___	___	___

IN GENERAL, UNDER STRESS, DO YOU:			
Remain steady and calm, at least externally?	Feel emotional, upset, or physically affected?	Welcome a passionate, open discussion full of sparks and fire?	Appeal to a trusted system such as psychology, religion, or philosophy to find an answer?
___	___	___	___
ARE YOU KNOWN FOR:			
Strong implementation skills and an even keel?	Caring for relationships and sensing the deeper identity issues?	Creativity, enthusiasm, and novel solutions?	Thinking and speaking quickly, being a great problem solver?
___	___	___	___
TOTAL:			
A	B	C	D
___	___	___	___

Totaling columns A to D on this table will yield different scores. Each column corresponds to an elemental type, as described below. The higher the total score, the more of that element you may contain. It is common to have two strong elements.

A: EARTH

Earth is connected to the physical. Those of us who are Earth people rely on our bodies and our five senses. We are observant and have a great gift of noticing subtle details. We are comfortable with the rational. We prefer to let things sit and are patient and diligent. We are strong at implementation and appear stoic or unmoved in crisis.

Earth's strength — and weakness — comes from holding ground. We can stand strong in the face of new ideas or overwhelming emotions. We slow down and calmly describe the world as we see it. Push me if you can. You can wear us down, but we move and change on our own schedule. However, we may wait too long or hold a position past its potential. We need ample time to process new information. In the story above, Edina is clearly an Earth person.

POSSIBLE STRENGTHS: Earth people are observant, pragmatic, and even keeled. They nurture and ground an organization and are loyal and supportive.

POSSIBLE WEAKNESSES: Earth types can be stubborn and hold grudges. They can procrastinate and let valuable opportunities pass by. They often thwart progress by denying that issues exist or by refusing to change.

B: WATER

Water is the realm of emotions. The well or pool has long been seen as a symbol of our emotional body; Water people dive into its depths. Those of us who are Water people are empathic and gentle. Of all four types we are the most able to flow with the situation. Water has the gift of changing form when pressed by fire (it becomes steam), air (it becomes ice or snow or it evaporates), or earth (it easily shifts and flows around the obstacle). In conflict, we know how to get out of the way: catch us if you can.

Trying to describe the force of our emotions can be very frustrating. Not only do we feel our own response but we are also tapped into everyone else's emotional landscape. This torrent of feelings can put us into a sullen or discouraged state. In general we hate conflict because of the emotional toll it takes on us, and we like to just flow away. We need freedom and lots of space before we'll engage. In the story above, Gene brought powerful Water energy to the business team.

POSSIBLE STRENGTHS: Water people are flexible and comfortable with chaos. Still waters run deep. They are tuned into the morale and emotional health of groups.

First we need to roam and learn from nature itself. To dabble, wade, dip, wallow, and splash. Toss pebbles or pick them up. Sleep by the water until it sounds in our dreams. See our faces in a pool and look beyond. Then, study hydrology.

— C. L. Rawlins

*Thus, pictures which wildfire
creates of itself are at least
bi-visual, part of fire's process
of procreating its meanings.
So as the fire at the top of
the ridge slithered through the
rocks, it stretched itself
out...using its tongue as
a torch to cut through
obstructions.*

— Norman Maclean,
Young Men and Fire

POSSIBLE WEAKNESSES: Water types have a tendency to bail out of relationships or to become depressed when conflict hits. Highly sensitive, they interpret everything as a personal assault. They are sometimes unwilling to be honest for fear of damaging feelings, and thus they withhold valuable information.

C: FIRE

Fire is a symbol of the spirit and of creativity. If we are Fire types we are enthusiastic players who are passionate about our relationships and ideas. We are unwilling to be pinned down. Once ignited, we love a wild and exciting battle, complete with sparks and flames. Blaze, the protagonist of the story above, is full of Fire.

Since fire is formless, we are always looking for the biggest picture or a boundless container. A battle is never just a battle; it is part of a larger issue that can be a bit overwhelming. If fed carefully, fire burns bright and warm, but stand clear when we heat up, or you'll get burned. We attack and are surprised when we run off the other players. We need to have our perspective acknowledged to remain vibrant and under control.

POSSIBLE STRENGTHS: Fire people are imaginative and enthusiastic. They bring life into failing projects or organizations and care deeply about the group and its future.

POSSIBLE WEAKNESSES: Their frustrated ranting can offend or incite others. Fire people may move into others' territories without respect for boundaries. They are easily overwhelmed and hard to predict and can be explosive.

D: AIR

Air is associated with the mind. We Air people are recognized for objective rational thinking; we understand the world using structured systems such as law, philosophy, mathematics, or psychology. We understand how to create processes and organization. We wish to resolve disputes quickly. We are sharp, fast-talking, and love lively debate. In the story above, bright and busy Amy has strong Air energy. Like a dog after a bone, our minds gnaw on a dilemma and are unwilling to let it go. An issue can occupy all our thoughts and attention, becoming an obsession. We talk first and ask questions later. It is often difficult to understand the emotions of others since we rely on our minds to make sense of the world. We need others to fully engage and match our arguments in conflict.

POSSIBLE STRENGTHS: Air people are great communicators and problem solvers. They can fit complex situations into applicable frameworks and are articulate and willing to offer an opinion.

POSSIBLE WEAKNESSES: Air types may need a reality check on the viability and emotional implications of proposed solutions. They may not realize that others disagree with or misunderstand their reasoning.

I loved the prairie, even while I feared it. . . . Still in my dreams I can feel the force of that wind.

— Pearl Price Robertson,
"Homestead Days
in Montana"

CHAPTER 2

Identifying the
Team's Personality

We don't accomplish anything in this world alone . . .
and whatever happens is the result of the whole tapestry of one's life
and all the weavings of individual threads from one
to another that creates something.

— Sandra Day O'Connor

When people gather together for any reason, they form a team. In some cases, a group comes together only to discuss or resolve an issue, and then it disperses. On a playing field, for example, athletes gather into squads, play the game, then head back to the lockers. With families, corporations, and other communities, however, a single team might stay connected through countless experiences and challenges.

Like individuals, teams also have elemental personalities. One collective might choose generally to avoid conflict, while another will be all sparks and bickering, and another might need large blocks of time to process information before acting. When we are lost in conflict it is helpful to back up and look at the forest through the trees, to see the entire team beyond its individuals. When I am consulting or mediating a dispute I begin by mentally "backing up" to see all the participants as a single entity, even if they are taking opposing sides of an issue. Because a team acts like a living, breathing creature with its own distinct personality, I treat it as another player in conflict.

To give an example, our friends the Smith family love to be outdoors. Their home is welcoming, and they are great hosts. They enjoy hanging out reading, watching TV, or playing games. If you wish to create conflict with this family, be consistently late. If you'd like their company, give them ample notice, and they'll know you respect their commitments and calendar. Once I understood that the Smith family was an Earth "team," my relationship with them improved drastically. Time integrity, a strong Earth trait, is as important to them as being connected to the outdoors.

To use another example, Selby Tool is a creative, responsive organization. If the customer says she needs a new type of screwdriver, they'll make it. Unfortunately, that might be the only screwdriver of that type that anyone will ever need, so Selby must absorb significant retooling costs. Regardless of who runs their operations, Selby Tool seems to enthusiastically follow their customers down wild rabbit holes, which drives some of Selby's employees crazy and out the door after a few years. When I consulted with Selby, knowing that they led with Fire, I knew it was critical that the company articulate and commit to a clear direction to hold onto employees and bring back customers.

When I am mediating, knowing the group personality helps me to determine how to pace the discussion and address the group. In general, if a group carries strong Water energy, I will assume a gentler and more relationship-based approach. With a fiery group I am more direct and involved.

Our bodies change over time as we grow from infants to children and into adulthood. However, through these changes we keep lasting personalities. This is also true with teams. Even as members come and go, barring a major event, a group will maintain certain fixed characteristics. To understand this lasting group personality, notice how the group treats others, how quickly the collective makes decisions, what it is attracted to and what it seems to attract. Regardless of the circumstances, some teams easily gain support, while others seem to turn folks off or frustrate them, no matter who is in charge. Some teams are always late; some are just plain fun to be around.

During its two-hundred-year-plus history, the United States has been a Fire "team." A passionate and idealistic nation, the United States is a continual source of new and creative ideas, excitement, and enthusiasm. Jacob Needleman, author of *The American Soul*, ascribes this enduring focus on Fire to its founding fathers. He said, "These founders were deeply concerned in one way or another with questions of the heart, of the spiritual search." This country is also often perceived as harsh, coarse, and unrelenting, which can also be fiery attributes. It is known as a hawkish and violent culture that struggles with its boundaries. Other Fire-based personality traits of this nation can be seen in an expansive gathering of territory throughout the North American continent over its history and in the stereotype of the "ugly American" who travels throughout the world speaking too loudly and brashly criticizing his native hosts.

The test offered below will help you to determine the character of a team so you might understand the greater player against whom you are matched. Knowing your family is an Earth team, for example, will help you set realistic expectations about how quickly that system might change. If you work with a Water team, to make progress you might wish to address it gently. Also, within larger teams exist smaller subteams. For example, the marketing department might be a fiery group that will need to be treated differently from the slower-moving service department, while the master organization will carry a personality of its own.

When determining a consistent team personality, it is important to examine the consistent patterns over time and in different situations, since each conflict will bring out different facets of your team. It is also important to remember that everything changes. When mapping the personality of your team, look for ways in which it may have shifted. For example, if you expect your family to react in conflict the way it did when you were a child, you may be caught off guard. That family as you knew it may have died long ago. Although all the players in a family may be the same, this collective may not be the same animal you were working with before a divorce, a death, or some other major event shook it to its core. A system can be pushed so far that it loses fixed personality attributes. When working to form metal, this is called being stretched beyond the elastic limit, that point past which the metal can no longer return to its original state. If a team is taken beyond its elastic limit, it may be a completely new entity, quite different from what you remember.

IDENTIFYING THE ELEMENTAL TEAM STYLE

For each response, enter a 3 if the statement is a frequent response, 2 if it is an occasional response, and 1 if it is an infrequent response in the boxes on page 21. Then add up the A, B, C, and D columns to find the team score for each. Use the test first to track where the team is today and then how the team has reacted consistently over time.

19

WAY OF CONFLICT
TEAM PERSONALITY INVENTORY

My team is:

1. On time to meetings or other engagements.

2. Worried about how others will perceive them.

3. Geared toward bold aspirations.

4. Great at communicating.

5. A creator of well-organized events.

6. Able to laugh at themselves and their failings.

7. Full of great new ideas and plans.

8. Interested in talking through issues and concerns at length.

9. Detail oriented.

10. Spacey.

11. Enraptured with travel and excitement.

12. Intelligent and quick talking.

13. Completely aware of the current situation and able to describe it with keen accuracy.

14. Focused on making the world a kinder place.

15. Animated, theatrical, sometimes explosive.

16. Very confident.

17. Slow to change or implement new strategies.

18. Flexible, easily changing plans or format.

19. Enthusiastic to commit but capable of changing their minds.

20. Drawn to rules, guidelines, methodologies, and structures.

21. Voracious about research.

22. Caring of everyone's feelings.

23. Passionate and fond of giving advice.

24. Known to debate issues.

25. Set in their ways.

26. Often worried or morose.

27. Happy to make quick gut decisions.

28. Sure they know a right way of being or approaching a situation.
29. Grounded and easygoing.
30. Emotional.
31. Fun and lively.
32. Happy to engage in competitions and to play games together.
33. Generous but struggles with being taken advantage of.
34. Gentle.
35. Dynamic, expansive.
36. Fond of telling stories and jokes.
37. Focused on financial and physical well-being.
38. Focused on relationships and being a caring team.
39. Focused on new creative ideas.
40. Focused on developing a solution and strategies.

A	B	C	D
1.	2.	3.	4.
5.	6.	7.	8.
9.	10.	11.	12.
13.	14.	15.	16.
17.	18.	19.	20.
21.	22.	23.	24.
25.	26.	27.	28.
29.	30.	31.	32.
33.	34.	35.	36.
37.	38.	39.	40.
TOTAL	TOTAL	TOTAL	TOTAL

A: EARTH TEAM

Teams with strong Earth energy focus on the details. They pay attention to time and space. They are generally on time for meetings or gatherings. They remember to bring their raincoats to the well-organized company picnic. In conflict they will be perplexed by passionate ranting, intimidated by fast-talking folks, and turned off or bothered by any emotions displayed. They want to asses the problem and get those other people to stop all that commotion.

Although not focused on strategic thinking, Earth types will roll up their sleeves and implement the day-to-day aspects of a greater plan. Earth families create annual traditions or dinner time rituals, which they diligently follow. They pay attention to what is happening around them and are not always interested in change. Some may perceive them as simple folk, but they are a solid team with solid values.

Earth teams are also great nesters. They focus on a comfortable, nurturing environment and will spend hours in that space. These are the families that create welcoming, comfortable homes. Under stress, Earth teams slow down and can become mired in details. They want data and time to incorporate it.

B: WATER TEAM

Water groups worry about their members and how they are perceived. They are sensitive, fluid groups who grow concerned when one member is out of whack or unhappy. In a business setting, we often assign watery tasks to personnel management. Water families invite wayward souls, extended family members, and friends to move in and out of their homes. Water teams spend a lot of time trying to figure out what they did to make another angry, or they may devote hours to gossiping about the one who wronged them. These collectives are always working to ensure that everyone on the team is treated fairly so no one gets their feelings hurt; issues of equity seem to predominate. They teams want to make the world a kinder and gentler place. Small subgroups often form when things are in chaos, and if left unattended, they will wage emotionally charged wars.

In conflict, Water teams disappear. They aren't interested in direct, fiery conversations. They flow into corners or behind closed doors to discuss the vexing problems, or they appear comatose. To move their current in your direction, you will need to give them quiet nurturing and ample space. Lots of low-key, flexible, and open meetings without a firm deadline or outcome will keep them around.

C: FIRE TEAM

Fire teams love ideas. They will get charged about something and make commitments that they later need to rescind, which can drive friends and business alliances crazy. A passionate, creative group, they'll fight wildly about concepts without much need of proof, which will make the Earth and Water people in the mix cower in confusion. They are often blind to facts and figures, relying instead on their instinct. For example, they'll "know" they are best in the business and yet can't tell you what their competitors' products look like or exactly why they are superior. Often they are right! Fun to be around, fire families always have a new adventure or project cooking. There's lots of arm waving and flying superlatives with this group. They'll supply lots of advice to anyone who asks, and even to those who don't!

Fierce fire reveals true gold.

— Chinese proverb

In conflict, the *issue* is everything. They want to bring it on and discuss it with enthusiasm until closure. They need the issue to be articulated and acknowledged *as important.* It needs to be given priority, tracked, and moved forward. Members of this group will have lots of ideas but will need structure and boundaries to implement a resolution.

D: AIR TEAM

Do you need a new system for monitoring the production schedule? Are you looking for guidelines to parenting a teenager? If so, go to an Air team. They love developing strateges and campaigns. For example, Air families might have a six-point morning checklist or a posted chore matrix. They talk quickly and fall in love with their new and efficient approach to market penetration or team success. Disregarding the fact that their theory hasn't been proven, they just love systems, strategic

Twenty years from now you will be more disappointed by the things that you didn't do than by the ones you did do. So throw off the bowlines. Sail away from the safe harbor. Catch the trade winds in your sails. Explore. Dream. Discover.

— Mark Twain

frameworks, and methodologies. Air teams don't have patience for those not along for the ride. They don't understand the worries of the Water folks or the frustrations of their Fire team members and will happily create an employee improvement plan to get rid of those morose and wild folks ASAP. Sometimes a predominantly Air team will decide that slower-moving Water and Earth people should be gone tomorrow if they don't get with a new program.

Air teams love objective, clear communication. Ask members of this team how a problem affects the larger organization, how it affects the framework, and how it can be solved. Honest and continued communication in a structured, repeatable format will be most effective with this group. They love facilitated meetings, and in a family setting, they will appreciate weekly planning sessions. They enjoy lots of banter, and engaging in a verbal Ping-Pong match is one of their favorite pastimes.

CHAPTER 3

Uncovering the Elements of a Balanced Team

The achievements of an organization are the results of the combined effort of each individual.

— Vince Lombardi

Many cultural traditions, such as Chinese medicine, that use the elements also map them onto different areas of the body. Earth is connected to the limbs, skin, and bones, or the body's physical matter. Water is our blood and guts, the two areas most associated with our emotions. And Fire is held in the heart and solar plexus as the seat of our passions or creativity. Air is associated with the head or mental capabilities and communication.

Just as we individually work to balance the four elements within us, balancing the four elements within a team makes it stable and productive. We see this in the team of Blaze, Edina, Amy, and Gene. When the team is stable, your earthy implementation gurus like Edina will act as its arms and legs, getting things done. The nurturing, flowing pack leaders like Gene, who hold the emotions or the lifeblood of the team, make sure that everyone feels happy and loved. Blaze, as the heart of the team, acts as its fiery visionary. And Amy becomes the brains of the organization as she creates structure and grabs rules "from the air."

In a balanced family, you'll find some caring for the hearth, others watching out for the emotional landscape of the members, those who are brave and enthusiastic, and still others who will speak for the group. Together, they act as a living, dynamic system.

A LIVING TEAM SYSTEM

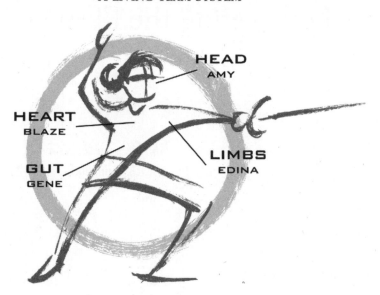

In a group dispute, we might focus on the individual players, seeing them as the problem. As a result, we miss the internal balancing act occurring within the team. We might say, "Oh, Amy is such a complainer. All she can do is bring up the negative. If only she'd calm down." We wonder how to cheer up Gene, to quiet Blaze, and to get Edina working productively again. However, these individual members are often just *acting* as the voice, ears, emotions, or limbs of the larger team. Notice what happens when you focus on the members instead of working with the whole group. Just when we think we've got Amy's issues addressed and under control, another dissatisfied member will rear its head. This team creature will also have legs and arms that, although they don't speak, will lash out in subversive ways.

Psychologist Monica McGoldrich writes that our culture typically assigns the expression of bereavement, a Water activity, to women. "As one woman put it, referring to the loss of one of her three sons, 'Through my eyes flow the tears for the whole family.'" Sometimes the roles we play fit with our elemental personalities. Other times, we are asked to take a position we would not naturally choose.

In any conflict, we will naturally seek balance. If one party in a team is being very emotional, then others will balance that person out by becoming stoic or by focusing on the mental or physical aspects of the conflict. We cannot judge a person's elemental conflict personality by how they are currently acting, since they may just be balancing someone else. If someone is focusing on the mental aspects of the situation, just see that person as the "head" or the Air energy of the dispute and treat them accordingly. Another's elemental conflict personality can be better deciphered by looking at the long-term patterns of that person across different relationships and environments.

THE PARTS OF THE TEAM

In the following grid place each member of the team who matches the criteria described in the quadrant. If the group is very large, instead place the leader of a subgroup, like Market Research or Human Resources, in the grid as it relates to the conflict in question. For example, Gene in our opening story:

1. Is clearly upset about how the team is being treated.

2. Is worried about the other employees.

3. Has been overheard backstabbing Blaze.

4. Has communicated his concerns to Edina.

Gene's name would be added to the "Internal" or Water quadrant, noting that he met three of the characteristics in that quadrant. Gene would also be added to the "Head" or Air quadrant, since he has been vocal about the issue.

WAY OF CONFLICT TEAM MEMBER INVENTORY

EXTERNAL: EARTH	INTERNAL: WATER
• Seems *oblivious* to the problem and surprised that folks are upset?	• *Personally bothered* or upset by the fighting?
• Willing to *support* or observe the effort to resolve the issue (will come to meetings)?	• Worried about *people* leaving and how this is upsetting others?
• Watches the battle but doesn't get involved?	• Wants everyone to get along, depressed about the situation?
• Has a good understanding of the conflict as it stands?	• Runs from the issue?
• *Angry* at those rocking the boat?	• *Quiet* or withdrawn?
• Uses current team policy to undercut another (turns off their email because of a minor infraction)?	• Subversively undercutting others and *backstabbing?*
• Likes it the way it is? Might appear stubborn?	• Harbors hurt and resentment toward others?
Names of those who fit the above, with the number of affirmative answers. Example: Edina 4	Names of those who fit the above, with the number of affirmative answers. Example: Gene 3
•	•
•	•
•	•
•	•
•	•
•	•
•	•

HEART: FIRE	HEAD: AIR
• *Passionate* about the issue?	• *Anxious,* wants the issue resolved?
• Has a *vision* for the team?	• *Communicates* the group problems and which players are upset?
• Feels as though no one appreciates his or her efforts or perspective?	• Takes a "heady" or *objective* approach to solving the issue?
• *Overwhelmed* or frustrated?	• Debates the merits of the ideas?
• Won't let any issue go, wants to focus on the problem and work it through?	• Works to destroy another's argument or credibility?
• Known to *blast* others in email or in person?	• *Confused* or spacey?
• Wants to brainstorm and be *creative?*	• Overly *controlling?*
Names of those who fit the above, with the number of affirmative answers. Example: Blaze 1	Names of those who fit the above, with the number of affirmative answers. Example: Amy 2
•	•
•	•
•	•
•	•
•	•
•	•
•	•

EXTERNAL: EARTH PLAYERS

Earth folks often like the situation as it is and are unhappy with those who are stirring the pot. They move more slowly than the other team members. Get them mad, and they are stout opponents: think of a giant suddenly given a club. Do you need a new printer? Suddenly the paperwork and procedures become thick and unwieldy. Earth players may not say much, but they are critical to the success or failure of a new idea, since they will gather the needed details and implement any new plan. They will watch to see what is decided. These players pay attention to see *if words are backed up by concrete actions*. They will test to see if you really mean what you say. Earthy team members will purposely keep coming in late, for example, to see if you really mean that everyone has to arrive to work on time.

INTERNAL: WATER PLAYERS

Water players feel the emotional content of the argument. They may be personally affected and unable to sleep, and they may wish to leave the group or subversively try to remove others. *Gently and objectively describing the disruption* will bring Water players out of hiding and back to your side. Find out who they don't like and why. This information will lead you to the core issues of the dispute. Although they may appear volatile and petty, Water folks actually care about the emotional well-being of the entire team.

HEART: FIRE PLAYERS

Fiery team members are focused on the "heart" of the issue. They care about what is at stake and the future of the team. These participants will be personally invested in creating a vision, often fighting wildly for it. Sometimes they will blast you with their intensity and will not give up, even when it appears that they are whipping a dead horse. At other times, these passionate players will brood silently as they become frustrated or overwhelmed. By *recognizing their ideas*, you can allow Fire players to fuel the entire organization.

And forget not that the earth delights to feel your bare feet and the winds long to play with your hair.

— Kahlil Gibran,
The Prophet

Love the earth and sun and animals,
Despise riches, give alms to everyone that asks,
Stand up for the stupid and crazy,
Devote your income and labor to others.

— Walt Whitman,
Leaves of Grass

Be glad of life, because it gives you the chance to love and to work and to play and to look up at the stars.

— Henry Van Dyke

HEAD: AIR PLAYERS

Air participants will describe the situation and communicate the practical issues. They are communicating for the team and can be viewed as its messenger or "mouth." Since they are the only ones talking, don't mistake them for the only people involved in the conflict or think that the opinions they state are theirs alone. They may wish to stay in the mental or rational and will want the heart folks to stop screaming, the watery internals to stop sniveling, and the externals to get moving. When confused or anxious, Air players will beat you about the head with their verbal arguments. They can become overly controlling, since they want to *work through this issue* and get it resolved.

The moment one definitely commits oneself, then Providence moves, too. All sorts of things occur to help one that would never otherwise have occurred.... Boldness has genius, power, and magic in it. Begin it now.

— Johann Wolfgang von Goethe

CHAPTER 4

Playing Well with Others

Ask not what your teammates can do for you.
Ask what you can do for your teammates.

— Magic Johnson

Every person views a battle differently. To create a balanced solution we need to recognize that we typically can hear only a limited range of information in any conflict. At a minimum, a person who relies on Air energy, like Amy, may only be tuned into the mental aspects of the conflict. She may discuss the strategic pros and cons of removing a product and the associated layoffs. A Water person like Gene, engaged in the same battle, may just perceive the emotional and interpersonal implications, information to which the Air person might be oblivious. It is as though each natural element is tuned to a different radio frequency. Amy and Gene will both receive valuable and different information. The more data we receive from the widest variety of folks, the better equipped we will be to develop a solution.

BEING A TRANSFORMER

Do you remember when the teacher of your high school physics class brought out two wave machines that created differing wavelengths? She first showed you how when the wave of one hit the other, its energy would bounce off of it. In difficult conversations it can often feel like what you are saying is not being heard or understood by your opponent, and vice versa. To use a common phrase, you are operating on different wavelengths. To complete the experiment, the teacher then added a *transformer* that modulated the energy of one wave so that it could be accepted and absorbed into the other. Those two wave machines were initially in conflict. When a transformer was added, they were able to understand or absorb and thus use the energy of the other.

All kinds of transformers are available to us in conflict. For example, mediators transform a conversation by reiterating one disputant's perspective using vocabulary more suited to the opposing side. A favorite facilitator trick is to ask participants to change chairs throughout a contentious meeting to alter perspectives. Art, music, story, movement, theater, and silence can also act as transformers to alter and expand our perspective. The world's spiritual traditions all teach how four transforming tricks or "gifts" can be employed to match another's style and release the intensity of conflict. I describe these gifts as:

1. *Asking questions:* Who is a wise man? He who learns from all men (Talmud).

2. *Humility:* He who stands on tiptoe doesn't stand firm (Tao Te Ching).

3. *Acknowledging all viewpoints:* And cover not Truth with falsehood, nor conceal the truth when you know what it is (Koran).

4. *Honesty:* The Truth shall set you free (Bible).

In general team players will respond positively to anyone who acts as a transformer and tries to be on their wavelength. Each element has a cadence and pitch. If you are able to listen for and match that frequency, you will have a better chance of being heard.

Most people in conflict are infused with a strong dose of energy from at least one or more elements, and thus you will need a unique combination of techniques to let another know that you want to keep them around. Not to worry: you will note the frustration or increased emphasis in their communication if you do not get it right the first time.

The important thing is not to stop questioning.

— Albert Einstein

It is an interesting challenge to listen for the unique conflict style of another and work to match it. Guessing and matching conflict needs with the appropriate transformers can turn conflict into a more enjoyable game. We will begin to explore these skills below and will return to them in greater detail in part 3.

TRANSFORMER FOR EARTH PLAYERS: ASKING QUESTIONS

A person with strong Earth energy is observant and focused on information gleaned through the senses. She can give you a keen assessment of the current situation, describing the "lay of the land." To appreciate an Earth player is to acknowledge that you understand the landscape. Earth players need to know you have heard the facts. Focus on the content and recognize that an Earth person enjoys a slower cadence in conversation. Mountains move, but ever so slowly. Be methodical and listen carefully; Earth people have much to tell you about the battlefield and what is hiding in its peaks and valleys.

To give an example, a couple was driving across Canada engaging in a heated discussion about a previous exchange. As the wife described it, her Earth-based husband was angry and seemed to be stuck on a particular point from their earlier conversation. They had spent hours, it seemed, bantering back and forth, and yet he was still furious. The wife explained, "I arrived at a magic moment when I finally just stopped defending myself or attacking and asked him, 'What is making you so angry?'" She had employed one of the most critical transforming gifts, and an Earth person's favorite; she asked an open-ended question.

Earth players pay attention to the world around them; to them details are important. They can answer questions about who came to the last meeting, what was covered, and when the memo appeared on everyone's desk. If you ask them questions, not only will you gather valuable information but you will also honor an Earth person's gifts of observation and keep them willing to support resolution.

When you sincerely ask a question of anyone, regardless of personality type, others in conflict know you appreciate them and are thus more likely to stick around. The other players are also more willing to respond in kind by seeking to understand your point of view. Questions help

Be patient toward all that is unsolved in your heart and try to love the questions themselves . . . .
Do not now seek the answers, which cannot be given to you because you will not be able to live them.
And the point is, to live everything.
Live the questions now. Perhaps you will then gradually, without noticing it, live along some distant day into the answer.

— Rainer Maria Rilke

You can tell whether a man is clever by his answers. You can tell whether a man is wise by his questions.

— Naguib Mahfouz

everyone involved to feel safer. As the others answer your questions, you also buy time and give yourself a bit of breathing room. Additionally, questions raise our awareness and push us to see what we need to resolve our problems. Here are my top five questions:

1. How did we get here?
2. What do you wish you or I did differently?
3. How's it going? (a low-key inquiry into feelings)
4. In the best of all possible worlds, what would you like in the future?
5. What should we do now?

Stay away from questions that start with, "Why did you…?" The word *why* denotes blame and puts the other party on the defensive with a need to justify.

TRANSFORMER FOR WATER PLAYERS: HUMILITY

Water people flow and swim in the deep well of emotions. They feel deeply and are soft and smooth like dolphins. Watery folks may struggle with articulating their position since they are operating not from the head, but from the gut. Sensitive and aware of the emotional landscape, they notice how a conflict is affecting all those involved. They enjoy water and act as though they are liquid. You might find that they seem to ebb and flow without warning; now you see them, now you don't, although they are standing right in front of you. To get on a Water person's wavelength you need to note the emotional impact of a situation. Water players need to know you understand how they and those around them are feeling. A Water person should be given lots of space to maneuver, and gentle words should be used. Damming water can create all sorts of disasters.

Within my daughter, Senya, lies a pool of wisdom and emotion. She is often my gentle teacher about what a Water person needs and enjoys. Ever since Senya learned to talk, she has asked me to tell her stories about when I was little. Her favorite tales are those in which I laugh at

I believe that the first test of a truly great man is his humility. I do not mean by humility doubt of his own powers. But really great men have a curious feeling that the greatness is not in them, but through them. And they see something divine in every other man and are endlessly, foolishly, incredibly merciful.

— John Ruskin

how silly I was and describe what I learned from the experience. A subtle teacher, as should be expected from a Water person, Senya shows me that to connect with her is to demonstrate that I too was young, have made mistakes, and can be childish. My daughter flows to my side when I am humble and willing to laugh at myself.

In general, Water people appreciate humility. They are continually in touch, and often struggling with, the universal dance of self-esteem. If you can admit your failings and demonstrate that you know we are all in this together, they will swim to your aid. When a Water person is ready to give up, a story about your own struggles and humanness will open the gates of communication and will get them to laugh and come to your side. The word *humor* comes from a word meaning "water" or "fluid." Your ability to laugh at yourself will naturally bequeath you the ability to flow like water and will improve intimacy in all your relationships.

The word *humble*, however, comes from the word *humus*, or earth. A natural result of not taking ourselves too seriously is becoming grounded or humbled. Like water, we flow along the earth and stay connected to it. As R. L. Wing says about the way water is described in the Tao Te Ching, "It is used to describe the behavior of Evolved Individuals — those who spontaneously bring progress to situations without inviting resistance or resentment. Like water, Evolved Individuals do not compete to reach high places but, instead, hold to lower ones. This Taoist ideal runs counter to the common view that one must contend or struggle to achieve success." We think of humility as negative, as something that brings us off our high horses. Actually, humility reminds us that we are not better or worse than another but the same. We become approachable. Once connected to the earth, we can achieve success without struggle. So relax with a Water person and giggle at yourself.

TRANSFORMER FOR FIRE PLAYERS: ACKNOWLEDGING ALL VIEWPOINTS

Fire people jump up and down and widly gesture. Get them excited about a topic, and their stoves turn on. Fiery folks are intense, enthusiastic souls who can become ferociously angry. They live large and perform daring acts. Fire players need to know you see the strength of the

Too often we underestimate the power of a touch, a smile, a kind word, a listening ear, an honest compliment, or the smallest act of caring, all of which have the potential to turn a life around.

— Leo Buscaglia

fire within. Matching their enthusiasm, excitement, or passion about an issue lets them know that you hear them. You may need to get loud and big to match their blaze.

A long-time Basque activist explains the fire and the violence in his region this way: "We were an independent country until the mid-1800s. To lose our rights and sovereignty has raised the passions throughout our region. However, the Spanish government refuses to recognize our frustrations and to listen to us. I believe we are left with violence as one of the only ways to get the government to acknowledge our issues."

The act of witnessing or acknowledging makes an event and a perspective "real" beyond those involved. Quantum physicists tell us that the universe is a participative process based on relationship. For example, a rock is not heavy without a scale to measure it, and skin is not soft without our touch. We must observe and let others know what we have seen for it to be incorporated into reality. This may be why our religious traditions have long recognized the critical need to have others witness our marriages, bar and bat mitzvahs, baptisms, and funerals.

However, we often don't want to repeat or acknowledge another person's argument or beliefs. In diplomatic circles, to acknowledge is sometimes equated with validating the opponent's position. This action makes the other's position "real" in our own minds and gives it more power. We don't want to strengthen the force that threatens our current way of living.

Meanwhile, the universe seems to work hard to assure that its components are seen. Terrorism is a good example. A dismissed participant's acts become bigger and louder until someone "sees" them. Although it may appear counterintuitive, one of the best things we can do *for ourselves* in conflict is to acknowledge the other. Not only does this keep everyone relaxed and willing to play the entire game of conflict, it also gives our own perspective more fuel. We don't have to agree, but once we acknowledge the existence of the opposing argument we are more able to use the information and energy within the position and create a bigger picture, which makes *us* stronger. This is the concept of "interpenetration" in physics, that acknowledgment allows us to come close enough to exchange and use energy from another system.

Silent gratitude isn't very much to anyone.

— Gertrude Stein

You give but little when you give of your possessions. It is when you give of yourself that you truly give.

— Kahlil Gibran, *The Prophet*

To acknowledge is to notice:

1. what was said,

2. the underlying emotions, and

3. how it affects the speaker.

For example, if I worriedly add, after telling you about an exciting trip I have planned, "My mother is ill," and you parrot back "Your mother is ill," in monotone, I will not feel heard. If you respond, "You seem very worried," I will probably still not feel heard. When you acknowledge what is happening and its impact with, "Wow, your mother is ill, you seem really worried, what does that do to your vacation plans?" the conversation and the relationship will move forward.

One of the most effective forms of acknowledgment comes when we apologize for the negative impact of our actions. Sincere apologies often instantly transform its participants and lay a solution in holiday robes at our feet. Fire people *love* apologies! Master negotiator William Ury notes, "One word of caution: your opponent will usually be able to tell whether or not your acknowledgement is sincere. Your intent, as expressed in your tone and body language, counts just as much as your words." Honesty, as discussed below, is usually the best policy.

When the heart is full, the tongue will speak.

— Scottish proverb

TRANSFORMER FOR AIR PLAYERS: HONESTY

Air people love the patterns or framework of an argument. Often very cerebral folks, they are focused on the underlying structure of a situation. This structure may be a philosophy, a mind-set, the corresponding laws, or a defined system. Air people talk and think fast. To engage an Air player is to understand and match the reasoning in their underlying argument and philosophy. Air players are always looking for resolution. They search for the truths on which they can construct their solution. So to keep them in the game, tell the truth.

We might think it best to withhold information and shield others from pain or ourselves from embarrassment; however, doing so is betrayal. Pick any presidential scandal, the Johnson administration's actions regarding Vietnam, the Watergate hearings, or President Clinton's sexual indiscretions, and note that it was the cover-up and lies that exacerbated each conflict. Spiritual traditions acknowledge that to learn we must make mistakes. However, in every tradition I have studied, the advice on this point is clear: *complete honesty is the best policy.*

It would be incorrect to say that honesty is *always* best because, just as with any trait, its opposite also can play a valuable role under appropriate circumstances. For example, *The Art of War* describes deception as a possible strategy when seeking a win-win solution. However, a small yet personally illuminating example of the power of honesty came one winter holiday break. A week before she was to arrive at my house, my sister Tara called to announce that she was pregnant. We were both thrilled, but because it was early in the pregnancy, and she wanted to share the news herself, she asked that I not tell anyone. Another of our sisters, Bevin, noticing a pile of baby books left in the guest room, asked, "Is Tara pregnant?" Not wanting to lie I said, "Yes, but let her tell you." When Tara and her husband landed in town for the holidays, she asked me if I had told anyone about the pregnancy. Not wanting to anger my newly pregnant sister, I said no.

What a mess! Later that day I went for a run with my stomach in knots. I realized I needed to tell Tara the truth for Bevin's sake, if nothing else. At the beginning of my route, I thought of all the reasons why I had said what I said, how I was intimidated, and how I had been caught off guard by both sisters' questions. Halfway through my running route, I had created a boring, whining fifteen-minute monologue. I then realized to tell Tara the truth was simply to say that I had lied to her and that I was sorry. No excuses. Then I was terrified.

After staking my ego on studying conflict and communication I knew that I had to tell her the truth. On my return I found Tara alone in her bedroom. I asked her if she had a minute and then, not as gracefully as I would have wished, I explained succinctly, "When you asked me if I had told anyone, I lied to you. I told Bevin. I am sorry; I shouldn't have lied to you." Instead of the expected anger or disappointment, I met compassion and understanding. My honesty was heard and appreciated. My overriding desire to have a strong and trusting relationship with my sisters had shown through.

Study nature, love nature, stay close to nature. It will never fail you.

— Frank Lloyd Wright

I know now that if I had tried to make excuses or chosen to ignore the situation entirely, anger and distrust from my sisters would have been the logical response, since my underlying motivation would have been skirting responsibility instead of mutual respect. This story illustrates three facts about searching for the truth and making respect an underlying motivation in every conversation. The three key tenets of honesty are:

1. *The truth is short.* If you find that your description rambles on through lots of excuses, background information, or sidebars, you haven't arrived at it yet. Truth is succinct and sometimes comes with a dose of embarrassment or humility.

2. *Truth includes the acceptance of responsibility.* When we accept responsibility for our actions, we not only show respect to another, but we also respect and acknowledge ourselves. We accept ourselves as we are and become empowered to make changes.

3. *The truth has to be said.* Truth has a way of making itself known. Either you can listen for the right time and present the truth when it is best for all parties, or it will find a way to present itself at a less-than-opportune moment. Since so much of our communication is nonverbal, we actually convey the truth, even though our words and actions may not match.

Since we all have the four elements within us, we will always appreciate any of the four transforming gifts of asking questions, humility, acknowledging all viewpoints, and honesty bestowed upon us. Give these gifts lavishly, and notice the difference this makes in your understanding of the conflict and in your communication.

SUMMARY

The following table is a quick reference guide to identifying and further understanding your or another's elemental personality. It summarizes each type's characteristics, as detailed in this section, by giving some dominant traits, a common role, and a few real-world examples. This is provided with an understanding that no one can be put into a box, let alone ever be fully summarized in a table.

ELEMENTAL PERSONALITY STYLE SUMMARY

	EARTH	WATER	FIRE	AIR
STRENGTHS	Persistent, attends to details, observant	Flexible, sensitive to others	Enthusiastic, creative	Logical problem solver, quick thinking
WEAKNESSES	Stubborn, denies problem	Runs away, feels victimized	Harsh, prone to outbursts	Controlling, anxious
CONNECTION	Physical	Emotional	Spiritual or creative	Mental/rational
DEFINING CHARACTERISTICS	Grounded	Gentle	Strong	Sharp
PACE	Slow	Fluid	Fits and starts	Fast
FAVORED APPROACH	Wait	Watch at a safe distance	Confront	Talk
NEEDS	Time	Space	Understanding	Presence
FAVORITE GIFT	Questions	Humility	Acknowledgment	Honesty
ROLE	Worker	Relater	Visionary	Designer
SUPPORTS	Implementation and nurturing	Harvest and releasing	Development of future	Creation of new structures and forms
ENERGETIC EXAMPLE	Maria Montessori and Edward Abbey	Mahatma Gandhi and Mother Teresa	Hildegard of Bingen and Carl Jung	Martin Luther King Jr. and Sandra Day O'Connor
TYPICAL DEPARTMENTS	Information Systems, Facilities	Human Resources	Research and Development	Financial Systems and Quality Assurance

As you confront an individual or group, watch their rhythms and patterns to identify their innate elemental styles. A person's relationship with time and space will also provide valuable clues into their elemental proclivity. The following matrix defines the connection an elemental personality has with each of these concepts:

WAY OF CONFLICT TIME/SPACE MATRIX

EARTH	AIR
Slow speaking, not affected by tight schedules, and usually punctual. Very aware of, and often attached to, current environment.	Is very aware both of schedules and of external constructs. Talks fast, loves data.
WATER	**FIRE**
Often doesn't care about time; relationship centered. Not focused on external but instead on internal issues.	Fights with time; there is never enough, and he or she is often late. Deals in the creative and the conceptual, not with the day-to-day details.

SPACE ↑

TIME →

If a player is always fighting with time, he or she is probably a Fire person. When someone becomes attached to "the way things are," or connected to space, they are bringing Earth to the table. The person who appears "out of it" or unattached may be a Water soul. Air folks with a strong connection to both space and time love organizers and use clear structures or philosophies to make things bearable. Again, we each carry all four elements within us and all their potential strengths and challenges.

In part 2 we will apply the elements not only to engaging the players but also to deciphering conflict itself. Following *The Art of War,* we have now explored an approach to "know the other and know oneself, [so] victory is not in danger." Next we will explore the "heaven," or the basic cosmic laws of conflict, so that "then victory can be complete." The directions to part 2 might best begin: "The Game of Conflict. To be played from birth to death. Played every day by every thing across the universe."

PART 2

THE RULES

When a quarrel heats up,

pretend it is a game.

— Hasao proverb

This story, a parable imparted by Buddha and famous Sufi poets, is an often-shared tale from long, long ago. Some say it originates with the Jainists of India. The tale has been reshaped during at least twenty-five hundred years of telling. It begins: Once upon a time three blind men were trying to find a path through a dense jungle. They stumbled along over fallen branches and around vines until they came upon a great elephant.

Never having been introduced to an elephant before, the first man standing at the trunk screamed, "We found a snake!"

The second blind man, touching the expansive side of the beast said, "Calm down. There is no snake. This is simply a great wall around which we must find our way. It is solid and long. We must inch along it."

The third man, holding onto the tail, replied, "I have found a rope. Let us use this to climb over the wall."

Individually they could find no answer to their dilemma. Only together would they find their way.

CHAPTER 5

The Object of the Game

Out beyond the ideas of right doing and wrong doing,
there is a field.
I'll meet you there.

— Jelaluddin Rumi

Once upon a time, beginning in the seventeenth century, scientists believed that the world operated like a machine made up of independent parts. Things were to be taken apart and dissected to be understood. If we didn't like a part, we could simply remove it without affecting the whole. In this Newtonian viewpoint anything "real" had to be seen or experienced through one of the other five senses.

Then in the twentieth century along came the "new scientists." There were biologists, chemists, physicists, and mathematicians who began to focus on the *whole*, or what they called the *system*. These thinkers demonstrated that it is the invisible, things like relationships and potential, that runs the universal show. These new scientists described the universe as a *living system made up of interdependent, interrelated systems*. In other words, they maintained that, if we see only the parts of something, as the blind men did, we miss reality.

Any group of people, be it a married couple, a family, or a community, is a system. As a human being you are a complex, intricate system comprised of other subsystems such as tissue, a circulatory system, blood vessels, organs, emotions, and beliefs. The story above describes a system of interrelated jungle, blind men, and elephant subsystems. As a system the Universe contains unified galaxies, which include planets, which may have integrated ecosystems holding communities, which include families, and so on. And systems are the playing fields of conflict.

A system can be defined as a *complex grouping of things*. As has been done cross-culturally for millennia, for our purposes we will use the circle to symbolize a system.

Tribal cultures build their homes and conduct community meetings in a circle, the recognized symbol of wholeness and unity. In the Japanese tradition, the round symbol denotes "mu" or "no-thing," which recognizes that we can see only a small piece of what a system actually encompasses.

Whenever I draw a circle,
I immediately want
to step out of it.

— R. Buckminster Fuller

Systems constantly emit and receive energy. When two or more living systems come into contact, the energy or "information" of those systems begins to interact. If any of the information exchanged between the interacting systems is disparate, if something doesn't fit, their co-created system or relationship moves into a state of change or conflict. This disruption will intensify until one or more of the participating subsystems evolves and the information they share can become harmonious. Then the co-created system returns to a state of stability. For example, in nature, water, heat, and atmosphere often meet and disagree. Together these elements exchange energy and in conflict create clouds. In their chaotic battle to find stability the clouds may be transformed into gentle rain or turbulent storms. After a time, homeostasis or balance is found, and clear skies once again bring peace.

A WORLD OF SYSTEMS WITHIN SYSTEMS WITHIN SYSTEMS

INTERCONNECTED SUBSYSTEMS

All systems constantly dance between chaos and stability. For example, my husband and I have different beliefs about purchasing cars; he likes to buy new cars, and I don't. Each time my husband has presented the possibility of a new car purchase over the past twenty years, our relationship system usually moved into conflict. These purchases are not only related to whether or not we need a new car (in the iceberg analogy, what is seen above the surface) but are connected underneath to issues about joint decision making, control of common finances, and our individual priorities. Our differing beliefs about money and cars, formed far before we were married, are tested and refined each time.

Over the years, we have tried different tactics. I have compromised, and we've bought a new car I did not want. Other times, my husband has relented and not bought the car he desired. When we chose to ignore our

To you I'm an atheist. To God I'm the loyal opposition.

— Woody Allen

differences or to try to intimidate the other into silence, our subsequent car conversations were more intense and uncomfortable. We have become stuck in conflict over this issue from time to time, something we will address in a later chapter.

However, our most lasting and beneficial solutions have not included compromise or coercion. It is a continuing process, but I can say that when we are willing to incorporate one another's perspective and seek an answer that meets both our needs, our relationship improves. It becomes easier to determine whether we should buy a car or not as our belief systems become broader and more aligned. And we've learned that our initial positions often hide other wants and needs underneath that can be met independent of buying or not buying a car. This issue has created a valuable playing field for us to discover more about marriage and finances.

A SYSTEM IN CONFLICT

In conflict, systems are active. Conflict creates energy, or *creative tension*, which encourages the participating subsystems to move and evolve.

Meanwhile, all systems seek a balanced, stable state. In human terms, when a relationship is disrupted by conflicting needs or events, when it is filled with creative tension, it pushes its members to "figure it out!" Creative tension is that nagging feeling that keeps you up at night and pushes you to resolve outstanding issues. Think of creative tension as an invisible visitor who stands between distinct systems and prods them to learn from one another. It is the energy of the relationship system at work. Creative tension coaxes perceived opposites to dance together until their "information" becomes harmonious.

Each system holds a unique and important perspective on their particular problem. Depicting with circles how this initially appears in the elephant story, we might draw the systems as separate entities:

God is day night,
winter summer, war peace,
satiety hunger.

— Heraclitus of Ephesus

MAN AT THE TAIL   MAN AT THE MIDDLE   MAN AT THE TRUNK

They each believe that the other is simply wrong. The other travelers are seen as stupid, as having faulty reasoning, or as "blind" to the truth. We see this vision in many arenas of our daily lives. For example:

We are led one thing
at a time to that pure gain
— all that we lose.

— William Stafford

Pro-life   Pro-choice
Logger's use of forest   Hiker's use
Boss's strategic plan   Employee's vision of the future
Father's parenting style   Mother's approach
Parents' favorite dinner   Children's favorites

However, in the case of the blind men, and indeed in every conflict, one perspective or solution that encompasses the whole of all sides exists. It is a solution in which everyone can be right and allowed to remain in one piece. The elephant story teaches that since we are blind yet interconnected, we must listen to and incorporate as many different voices as possible to understand the greater reality and find an appropriate solution. The sages purposely do not end the tale so we may recognize ourselves that the only action the blind men can take to reach resolution is to work together.

The cross-cultural definition of a win-win solution is to arrive at an overarching, encompassing viewpoint. This conflict resolution approach is described in every tradition I have studied and is depicted in a number of the major religions' foundational sacred symbols. The symbols picture a conscious meeting of impossible opposites until transformation can occur. The Christian tradition uses the almond-shaped intersection between circles called a *mandorla* to represent an attitude that allows all sides to be right and develop something larger than any side could create alone.

Using the *mandorla* symbol, a resolution to the tale might be illustrated as such:

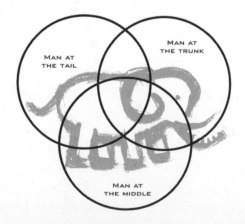

No man is an island, entire of itself; every man is a piece of the continent, a part of the main . . . any man's death diminishes me, because I am involved in mankind; and therefore never send to know for whom the bell tolls; it tolls for thee.

— John Donne, *Devotions upon Emergent Occasions*

The *mandorla,* the Italian word for "almond," has been used throughout the history of Christianity to describe the *resolution between impossible opposites* such as light and dark, heaven and earth, God and human, and male and female. Medieval church windows place the Virgin Mary and Christ within the *mandorla* to signify those who integrate the perceived irresolvable opposites of heaven and earth. Probably a pre-Christian symbol, the *mandorla* adorns the tops of wells in the British Isles and was used by early Christians as a secret sign that one was among friends. It has reminded us for centuries that we can always find common ground between the most unworkable differences.

In this process, we must remember that all win-win solutions are also win-lose. At a minimum, to find the elephant or to create a *mandorla,* each blind man must relinquish his initial solution. For example, what the man at the tail experienced could be true, that is, that he found a long, rough, cylindrical object, but he must be willing to let go of his assumption that he is holding a rope. He will also have to abandon the belief that he can resolve this complex problem alone.

Multiple *mandorlas* create the Buddhist symbol of the lotus flower. We intersect circle after circle of multiple parties, expert opinions, community perceptions, history, and more to build the almond-shaped petals of this sacred image. The lotus flower as a whole then represents the largest view of reality, or in Buddhism, it becomes life itself.

The *mandorla*'s Chinese equivalent is the Taoist yin/yang symbol. The intersection of the opposites of black and white honors unity in diversity and forms the philosophical foundation of this ancient Asian tradition. The methodology of Sun Tzu's *The Art of War* is based on Taoism and this symbol.

The Art of War's terminology of battle and destruction (*taking the enemy,*

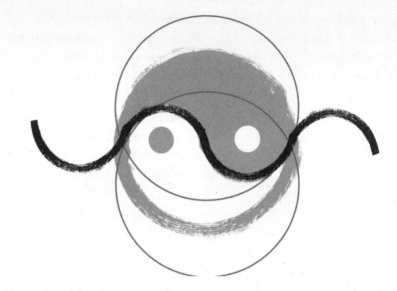

You never change things by
fighting the existing reality.
To change something,
build a new model that makes
the existing model obsolete.

— R. Buckminster Fuller

We have the means
and the capacity to deal with
our problems, if only we can
find the political will.

— Kofi Annan

commander, and *army*) can be confounding; however, its philosophy is one of lasting peacemaking and win-win solutions. Sun Tzu describes the *mandorla* approach: "The object of all conflict should be to take the enemy whole." This point encompasses not only taking the physical body but also preserving the enemy's perspectives, stories, and other resources. "Taking the enemy whole" is to let everyone remain whole. Instead of annihilation, it is holding the belief that you *and* your opponent are correct, that everyone's wants and needs are relevant, and that all this information can create an expansive, lasting solution. All parties are respected and incorporated into the resolution. The objective is to find a result in which everyone comes out whole and satisfied.

When everyone is protected the greater system, of which the opponents are an integrated part, is nurtured, which keeps not only your enemy but also you safe. However, following this objective is more than an act of self-preservation. Only when you completely incorporate the other into a solution is the battle truly won and stability again brought about. Sun Tzu knew that you might win a battle through destruction, but to win the overall war you must incorporate the enemy and leave them whole. This was a painfully clear lesson when the world left Germany in financial ruin after World War I. The Third Reich quickly waged war once more in an effort to return to economic wholeness. This result not only wrought World War II but eventually necessitated a new policy of reconstruction and the development of the United Nations.

By taking the enemy whole, Sun Tzu believed that resolution could bring everyone to something *larger than either side.* It is said that when one intersects a white and a black circle using this approach, the resulting *mandorla* is never gray but is a *pavanis,* or the colors of a peacock's tail. Resolutions created with the *mandorla* objective always leave the players

in a better position than either could create alone. When taking the enemy whole is the object of the game, the players complete play feeling energized and transformed. Sometimes we are only able to see a small *pavanis mandorla* at first and might decide to agree to disagree in other areas. Regardless, it is within the *mandorla,* the place of "both/and," that wholeness occurs and relationships are nurtured and strengthened.

The almond-shaped *mandorla* also symbolically represents the entrance to the womb or cave. Spiritual teacher Sobonfu Somé says that the African Dagara tribe believes there are portals to other worlds or universes hidden in rocks and caves. Caves are commonly used to symbolize doorways to new worlds and possibilities, as we can see in the Christian resurrection story. In quantum physics, we have the theory of multiple universes that exist and continue in unison. By entering the *mandorla* doorway, we can jump into a new universe. This mind-blowing concept allows that anything is possible, since we have millions of universes from which to choose.

Win-win solutions that serve as entrances into new realities can be hard to fathom. Think about the world we lived in before the invention of fertilizer and irrigation. Our entire perception of how civilizations could be fed, the necessary size and location of a planting field, and overall human health standards drastically shifted after we developed these expansive and creative solutions to our food-production conflicts. Other

The most exciting phrase to hear in science, the one that heralds new discoveries, is not "Eureka!" but "That's funny…"

— Isaac Asimov

We cannot solve our problems with the same thinking we used when we created them.

— Albert Einstein

examples of famous win-win solutions that have created global quantum shifts are the invention of penicillin and the confirmation that the sun, not the earth, is the center of our solar system.

When we take the enemy whole, conflict becomes a vehicle for traveling to new and better worlds. Systems working together, represented by two circles creating a *mandorla*, become the portal, or the wormhole, as it is known in physics, to take us there.

CHAPTER 6

Introducing Conflict's
Four Quarters

I exhort you also to take part in the great combat, which is the combat of life.

— Plato

A mother and teenaged son lived in a small apartment. This arrangement worked well until the son fell in love with grunge music and brought it into the apartment. The mother, up to this point, had enjoyed listening to classical music and meditation tapes on their common stereo. Since she relished spending her free time with her son and listening to music together, the son's new musical choices disrupted the balance in this household and created conflict.

Over the following weeks mother and son battled back and forth about the merits of their respective musical preferences. The battle continued to intensify and moved their relationship into a chaotic state. The son believed that his mother was valuing neither him nor his choices. The mother felt disrespected, misunderstood, and frustrated with the "horrid" music her son continued to play. Neither wished to speak to the other or be in the same room.

Then a creative whim took hold. In an effort to break their impasse, the son decided to mix a tape containing selections from his favorite music that he believed his mother might also enjoy. *The relationship returned to stability as the pair listened to this tape together. The mother realized that she had been miscalculating not only her son but also his choices. They laughed together as the young man was only able to find a quick stanza in some songs that suited his mother's tastes. The tape allowed them to feel newfound respect for each other and created a doorway to sharing the stereo, their common space, and each other's company.*

Chaos is necessary to new creative ordering. This revelation has been known throughout time to most human cultures; we just needed the science to help us remember it.

— Margaret Wheatley

With all the systems of the Universe, the path to conflict resolution is a journey through four distinct stages. First, when any discordant information is introduced into the current system, for example, the grunge music in the story above, it *disrupts* and begins the conflict process. Next, the system moves into some degree of *chaos* as it attempts to understand and adjust to the information. In the third stage, the system creatively adapts or *evolves* to the change. Last, once the information is fully incorporated, it will return to *stability*. From galaxies to groups of people to bacteria, this familiar cycle repeats itself throughout the Universe.

CONFLICT PROCESS

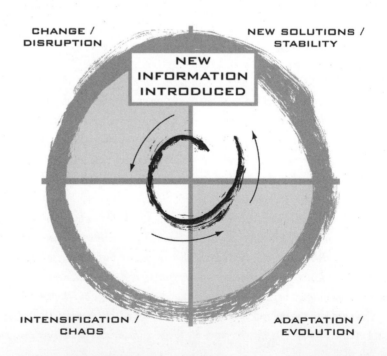

Place a half-full glass of water on a table, letting it settle into equilibrium. Then change the water "system" by adding another drop. Watch how the waves bounce off the glass's edges and into one another, creating chaos. In the third stage, the water adapts and finds new stability as it incorporates the new droplet and moves into balance once again.

Some systems, including human beings, can refuse to adapt or can be unable to incorporate a change. The elephant disrupts the system of the three blind men. The story ends before the blind men are able to incorporate this change and adapt. As we read this story, we are all left stuck in the second stage of conflict without a solution. In the next chapter we will discuss how to cope with "getting stuck" in one stage. For now we need to recognize that only when we make it to the fourth stage, or stability, can a conflict be considered complete.

In nature we often see conflict. Chaotic systems create *fractals*, or infinitely complex objects, when their disrupted elements push against one another. For example, a cloud or a hurricane is a fractal created between air, heat, land, and water. Galaxies are also fractal spirals created as gravity and matter push and shift. Wherever you find a fractal spiral in the natural world, change, conflict, and chaos are at work.

We often try to get control of a dispute by focusing on the details. Scientists teach us that this is an unproductive and frustrating pursuit. Documenting conflict is like trying to measure a coastline, the classic fractal example. From afar, it looks easy, but as you work to map even a square mile, you find unique bends and curves within each bend and curve, which are comprised of even more similar yet ultimately immeasurable shapes. With conflict, documenting past discussions, memories, and interconnecting relationships will quickly get you mired in data with no hope of understanding the overall picture.

To work with conflict, we will use the same methodology that scientists use to study fractals. Since all chaotic systems are too complex to quantify, systems theorists do not focus on discrete data but instead work with *rhythms* and *patterns*. The beauty of fractals is that they are self-similar. A small portion of a greater fractal will display patterns that are similar to the greater system. So even when we can see only a small part of a conflict, we can gather information on the greater whole. An implicit

Fall seven times.
Stand up eight.

— Japanese proverb

To see a world in a grain of sand and a heaven in a wild flower, hold infinity in the palm of your hand and eternity in an hour.

— William Blake

order or personality appears when we monitor any portion of the system's flow and response.

Like the hurricane and the galaxy, the fractal image that best represents human conflict is also a spiral that moves through four distinct phases. Sometimes, as change is introduced and incorporated, systems may return to partial stability and will continue around the conflict wheel an additional one, two, or, as in my spousal battle over automobiles, six or more times. Complex or intense conflicts most often demand multiple turns around the dance floor.

The human mind always makes progress, but it is a progress in spirals.

— Madame de Stael

CONFLICT'S PATTERN THROUGH FOUR PHASES

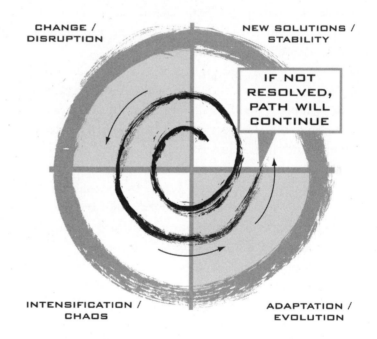

And there is the circle or the cycle, without which there is chaos, meaningless succession of instants, a world without clocks or seasons or promises.

— Ursula K. Le Guin,
The Dispossessed

I have confirmed the relevance of the spiral pattern not only by observing thousands of conflicts but also by researching the epic stories of heroes facing challenges. For example, pick any great folktale or myth. A typical story begins as the hero is disrupted or put to a test. He or she then endures great trials and chaos, and the situation appears hopeless. Next, the hero becomes enlightened in some way, overcomes the challenge, and is then finally able to "return home" to stability. This four-part model forms the core of every great drama, from the Greek plays to modern movies and novels. These phases also appear in the Four Paths of Creation Spirituality as developed by Matthew Fox, as well as in Angeles Arrien's *The Four-Fold Way*. Through extensive research Fox and Arrien have documented four main spiritual themes or paths found respectively through the Christian mystical tradition and indigenous cultures. In the appendix I describe how these methodologies connect to the conflict process.

Cross-culturally, the spiral is considered the archetypal symbol of change whose result is "a new perspective on issues, people and places," according to Arrien. It is also a classic symbol of death and rebirth, celebrated in ancient dance, carved on pre-Celtic passage graves, and depicted in many ancient societies in the symbol of the coiled serpent. Each conflict will send its participants along a unique yet predictable path, just as each tennis match is one of a kind yet follows a similar game pattern. With some conflicts we may spend more time in a certain phase. Some disputes will loop multiple, maybe hundreds of, times through the four states, whereas others might disappear quickly as change is deftly incorporated into the system.

CONFLICT'S PATTERN THROUGH FOUR PHASES

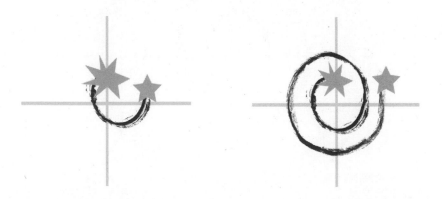

THE ELEMENTAL CONFLICT LIFECYCLE

The only important thing is to follow nature. A tiger should be a good tiger; a tree, a good tree. So man should be man. But to know what man is, one must follow nature and go alone, admitting the importance of the unexpected.

— C. G. Jung

Each conflict can be perceived as a fascinating stranger. It will have its own unique path and personality and, just like the disputants involved, it cannot be fully quantified. For thousands of years Eastern and Western cultural traditions have used earth, water, fire, and air to describe what we can see. For example, when we take a river sample, we find a unique combination of *water*, small pieces of *earth*, bubbles of *air*, and an inherent temperature, or heat *(fire)*. A plant, mountain, or cloud could be described in the same manner. Just as we have used the natural elements to discover the rhythms and patterns of the players, we can also apply them to uncovering the "personality" or components of a conflict.

As I studied the conflict process in detail, I noticed that each natural element's characteristics mapped well to each of the four conflict stages. Through its fractal spiral pattern, each conflict then becomes a unique combination of earth, water, fire, and air. Alchemy, the precursor of modern chemistry, uses simple symbols to denote the natural elements, which we now add to our conflict picture below:

The spiral is a spiritualized circle. In the spiral form, the circle, uncoiled, unwound, has ceased to be vicious; it has been set free.

— Vladimir Nabokov

CONFLICT'S PATTERN THROUGH ITS FOUR DISTINCT PHASES

EARTH
DISRUPTION

AIR
STABILITY

WATER
CHAOS

FIRE
CREATIVITY

Mapping the conflict phases to the natural elements makes it easier to recognize our location in conflict since each stage "feels" different. Every phase requires different techniques to move to resolution. In part

3 we will explore each phase's characteristics and required techniques in detail. Below I offer a brief overview.

PHASE 1: EARTH — CHANGE AND DISRUPTION

EARTH DISRUPTION

In this initial phase, we realize that we are in conflict. Here we must gather information and work with what *physically exists* today. We will solidify our positions, focus on our differences, and find critical sticking points. We often begin by trying to convince one another that our initial position is the best solution.

A common example is when an aging parent can no longer live alone. In one case I coached, three siblings gathered to discuss options after their father passed away, leaving their mother alone, who had begun to exhibit signs of dementia. The eldest wanted high-quality care for their mother and believed she should move into an assisted-living facility. The middle child wished to create consistency and proposed instead that a nurse visit their mother's apartment. The youngest sibling could not bear the thought of their mother being with strangers and thought that she should take turns living with each of the siblings. In this first phase, these grieving siblings spent hours on the phone, trying to convince one another of the merits of their respective approaches.

PHASE 2: WATER — CHAOS

WATER CHAOS

At this point, things take a turn for the worse. In the second stage no solution is evident, and some original gains can be lost. We might become confused, frustrated, or awash in emotion. This phase might be a quick shifting of gears, or it can become a drawn-out experience when we seek to destroy the opponents, feeling lost in a dark well and stuck with no escape in sight.

In the above example, at this stage the three siblings came to understand that none of their proposed options were feasible. After a medical consultation they realized that their mother was too ill to move into assisted care. Full-time home care was too expensive, and none of the

The science of alchemy I like very well, and indeed, 'tis the philosophy of the ancients. I like it not only for the profits it brings in melting metals, in decocting, preparing, extracting and distilling herbs, roots; I like it also for the sake of the allegory and secret signification, which is exceedingly fine, touching the resurrection of the dead at the last day.

— Martin Luther

children was able to care for their mother full-time. It is in this phase that the participants become discouraged or depressed, since there appears to be no answer to the dilemma.

PHASE 3: FIRE — EVOLUTION OR CREATIVITY

FIRE CREATIVITY

In the third phase necessity becomes the mother of invention and the *creative* juices start flowing. The opposing views are burned down to their core wants and needs. This information fuels the creative process, and new solutions begin to emerge. Time appears to speed up as an urgency to resolve the situation takes hold. This evolutionary phase may become overwhelming as the new ideas are matched with existing constraints in the search for a possible solution.

Returning to the three siblings, the mother eventually started a small kitchen fire when she walked out of her apartment while cooking eggs on the stove. In talking to the apartment supervisor, the children realized that this had happened three other times and that a change had to be made quickly. However, none of the children wished to place their mother in a nursing home. They began to piece together a plan in which the youngest committed to having their mother live with her on a trial basis if the other two would agree to adding a guest bedroom and paying for a part-time nurse. The eldest agreed to meet with an attorney to strategize on paying for their mother's care. The middle child took on the task of finding a competent nurse.

Many of us spend our whole lives running from feeling with the mistaken belief that you can not bear the pain. But you have already borne the pain. What you have not done is feel you are beyond that pain.

— Kahlil Gibran

PHASE 4: AIR — STABILITY

AIR STABILITY

In the final phase of conflict, we translate creative ideas into action, developing a solution or simply an expanded perspective. If we keep focused and communicating, the conflict may be resolved, or we may begin again at Phase 1, gathering more information and delving deeper. This phase holds the "winds of change." Implementation can feel daunting, but if we courageously stick with the details, a solid solution takes form.

It is in this phase that the three siblings will implement their strategy to care for their mother. They will add a guest bedroom and hire a part-time nurse. They will all try to make the agreed-on solution work. However, if the mother's health deteriorates or other changes occur in this family system, the siblings may begin another loop through the four phases to revamp or redevelop a proposed solution.

The overriding trick to the win-win method is to ensure that everyone playing feels safe enough to hold the creative tension through all four phases without seeking to run or to destroy the opponents. However, constant dangers wish to thwart progress. For the remainder of the book, we will spiral deeper and deeper into the game of conflict to gather techniques for keeping all its participants moving toward a balanced solution.

CHAPTER 7

Time on the Sidelines:
Getting Stuck in a Dispute

Prosperity is a great teacher;
adversity a greater.

— William Hazlitt

Like the blind men walking through the jungle, we too stumble along the
path of conflict as we confront different challenges. When the challenge
is too great we can fall off the conflict spiral and get stuck for a time in
a particular stage. All sorts of elephants will stand in our path; they are
part and parcel of the journey. Luckily, many lasting cultural traditions
have experienced these obstacles for thousands of years and have developed principles and practices for overcoming them.

We all have our unique physical, emotional, spiritual, and mental
comfort zones in which we feel confident and strong. For example, I can
walk at a certain pace without too much effort, and there are subjects I
can debate without much thought or emotional impact. However, if we
never push ourselves beyond or *to the edge* of our comfort zones, we never

improve or grow. David Gershon and Gail Straub, in their book *Empowerment*, call these boundaries our "growing edges." "Like nature, human beings who are vital and alive are always pushing out in new directions — they are growing.... *The growing edge is the point that our ever-evolving self is moving toward next.*" I find my growing edges when I try new activities, train at the boundaries of my physical capacity, or discuss polemical topics that stretch my emotional or intellectual boundaries. The job of the sports trainer and spiritual master alike is to take us to our limits and work us there until we improve. They create conflict so we may grow. "Stress exposure is the most powerful stimulus for growth in life," says fitness and professional trainer James Loehr.

The human brain is often described as a record of our physical evolution. The primary, reptilian, or survival-focused portion is located at the base of the spine. The secondary brain system is called the old mammalian or limbic system and houses relationship and emotion. The neocortex is the largest portion of our brain, consisting of the left and right hemispheres. Where the primary, reptilian brain focuses only on the present, and the secondary limbic system works in the past and present, the neocortex possesses awareness of past, present, and future. The neocortex hemispheres allow us to imagine and develop creative solutions and are the source of language and expression. Last to develop are the prefrontal lobes resting just behind the forehead, which appear to be connected to higher human values, such as compassion and empathy. Each system works with the other, and depending on our reaction to a situation, any of the four can act as the brain controlling our actions.

For example, on the edge, our reptilian, survival-focused brain and the ariagdala, a part of the limbic brain that stores memories of threatening experiences, try to take control of our actions and wrestle with the more developed neocortex. The fear system of our brain yells "stop," "too much," "run," or "fight," while the neocortex knows that the edge is the only place from which we can expand and learn. Through our daily practices and attitude toward conflict, we can determine which portion of our brain will run the show.

It is said in yoga that our limits reside where more of a stretch would

Should you shield the canyon from the windstorms you would never see the beauty of their carvings.

— Elisabeth Kübler-Ross

be too much and less would be not enough. This avenue of transformation holds the path through conflict. Conflict will take us to our boundaries to change us. The danger is that if we don't reach our edge we will stagnate and lose our ability to adapt. If we stretch beyond our edge, we cause injury. Luckily, a continuum of growth is available on the edge. We can stretch a little and grow a little, or we can stretch a lot and grow a lot.

Extending beyond our limits, we begin to rely on the reptilian brain or to move into survival mode, which operates only from a fight-or-flight state. Beyond our edges reside the actions of revenge, destruction, or escape. These are states of great stress that put our health and well-being at risk. Although it is natural to spin out, it is imperative that we take steps back toward center as quickly as possible.

Healing traditions that work with the elements would call going over an edge an *imbalance*. So if you are in the Water phase of conflict and you are pushed beyond your emotional edges, you will become imbalanced and stuck in the Water phase. You will simply have too much Water. Too much of any element can be destructive. We become mired in what Chinese medicine calls the "vices" of the element. Elemental imbalances throw us off the conflict spiral. In the Chinese and Indian healing traditions, when someone has too much of a particular element, activities or diets are prescribed to bring her back in balance and get the neocortex back in the "driver's seat." In the following chapter we will discuss some balancing techniques for when we fall over an edge and back into the reptilian brain. But for now let's examine what it looks and feels like to get stuck in each phase of conflict.

Conflict begins in the Earth phase. When too much change or disruption is introduced, I may react with a stark refusal to change. I cross my arms and say, "No, I am not moving." I become furious at those who present the new information. Inertia takes hold. If, for example, after I had been living in a committed relationship for years, a friend were to tell me that my partner had an affair, that might be more information than I could handle. My natural reaction would be to become angry at my husband and my friend or simply to refuse to accept the information. I could also spend months or years in this phase filled with rage or denial, becoming progressively more stagnant and fragile.

Unfortunately, the balance of nature decrees that a super-abundance of dreams is paid for by a growing potential for nightmares.

— Peter Ustinov

Next, the Water phase brings the powerful emotions of loss. When I have a lot to lose, I can become mired in hopelessness and despair. I believe there is no hope, that we are doomed, and that I am a victim of my circumstances. Think of common sentiments related to our environmental crisis: "What is the use of trying? There's six billion people eating up this planet — we are sunk." When stuck in Water, I refuse to look for solutions and choose to become a victim instead. Depression is a common by-product of being stuck in the Water phase.

OVER THE EDGE: STUCK IN THE FOUR ELEMENTAL PHASES

PHASE I - EARTH
DISRUPTION
REFUSAL TO CHANGE
DENIAL AND INERTIA

PHASE IV - AIR
STABILITY
REFUSAL TO IMPLEMENT
FEAR AND DOUBT

PHASE II - WATER
CHAOS
REFUSAL TO ENGAGE
HOPELESSNESS AND DESPAIR

PHASE III - FIRE
CREATIVITY
REFUSAL TO ADAPT
FRUSTRATION AND VIOLENCE

In the Fire phase, everything heats up, and I can become overwhelmed by the intensity of conflicting information. With too much pressure I might strike out and become verbally or physically violent, or, unable to see a way out, I may find refuge in my anger. W. E. B. DuBois, in the 1903 classic *The Souls of Black Folk*, described the pain of this phase through an internal battle of opposing belief systems: "One ever feels his twoness, — an American, a Negro; two souls, two thoughts, two unreconciled strivings; two warring ideals in one dark body, whose

When a man finds that it is his destiny to suffer, he will have to accept his suffering as his task, his single and unique task. . . . No one can relieve him of his suffering or suffer in his place. His unique opportunity lies in the way in which he bears his burden.

— Viktor Frankl,
Man's Search for Meaning

He led a double life. Did that make him a liar? He did not feel a liar. He was a man of two truths.

— Iris Murdoch

dogged strength alone keeps it from being torn asunder." It is here that tempers flare and I say all those things I swore I wouldn't. Stuck, I choose to oppress those who created the conflict.

In the Air phase, I need to try out the ideas found in the Fire phase so I can return to stability. I can "spin out" here if I am unwilling to implement. When the rubber meets the road and I want to apply a new idea, I can falter in self-doubt. If the stakes are high and much courage is demanded, this struggle with insecurities and anxiety can be stifling. We may become controlling and "fix" everyone else instead of taking personal responsibility. In a family conflict over alcoholism, if I spin out in this phase, I might try to reform the alcoholic, dissect the failings of other family members, and refuse to change my own behavior. Stuck, we will try to rescue instead of evolving.

In part 1, we identified our elemental conflict personalities. We learned that we each have proclivities or tendencies toward particular elements. You might lead with Water, and I might have more Fire. As a result of my connection to an element, I will also be attracted to the corresponding stage of conflict. For example, an Air person will naturally love the Air phase of conflict. It is where we focus on the mental aspects of a conflict and develop solutions, an Air person's strong suit.

Yet we do not seem to have these virtues without some vices as well. As an Air person I will also be more apt to get stuck in the stage to which I am most attracted. Air people obviously carry a lot of Air, or mental energy. The Air phase adds more of this energy. With too much of it Air folks can be pushed over their edge into high anxiety or imbalance. In the final phase an Air person is more apt to become overly controlling in an effort to hide their anxieties and doubt. They are the most likely to falter when it comes time to implement a new solution.

Using the four transforming gifts of asking questions, humility, acknowledging all viewpoints, and honesty can help bring those stuck on the sidelines back into play. The equidistant cross, which demarks the four phases and is this chapter's symbol, depicts balance. When we venture beyond our growing edges and move into a fight-or-flight response, we must rebalance. When we are off balance, it is tough to move. In the next chapter, we place another symbol at the center of the equidistant cross to foster our equilibrium as we search for a durable solution.

If you tell the truth, you have infinite power supporting you; but if not, you have infinite power against you.

— Charles Gordon

Vices are sometimes only virtues carried to excess!

— Charles Dickens

CHAPTER 8

Home Base:
The Power of the Center

*All life is interrelated. All men are caught in an inescapable network of mutuality,
tied in a single garment of destiny. Whatever affects one directly affects all
indirectly. I can never be what I ought to be until you are what you ought to
be, and you can never be what you ought to be until I am what I ought to be.*

— Martin Luther King Jr.

One day I attended a morning business conference in San Francisco with
my mother, who is an international management consultant. Looking
around I was impressed and fascinated by the pedigrees of the forty-five
business and nonprofit leaders, international speakers, and recognized
authors. I believed myself to be in good company, hanging out for the morning with folks working actively to be professionally and personally on top
of their game.

As we sat as a group, one participant, Travis, lamenting a possible
war in Iraq, said, "I think that win-win is simply rhetoric. It is not
possible; conflict is always a win-lose proposition." I was crushed. Not
here, I thought. How could he, as part of this group, buy into that

disempowering notion? How could this group "believe" that destroying or being destroyed was our only answer? This man was a force to be reckoned with: he was statuesque, well spoken, with solid credentials and a compelling British accent. What if all the other people believed him? Is it true that there is no hope?

I was filled with the fear that all these movers and shakers would give up and that there would be no hope for finding creative solutions to our current international and environmental challenges. I believe that we have to be willing to work together, or we place ourselves in great peril as a species. *"They should not believe him,"* I thought. Being all about win-win, my mother whispered, "You should say something," thereby assuring that I would jump into the fray.

"I disagree. I deeply believe in win-win solutions," I began. "I've seen them again and again in mediation and in my own life — solutions that are larger than either side can imagine." I added, "I'm trying to find a way to prove to others that win-win works." After a bit more rambling, I finished, feeling quite stupid, alone, and embarrassed.

I had fallen over the edge and was stuck in the Earth phase. I felt I had gone for a "win" by trying to discredit and destroy Travis's statement. When over my edge, I don't particularly like the other person, belief system, or situation that is pressing on my comfortable, stable world. When we have fallen over the edge, win-lose is our initial gut reaction. The beautiful irony is that my gut reaction partially proved the truth of Travis's pronouncement that all conflict was win-lose. Conflict frequently begins as a win-lose proposition.

In my better moments, I like to use the metaphor of the Universe being a massive window-filled tower. Every being is assigned to look out one window. Only by communicating what we see, what we know, will the larger vision of reality emerge. When I am standing in this tower, my opponents are usually looking at the windows opposite my own. I might see a sunny day, while others might see a tornado. In my example, looking out on the conflict landscape, I saw "win-win," and out of his window Travis saw only "win-lose."

A win-win solution holds a unifying objective at the center. We recognize that our enemies can be our allies. When we are willing to move

A person who never travels believes his mother's cooking is the best in the world.

— Kiganda proverb

The Earth is but one country, and we its citizens . . . you are the fruit of one tree and the leaves of one branch.

— Baha'u'llah

to the center of our grand tower and to combine our realities, a solution larger than both sides emerges. We are able to follow the Christian tradition's path of loving your enemy as yourself. Martin Luther King Jr. and Gandhi both based successful nonviolent win-win campaigns on their respective religious disciplines. Gandhi drew his strategies from the sacred Hindu Bhagavad Gita. King drew both from Gandhi and the Bible. Deeply religious men, they both attributed their ultimate success not only to the texts but also to the fact that they diligently followed daily spiritual practices.

So what separates a Gandhi from the Grand Inquisitor, who used religion as an excuse for torture? What separates win-win from win-lose solutions? In the mid 1960s the predominantly African American Memphis public works employees walked out over basic workers' rights. It was to their aid that Martin Luther King Jr. came, and it was there that he was ultimately assassinated. Protesters carried signs bearing the words "I AM A MAN," which became a unifying slogan for this battle and a cultural icon of that time. This slogan, embodying the truth that all human beings deserve equal treatment under the law, is a manifestation of the belief in the tower. We all deserve to be respected. Author and activist Matthew Fox calls this a belief in "royal personhood," when we are participating in interpersonal conflict.

To remain in balance during their journeys through conflict, both Gandhi and King placed this belief in royal personhood at the center of every protest and action to transform their countries. They believed that everyone was equal and had valuable information to share. Although our opinions may differ, they believed that we are all fundamentally the same, that we are all valuable and should be allowed to come out whole. To walk with Gandhi and be a nonviolent protester, or *satyagraha*, one had to make a commitment never to hate or disrespect the people against whom they protested so as not to render the campaign ineffective and damage the cause.

The moral of the elephant story is that only by collectively going toward the center will the three blind men find an answer. Each must see the other as an equal and critical contributor to the solution. They must recognize their interconnectedness. We, in effect, become the fourth entity in the story, which says, "It is only together that we will find a way

We hold these truths to be self-evident, that all men are created equal; that they are endowed by their Creator with certain unalienable rights; that among these are life, liberty, and the pursuit of happiness.

— Thomas Jefferson

*His life was gentle,
and the elements
So mixed in him, that Nature
might stand up,
And say to all the world,
This was a man!*

— William Shakespeare,
Julius Caesar

out of this jungle and understand what lies in front of us." In every conflict I have a choice. I can move away from the center and see myself as separate from another. I can hate and wish to destroy. Or I can remember that we are all equal and interconnected and strive to return to a balanced state. By remembering the core, along with its connectedness and equality, I am able to find the win-win solution. Without the center, everyone suffers.

This belief brings about a feeling of tranquility and relaxed concentration, which many of us would call "being centered" or being in balance. It is peaceful awareness, a state of grace and connection to the neocortex. It is when all feels right with the world and we feel that there will be enough time and space to arrive at a solution. Tom Crum, in *The Magic of Conflict,* states, "Centering is a real psychophysiological experience....It occurs when the mind, body and spirit become fully integrated in dynamic balance and *connectedness with the world around us.*" It is also when we perform best. Sports trainer James Loehr found that athletes give optimal performances during stressed conditions when their mental states can be described as relaxed, calm, energized, positive, automatic, effortless, confident, and focused.

By initially losing center, my gut response of destruction will get me nowhere except upset. I feel fragmented, alone, and miserable. I am afraid. When I am centered, finding answers becomes effortless; indeed, solutions seem to find me.

At a break during the conference, I walked around the meeting room. I noticed my internal conflict from this exchange with Travis. Taking a deep breath, I decided to practice what I preach and recognize that Travis was the best teacher I had had in months. As I shifted closer to center, new answers emerged to explain my definition of "win-win" and how conflict works.

At the center of our conflict drawing we now add a six-pointed star. Throughout the world, the six-pointed star symbolizes unity or harmony among perceived opposites. It is related to the *mandorla* and yin/yang symbols. The six-pointed star is a central symbol of Islam, Judaism, and Christianity that displays union between heaven and earth. Central to this symbol is the spiritual belief that all beings are sacred and that an inherent oneness connects us all. The star depicts an undying connection to unlimited possibility and a promise that a win-win solution exists to every problem.

Cross-culturally, the star describes a centered state where Earth, Fire, Water, and Air exist as one. In alchemy the star symbolizes a fifth element, *quintessence*, which is the union of the four elements and is always greater than the four separately. What my enemy sees and knows may be critical to my survival or sanity. The other sees what I cannot.

Buddhist monk, activist, and author Thich Nhat Hahn says, "Love is understanding, understanding is love." Travis and I are intimately interconnected as we stand in our single tower. To love him is to seek to understand and incorporate his perspective. At the conference, my "enemy" was speaking my own doubt and confusion, which my ego would not allow me to recognize. Travis was a brave voice that needed to be heard, since up to that point I had been tightly hanging on to my limited vision of "win-win" and I didn't want to hear about loss.

Travis was right; all conflict is win-lose. To find a unifying and satisfying solution, all parties must at least let go of their initial positions and their limited beliefs. I too was correct; win-win solutions are also real. By being willing to adapt his seemingly opposite beliefs and stay with the creative tension, I was able to embrace an expanded view of reality in which we both were correct. I evolved a bit at that conference, and I am grateful to Travis.

To maintain elemental balance, to return to the center, as I needed to in the above story, we must give equal value to all four elements. To bring a patient back into balance practitioners of Chinese and Indian medicine call on the opposing energy in the conflict picture. Note how a diagonal line connects each two opposing elements, Earth and Fire and Water and Air.

If you have spun out in the Earth phase, as I had with Travis, the energy of this element is very strong. You become like a mountain or an earthquake. You don't care about the future and are unwilling to change. You become overly righteous. To rebalance, we need to use the continuum between what is today or reality (Earth) and what is possible in the future (Fire). Fiery centering techniques can help move you from an Earth imbalance back toward the center.

Be assured that if you knew all, you would pardon all.

— Thomas à Kempis

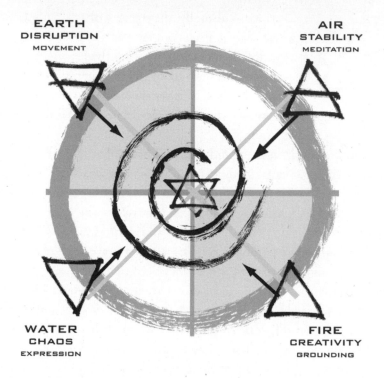

CENTERING PRACTICES FOR THE FOUR ELEMENTAL PHASES

EARTH
DISRUPTION
MOVEMENT

AIR
STABILITY
MEDITATION

WATER
CHAOS
EXPRESSION

FIRE
CREATIVITY
GROUNDING

Nobody cares if you can't dance well. Just get up and dance. Great dancers are not great because of their technique, they are great because of their passion.

— Martha Graham

Since any movement is considered a fiery activity, I most often go for a run or a walk to dislodge myself from the Earth phase. It opens my heart, the physical center of Fire. In contrast, when I am stuck in the Fire stage and overwhelmed with information, I call on the physical, or Earth, to bring me toward center and back into play. I ground myself. Just as in nature, Earth quiets the intensity of Fire, just as Fire transforms Earth.

The continuum between Water and Air holds the balance between emotions and rational thought. In Water we can become mired in feelings or our gut. In Air we can focus only on what is happening in our minds, becoming anxious and fearful. To balance out Water we use mental activities to draw us up from the depths. With an Air imbalance, connecting with our watery, emotional innards draws us down from restless mind games.

Below I offer four techniques for moving out of stages in which we are stuck and moving back toward center.

FOUR CENTERING TECHNIQUES

WHEN STUCK IN EARTH, MOVE!

When we are stuck in Earth, we cross our arms and say we're not moving. To progress from a refusal to change and jump back into the conflict wheel, we can employ the fiery practice of movement. All spiritual traditions include some form of movement. Running, skiing, and other sports in which you find your rhythm and raise your heartbeat help us to shift. Around the globe dance is used to facilitate change. Dance can take many forms, from disco in the kitchen to the disciplined study of ballet to the graceful dance of the martial arts. Martha Graham once said, "Nothing is more revealing than movement."

In addition to making you feel better, movement wakes you up to the greater pulse of the Universe. In many African languages, the word for *dance* is the same word for *breath* and for *spirit*. Gabrielle Roth, dance educator for forty years and the developer of the rhythmic movement system called the Wave, describes the connection we create when we dance: "We move in [the Mystery], we act from it, and we feel amazing power pulsing through us. It's as if all of life were rhythmic and pulsing. When we dance, we're right inside that pulse."

The Sufi whirling dervishes spin in circles for hours as a meditation practice. As they look over their left shoulder with an arm raised, it is said that they are searching for the Beloved, who is just out of sight.

The practice of *randori* in Aikido, or the fending off of multiple attackers by a single student, offers a beautiful example of dance. As the student spins to gracefully receive and deflect attacker after attacker, she becomes completely enveloped in the energies surrounding her. As one Aikido teacher once told me, "There comes a point where you become one and flow with the larger world. I have had mystical experiences where I have felt golden light fill my body in *randori*." I have been told similar things by tango dancers, ballerinas, and those who ritually practice yoga together.

If you are stuck in the Earth phase, take a walk. Attentive walking is a simple exercise that can expand our perspective and foster our appreciation. It is the ecologist or biologist's best tool for surveying the object of study. They ask, "Who lives here?" "What is new?" "What is the same?"

In my darkest times I have to walk, sometimes alone, in some green place.

— Barbara Kingsolver

"What has changed?" Any form of movement, be it walking or dance, can help us to tap into a greater perspective.

WHEN STUCK IN WATER, EXPRESS YOURSELF!

During the Water phase we are asking to "die" to the old so that the new may take form. Here we are dealing with grief that can become depression and hopelessness. To reengage and return to the conflict wheel, we need to express. A quiet way to move out of our depths toward problem solving is to express ourselves through writing. The following is a personal favorite journaling exercise that has saved me from many a bleak moment.

First, take five minutes to write about what's bothering you. Write about the conflict without stopping, even if you repeat the same sentences over and over. Write what comes up, even what seems like the most inane thought. Then write the answer to the question, "What would I like to see happen in the best of all possible worlds?" Write with absolutely no limitations. Write your dream, your vision for the future. Just write; in writing we reengage and begin searching for creative answers to troubles.

Another form of expression that all cultures use is singing. The spirituals of African American slaves and the township music of South Africans under apartheid helped those suffering to give voice to their overwhelming grief and emotions. Belting out "Amazing Grace" or intoning our sorrows and prayers has great healing effects. It reminds us that we are not alone, that others have also suffered loss and survived.

You can also simply talk to a friend, another form of confession. What is eating you alive? What is too awful or upsetting to express? When we give voice to emotions such as grief and sorrow, they move from being dragons that overwhelm us to angels that remind us what we have loved and move us toward what is possible.

WHEN STUCK IN FIRE, GROUND!

As we spin out in the Fire phase, we can feel that we are being burned alive. The situation becomes overwhelming. To temper an intense flame,

Give sorrow words; the grief that does not speak Whispers the o're-fraught heart and bids it break.

— William Shakespeare, *Macbeth*

You must understand the whole of life, not just one little part of it. That is why you must read, that is why you must look at the skies, that is why you must sing, and dance, and write poems, and suffer, and understand, for all that is life.

— Krishnamurti

pour some Earth on it. Reconnecting to our physical body with its own fulcrum can move us back into the game.

Physics tells us that every object has a small point somewhere within it on which the entire object can be balanced. A human's center of balance or gravity is located approximately two inches below the belly button. In the Eastern practices of yoga or Chi-Gong, this point is named your *tantien,* or original *chi,* and is considered the center or base of all the body's energy. The actual balance point or body center is consistently changing as we move and shift but it is into this power point we will now tap. Martial art Aikido masters Terry Dobson and Thomas Crum have translated the philosophy into simple steps to find your physical center:

- To locate your physical center, place a hand two inches below your belly button. Relaxing your chest, bring energy and focus down from the head and move it through to the center of the body. Bring energy up from the feet, through the legs to this spot. (Dobson notes that it is sometimes helpful to pretend that the eyes are now located at this spot.)

- If you keep breathing, you will find yourself feeling remarkably more stable and stronger, no longer a "pushover."

- As you practice, try moving your focus from your center to your head and back to center, and note the shift in your strength and stability.

We are rarely allowed such controlled conditions in conflict as we try to get our bearings and respond to another's pushing. Continue practicing and integrating this centered state by having another tickle the top of your head as he or she presses under your collarbone in an attempt to push you over. Try this both focused on the head and centered. Since many of our conflicts are verbal, have your partner pretend to fight with you as she or he presses on your chest. Focus on the words without centering and see where they seem to land. Where do you constrict and hold your energy? Notice the difference when you move this energy down into your own power source. Connecting to your body will help keep your creative fire burning under control and toward resolution.

I'm not centered.
I don't even know what that is.
But, I'm always centering.

— M. C. Richards

WHEN STUCK IN AIR, GET QUIET!

We have the gift of consciousness, and along with it come fear, doubt, and uncertainty. If a battle rages on the inside, it can mire us in confusion. Stuck in this phase, we often become overly controlling or constricted. Frozen with fear, we refuse to test new solutions or behaviors.

Meditation, or quieting the mind, can help relieve the constriction and fear associated with the Air phase. Yoga is a Hindu practice of meditation through movement. Although it is a complex system that includes rules of conduct, breathing practices, and advanced meditation techniques, called the "eight limbs of yoga," for our purposes we will focus on one of the practices called the *asanas,* or postures. Yoga is known for its healing and calming results for those suffering from stress (read conflict) and high blood pressure.

Yoga was developed thousands of years ago to quiet the mind, enhancing meditation and our connection to life. Today there are many schools or styles of yoga, from Iyengar to Ashtanga. In yoga, the yogi or yogini (male and female practitioner of yoga) flows from one posture to the next again and again over weeks and months. Here I have included an *asana* to help relieve fear and constriction, called *Savasana,* or resting meditation. Although it appears easy, this yoga posture is the most difficult, since it is your mind instead of your body that must be controlled.

Lie on your back. If your lower back is uncomfortable, place a pillow or rolled-up blanket underneath your knees. Hands should lie open at your sides with palms facing up. Everything should be completely relaxed. Scan your body and let everything go. Make your belly as soft as a newborn's. Let any expression melt from your face. Quiet your mind, releasing all thoughts of the past and future. Welcome thoughts as they arise, and then send them away, keeping your mind as empty as possible. Pretend you are like water, without form. Seep into the floor. Use the breath as a focus for your mind, and release all other thoughts. Stay in what's also called "corpse" pose for five to fifteen minutes, taking in the benefits of your relaxation. To release this posture, roll to one side for three breaths before sitting up.

A peace that comes from fear and not from the heart is the opposite of peace.

— Gersonides

SUMMARY

To play the game of conflict, we follow the spiral through the different phases of change, chaos, evolution, and stability. Sometimes we'll fall off and will need to rebalance and return to the process. We may even back up before proceeding. What holds us on the wheel and brings us back when we leave it lies at the center.

The center star symbolizes that in conflict our intention should always be to take everyone whole. In one of my all-time favorite books, *Centering, in Pottery, Poetry, and the Person,* author M. C. Richards calls centering the "discipline of bringing in . . . rather than leaving out. Of saying, 'Yes, Yes' to what we behold. To what is holy *and* to what is unbearable." Everyone is equal, as every part of us is. Everyone deserves our utmost honor and respect, regardless of their actions. Everyone and everything is accorded royal personhood, everyone is considered a valuable member of your team.

The Sanskrit term for meditation — Samadhi — means literally "mental equilibrium." It refers to a balanced and tranquil state of mind in which the basic unity of the universe is experienced.

— Fritjof Capra

CHAPTER 9

The Oldest Game in the Book

Life has meaning only in the struggles.
Triumph or defeat is in the hands of the Gods.
So let us celebrate the struggles.

— Swahili warrior song

Conflict is a universal tango that has been part and parcel of existence from the beginning. Quantum physics says that this never-ending dance started in the first microseconds of the Universe when a great disequilibrium or fluctuation occurred. At that moment, the Universe went from being in harmony into conflict. The imbalance created diversity, and without it, there would be no existence. If everything is the same, nothing changes. If nothing changes, it stagnates and dies. The Great Disequilibrium assures that we will have conflict until the Universe expands into nothingness.

Meanwhile, since its beginnings, the Universe has also constantly searched for stability, or what scientists call homeostasis. We all truly seek peace. The constant search for homeostasis, along with the Great Disequilibrium's creation of difference, assures an eternal universal flow between stability and chaos. Differing forces meet throughout the Universe each moment and push on one another in a search for stability and harmony, and they evolve.

In other words, we have to play this universal game as long as we live. Fortunately, engaging in conflict is good for you. It is this pushing

I am always between two worlds, always in conflict. I would like sometimes to rest, to be at peace, to choose a nook, make a final choice, but I can't.

— Anaïs Nin

between systems that keeps us, like the Universe, alive and vital. As self-renewing systems we must grow to survive, and creative tension instigates all growth. Brian Swimme and Thomas Berry write in *The Universe Story* that not only is conflict a foundational part of the Universe, but it is also what enables planetary structures and living creatures to blossom: "Every being that thrives does so in a balance of creative tension." It is only through an intricate play of obstacles or conflict between systems that healthy new forms in our Universe emerge, be they mountains, galaxies, or you!

Think of the father who refuses to accept his daughter's job choice or his son's new partner. Think of the business owner who refuses to let go of the idea that her company is the best in the industry as her competitors run her over. These are examples of those who are engaged in conflict yet refuse to evolve. We can see their fragility and understand that their stagnation causes them internal strife. Creative tension is ruthless.

In comparison, think of those you know who welcome learning and new ideas. Think of those who have worked through divorce, disease, and other challenges. We enjoy their vitality, wisdom, and peace. They spark us to take on new challenges and to expand. Conflict resolution experts Robert A. Baruch Bush and Joseph P. Folger explain in *The Promise of Mediation* that creative tension also supports our interpersonal well-being: "A conflict is first and foremost a potential occasion for growth in two critical and interrelated dimensions of human morality. The first dimension involves strengthening the self.... The second dimension involves reaching beyond the self to relate to others.... This may be why the Chinese have a tradition of using identical characters to depict crisis and opportunity."

When bad things happen, that's good. When good things happen, you don't need a philosophy.

— Mike Mathers

Martin Luther King Jr. understood the importance of creative tension to the health of societal systems as well: "Just as Socrates felt that it was necessary to create a tension in the mind, so that individuals could rise from the bondage of myths and half truths ... so must we ... create a land of tension in society that will help men rise from the dark depths of prejudice and racism."

Think of each conflict as an epic journey or grand experiment. *The Way of Conflict* method entails sticking with the battle until it is complete. All we must do is remain with creative tension long enough without destruction or surrender, and transformation will eventually occur. It is the way the force of conflict works. We might pass through some unknown terrain along the way, and our destination will rarely be a place we've been before. If we remember that we are just along for the ride the experience can even be enjoyable.

To summarize what we have discussed in these chapters, conflict is:

- the constant dance between systems.

- a source of evolution and growth.

- a repeated four-staged process that upon completion yields a lasting, win-win resolution.

- a game played best when all parties are seen as equal, interconnected, and valuable.

I refuse to be intimidated by reality anymore. What is reality? Nothing but a collective hunch.

— Lily Tomlin

To describe the overarching tenets of a complex concept, many cultures employ images. From the Native American medicine wheel to Tibetan sand paintings, sacred pictures, or mandalas, provide graphic representations of notions that extend beyond words. Mandalas contain a central image enclosed within circles, squares, or crosses. They are found in Zen temples, inlayed into cathedral windows, and painted onto sanctuary ceilings. Tibetan Buddhist initiates are sometimes given mandalas upon which they meditate for years seeking enlightenment. We even see mandalas in science, for example, in the atomic drawings of physicist Niels Bohr.

I often drew pieces of the following picture on a whiteboard when I taught. I hadn't thought much about my chicken scratching until one day a wise workshop participant, Rosemary, said, "What a beautiful mandala." She went on to teach me secrets about conflict that she had found by meditating on my hasty drawings. I felt like the blind man standing at the elephant's trunk finally listening to my companion at the tail, and I was amazed by what I had not seen. Each symbol of the conflict picture held information that, until I had met Rosemary, I had missed.

WAY OF CONFLICT MANDALA

*Know earth and know heaven,
then victory can be complete.*

— Sun Tzu,
The Art of War

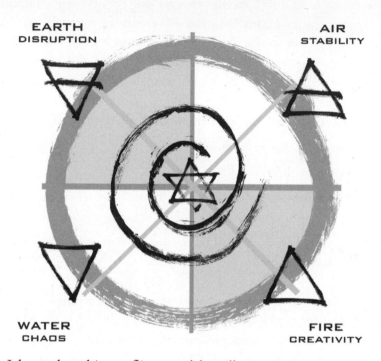

I hope that this conflict mandala will support you on your path through dispute. We will study this mandala in more detail in part 3 so that it can serve as a trusted map. Following Sun Tzu's advice in chapter 10 we will learn about Earth, or practical skills and techniques, to safely navigate stage by stage to creative resolution.

PART 3

THE ELEMENTAL PLAYBOOK

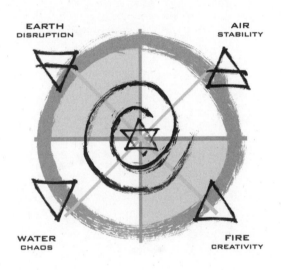

EARTH
DISRUPTION

AIR
STABILITY

WATER
CHAOS

FIRE
CREATIVITY

To the man who only has a hammer in the toolkit,
every problem looks like a nail.

— Abraham Maslow

My children play soccer, a fact that has assured that I'd be roped into coaching duty in our small town about a half a dozen times. However, I was always relegated to the primary-grade players since my babysitting qualifications far exceeded my knowledge of the game. From my husband, a fan of professional basketball and football, I've learned that every qualified coach on the sidelines owns a well-guarded playbook. It contains their favorite strategies, motivation tricks, and training techniques that they've refined over years of studying the game. They combine these pages with an intimate understanding of their players and their competitors and get paid the big bucks for their efforts.

In the game of conflict we are most often our own coach. Possessing a playing strategy with solid, practiced techniques is what separates the beginner from the master — much like what separates me from a World Cup coach. For millennia both professional warriors and spiritual sages, whose study was life's great struggles and challenges, have gathered their favorite conflict tactics in military and religious texts, in story and through symbol. I have broken down this part of the book into conflict's four stages, Earth, Water, Fire, and Air. Each chapter contains my favorite principles, skills, and tips taken from ancient sources and designed specifically for that stage. I have also included some scientific wisdom to demonstrate how ancient and modern thought are now merging in their understanding of the Universe.

Each phase of conflict contains the same elements of any good epic story. In any good grand tale, the hero must perform a task, for example, rescue the princess or discover the treasure. Using the conduct of the protagonist, the story teaches proper principles for conduct as he or she confronts challenges. The hero is also given magical gifts by an elder or stranger to make the journey easier. Following this multicultural model, each chapter in this part describes:

He who would know the world, seek first within his being's depth; he who would truly know himself, develop interest in the world.

— Rudolf Steiner

- a *task* to accomplish,

- an *elemental principle* to follow,

- the *challenges* to overcome, as introduced in part 2, and

- a transforming *gift*, as introduced in part 1, to help you and others through this phase's tough terrain.

Each chapter follows a similar format, including:

Seek not to follow in the footsteps of men of old; seek what they sought.

— Matsuo Basho

- a *folktale:* a classic story that highlights the key strategies and principles of the phase.

- an *introduction:* an overview of each phase's characteristics, tasks, and elemental principles.

- *practical tips:* simple techniques for applying the elemental principle.

- *art:* an easy art exercise, to make integrating the material more fun.

- a *real-life example:* a mini-biography of a leader who mastered the techniques and principles of this stage.

- a *summary,* in table form, of the chapter.

By combining information gleaned in parts 1 and 2 on playing styles and conflict rules with what you will learn in the following chapters, I hope you will find, as stated in *The Art of War,* that every victory is assured.

CHAPTER 10

Phase 1

Earth — Disruption

- TASK: Gather information
- ELEMENTAL PRINCIPLE: Appreciation
- CHALLENGES: Inertia and limited perception
- BEST ELEMENTAL GIFT: Ask questions

No man is wise enough by himself.

— Plautus

This is a story about King Arthur and his Knights of the Round Table. Fifteen hundred years ago, Arthur was riding through a forest in his search for the Holy Grail. Deep in this dark realm, he was surprised by a powerful man clad in black armor who pulled Arthur from his horse and pinned him to the ground.

"Arthur," the stranger says, "this is my forest and you shall die for your trespass. I will kill you myself, unless you can answer the question, 'What is it that women most desire?'" The king of this forest gave Arthur one year to answer the question.

Arthur went to his most trusted knight, Gawain, and told him of the agreement. Gawain promised to travel throughout the kingdom and interview every woman, from young maidens to aged crones, to find out what women most desired. And off he rode. Gawain did as he promised, speaking to every woman he could find throughout the surrounding lands. At the end of the year, he was satisfied that he had three sure

Peace cannot be kept by force. It can only be achieved by understanding.

— Albert Einstein

answers to this question. On his way home, he rode near the forest where Arthur had met the black knight.

Standing in his path was the ugliest woman he had ever laid eyes on. She had long stringy gray hair, funny warts all over her face, and a nose that came down to meet an upturned chin. And she smelled terrible! Gawain knew this must be Lady Ragnell.

"Gawain, you do not have the right answer to your question, you know," she remarked offhandedly. "Arthur is going to die." Gawain stood in shock; he had not told anyone his answers to the question, nor had he shared Arthur's possible fate. She must be a sorceress, a wise woman, someone to be reckoned with. "Gawain, I will tell you the right answer, under two conditions. First, you must include my answer with all the other answers. And second, if my answer is right, you, Gawain, will marry me. Within twenty-four hours of Arthur's pardon, we will be married. I want to ride in a golden carriage pulled by six white horses under garlands of flowers lining the streets to our new home."

Gawain said, "Oh, wait, Lady Ragnell. I already have three answers to the question, 'What is it that women most desire?' The most popular answer is, Women want to be respected."

Lady Ragnell sighed. "Yes, both men and women want to be respected just for who they are. That's a good answer, but incorrect."

Nervously Gawain replied, "Well, the second most popular answer is, Women want to be safe in their own homes."

Again Lady Ragnell sighed dreamily, "Yes, both men and women want to be kept safe. That's a good answer, but incorrect."

"The last most popular answer is, Women want to have sweet nothings whispered in their ear," Gawain blurted out. And Lady Ragnell replied with a tear rolling down her pocked cheek, "Yes, both men and women want to have sweet nothings whispered in their ears. That's a good answer, but incorrect."

Gawain thought, "She knows everything! And if her answer is the only right one, without it Arthur will die. But if her answer is the right answer, my life will be changed forever, perhaps forever ruined." For his love of Arthur, he agreed to the two conditions, and Lady Ragnell gave him the answer.

Gawain rode home with a heavy heart. He told the tale to Arthur, who then went into the forest to confront the king with four answers in hand. Arthur began, "What women want is to be respected." And the King of the Forest replied, "Yes, both men and women want to be respected. That's a good answer, but incorrect."

Arthur gulped and replied, "Well, the second most popular answer is that women want to feel safe in their own homes."

Just as Lady Ragnell had, the King of the Forest sighed with a far-off look in his eyes and replied, "Yes, both men and women want to feel safe. That's a good answer, but incorrect."

"Women also want to have sweet nothings whispered in their ears," said Arthur, noticing how similar to Gawain's experience with Lady Ragnell this was. The King replied with tears in his eyes, "Yes, both men and women want to have sweet nothings whispered in their ears. That's a good answer, but also incorrect."

With this, Arthur added, almost without thinking, "Shall we not forget that each woman most desires to get her own way?"

"You've been talking to my sister," screamed the King of the Forest. "You are free; now leave me in peace." Dumbstruck, Arthur left the forest. Sadly, Arthur and his wife, Gwenivere, broke the news to Gawain and began to plan the wedding. Within twenty-four hours, Gawain and Lady Ragnell rode in the royal carriage on cobblestone streets under garlands of succulent flowers. The villagers cried as Gawain rode by poised in his commitment to Arthur and to Lady Ragnell. That night in their new home, Lady Ragnell said, "Gawain, you now have certain duties to perform. Come here and kiss me." Gawain, again honoring the promise made, walked over to Lady Ragnell, and trying not to breathe through his nose, kissed her.

Instantly, in front of Gawain stood the most beautiful woman he had ever seen. And Lady Ragnell spoke: "Gawain, you have broken half of a wicked spell placed upon me. I can now be beautiful in the daylight and ugly at night, or I can be ugly by day and beautiful by night. Gawain, you decide."

Gawain thought and thought, weighing the advantages of each scenario. And then he spoke: "Lady Ragnell, this decision affects you more than me. Please, my lady, you decide."

And with that the spell was broken completely and they lived happily ever after, since . . . she had gotten her own way.

> Nothing in life is to be feared.
> It is only to be understood.
>
> — Marie Curie

INTRODUCTION

At the beginning of part 1, we met Blaze, Gene, Edina, and Amy as they discussed how they might save their company, Diamond Construction, from financial ruin. Their story, a composite of other real world conflicts, will serve throughout the playbook to illustrate each phase's characteristics.

Still sitting around the conference table with the team, Blaze was firm that he expected the problem resolved by the end of the month. He had been open to firing employees, but now he cringed as Gene told story after story about how a job loss would affect the young single parent, the man who cared for his ailing spouse, and the couple who had just moved from Iowa to join their firm.

Gene was clear that he could not work for a company that would fire thirty employees without a thought by month's end. It would be better to close up shop than to become another slash-and-burn business. He was tired of Amy's banter about profits and was not interested in Edina's litany about how they might scale back their annual holiday party.

Edina wanted to wait and see if their three outstanding construction bids were accepted. Edina and Gene had been dear friends for almost twenty years and had grown up in the same neighborhood. They had spent hours playing together with her younger brothers. But Edina was ready to fight Gene tooth and nail to keep the company alive. Secretly, she wondered if her marriage to Blaze would fail along with the business.

As they ran through different scenarios, Amy realized that firing thirty employees would not resolve their long-term problem, since their competitor, Ace Construction, had won all four major contracts in the city over the past year. They were in trouble — that much was clear. Sure, they had five construction contracts in progress, but with no new large projects booked, she was concerned. Deflated, she sat quietly, thinking of Ace's CFO and wondering what he might do in her place.

Over three days, the group gathered information on their financial and human resources situation. Each member threw out ideas to resolve their monetary challenges and just as quickly the others shot them down.

There is no security on this earth; there is only opportunity.

— General Douglas MacArthur

An adversary appears, and the Earth phase begins. We recognize the conflict, prepare for the battle, and engage. We then provide our different perspectives, often with an initial position on how to resolve the dispute. We assess our challenges and resources: What is the problem and what resources do we possess for solving it? The Earth phase continues until the parties recognize that no matter what they try, their individual positions alone will not create a lasting solution.

I equate the Earth phase with the opening scenes of a great story like the *Odyssey* or the *Iliad*. In the beginning of an epic tale, we meet the heroes and learn about their innate strengths and weaknesses. The stage is set with some sort of conflict or challenge, and the heroes must set off on an adventure. The Earth stage then continues until the heroes are lost and it appears there is no hope of returning home again. In Eastern, indigenous, and esoteric traditions "Earth" symbolizes our physical environment, or what exists today. This includes elements of the natural world (plants, birds, and trees), money, jobs, the physical body, and our current beliefs. As stated in *The Art of War*, it is the "high and low, broad and narrow, far and near, steep and level, death and life." During this phase, we find a disruption in our earthy environment and gather information from the world around us in order to better understand it.

From a sports perspective, in the Earth phase, a professional tennis player and a smart coach will watch videos of the opponent to understand his or her unique playing style. They note the "enemy's" rhythms and patterns, if he inadvertently indicates his next move and has favorite default shots. The coach and athlete also visit the venue or battleground and formulate a strategy. This initial stage continues as the players enter the court, acknowledge one another, and begin to play.

Initially, a wise military general keenly surveys the landscape. He identifies the potential opportunity and possible risks. The strongest army or warrior understands the enemy, the conflict, and the self. Quest stories of ancient warriors, like those of King Arthur, describe the tasks of the Earth phase. These tales are usually built around answering a question. The hero's success depends on keen awareness, the ability to objectively gather information, and a strict adherence to a warrior's code of conduct.

It requires a warrior's discipline to deal with our initial reactions to any confrontation. For example, as Gene models above, we usually would rather not hear our bothersome business partners' alternative perspectives. Everything would have been going along just fine up until this point, and our natural reaction is to deny the dispute or to be unwilling to participate. Just as we saw with our four friends, we often feel righteous indignation or anger toward our opponent. We struggle with a hope that our

Knowing the other and knowing oneself,
In one hundred battles no danger.
Not knowing the other and knowing oneself,
One victory for one loss.
Not knowing the other and not knowing oneself,
In every battle certain defeat.

— Sun Tzu, *The Art of War*

99

opponent and the conflict in general will just go away. Like Edina, we may wish to deny the issues and procrastinate if at all possible. The challenges of the Earth phase are formidable and require control and consistent self-responsibility.

The Earth phase is "warrior's work." *The Art of War* was a training manual on the skillful warrior's strategies and discipline. The archetype of the warrior can be found not only in military realms but also in the scientific and spiritual. An AIDS researcher, for example, can be defined as a medical warrior. Joanna Macy speaks of the ancient prophecy of the Tibetan Buddhist Shambhala warrior who uses the two tools of insight and compassion to fight injustice.

The sage warrior knows that we must prepare for battle. In *The Four-Fold Way* Angeles Arrien explains how cross-culturally the trained warrior always "shows up" for the battle and respects the positions of all concerned. The warrior archetype abides by a code of conduct. Gandhi, Martin Luther King Jr., Rosa Parks, and Jonas Salk were all disciplined warriors.

At the beginning of each chapter in this part, we will overlay similar cycles and symbols upon the conflict mandala to describe it in more depth. So that this conflict map may become a clear navigation tool, we will first explore how the four stages of conflict can be mapped onto a twenty-four-hour day, as seen in the figure on the following page. For example, the Earth phase of conflict can be described as occurring from noon to dusk.

During the top two stages, Earth and Air, we work with what is known or what we can see and touch. Here we focus on the existing structures, the physical constraints on our rational thoughts. Using the example of Diamond Construction, the task of the Earth phase is to understand the structure of the current situation, for example, in the case of our four friends, financial statements, employment contracts, and booked construction projects.

In comparison, the more chaotic and confusing Water and Fire phases concern what is yet unknown in the dark of conflict. We can associate the light with the conscious and rational and the night phases with the unconscious, or world of dreams, waiting, and potential. It may seem strange that conflict begins at noon instead of at the beginning of

Wisdom outweighs strength.

— African proverb

THE FOUR ELEMENTAL PHASES THROUGH A SYMBOLIC DAY

the day. However, in many cultures the beginning of change is ascribed to the afternoon, or to the fall, when things begin to decay. The dark, or night, then becomes the rich center of conflict. This model takes into account the potential of the night, of the Dreamtime, as it is called in the Aboriginal tradition. Morning in the last phase of conflict holds en*light*-enment, or the dawning of a new reality.

Returning to the iceberg analogy, the Earth and Air phases are above water, and Water and Fire reside unseen beneath the surface. Whereas the Earth and Air phases work with *form* we can see and touch, Water and Fire are connected with a conflict's underlying *essence*. Essence is the possibility or the *opportunity* hidden in a system. My "essence" makes me who I am, even though my "form" has changed innumerable times as I have grown from baby to child, from child to adolescent, and so on. Both form and essence are critical components of any system, be it a conflict or a human being.

Anthropology demands the open-mindedness with which one must look and listen, record in astonishment and wonder at that which one would not have been able to guess.

— Margaret Mead

In the Earth phase, we want to use the daylight to work with what lies ahead. The world is filled with information that can be helpful in the battle. Our Earth research began in parts 1 and 2 as we explored the unique personalities of the players and of the conflict. To take the fullest advantage of the opportunity hidden within the dispute, we will now gather information about the current situation. To keep everyone engaged, we commit to and abide by an internal code. We will "show up" and survey the battleground, searching for the conflict's Holy Grail. We will employ the elemental gift of asking questions, as in the story above when the question was asked, "What does woman most desire?"

ELEMENTAL PRINCIPLE: APPRECIATE

The more we know about our situation, the better prepared we are to resolve it. By gathering as much information as possible we can determine how to take everyone whole, or in the words of Lady Ragnell, how to *let everyone get their own way.* The better Blaze and his friends are able to understand their finances, market trends, customers, and one another's perspectives, the better prepared they will be to develop a lasting solution. So when in the Earth phase adopt the attitude of *appreciation.*

ap·prec·iate . . .
2. to be fully conscious of . . .
4. to increase in value . . . to appreciate — is to exercise wise judgment, delicate perception and keen insight in realizing the worth of something.

— Webster's Dictionary

The meaning of the word *appreciate* encompasses respect, keen awareness, and gratitude. To appreciate is to be open and astonished. We practice being fascinated with our object of study. Black-belt martial artists, our modern-day warriors, model this attitude in their opening bow. This salutation says, "Thank you for this opportunity to learn. You are a great teacher, and I am watching carefully. Teach me what you know."

Often in this phase we fight against an inherent disinterest in change. We are not willing to see our opponents as teachers, nor do we care about their perspectives. We want to destroy them, to run away from them, or to stay where we are without budging. *Appreciating* the situation and your opponents is a powerful counterbalance to the flight (denial), fight (anger/destruction), or freeze (inertia) responses. Recent neurological studies show that it is impossible for our brains to engage in a state of appreciation and a state of fear simultaneously. Although one may alternate between these states, they are mutually exclusive.

From a scientific systems perspective, appreciation is defined as *openness to new information.* The strongest systems continually exchange information with their environment. By being open and willing to gather new information, systems paradoxically will be healthier and more stable. Systems that practice appreciation are less affected by random changes in their environment and can more easily adapt. Systems theory analyst Margaret Wheatley states, "Openness to the environment over time spawns a stronger system, one that is less susceptible to externally induced change....Because it partners *with* its environment, the system develops increasing autonomy from the environment and also develops new capacities that make it increasingly resourceful."

The lasting cultural traditions use the interdependent disciplines of *gratitude* and *awareness* to teach appreciation. The Buddhist tradition calls appreciation "mindfulness." In mindfulness practice, we are taught to focus on the present moment, to take in all we experience with gratitude. In turn, by being grateful for everything in my situation, I am more aware of what surrounds me.

In many spiritual traditions we are asked to appreciate not just those who make life easy, but also those who make it difficult. His Holiness the Dalai Lama explains, "In Buddhism in general, a lot of attention is paid to our attitudes towards our rivals or enemies. This is because hatred can be the greatest stumbling block to the development of compassion and happiness....So, from this standpoint we can consider our enemy as a great teacher, and revere them for giving us this precious opportunity to practice patience....Just as having unexpectedly found a treasure in your own house, you should be happy and grateful towards your enemy for providing that precious opportunity."

In the Earth phase we explore the differences that caused the conflict to learn more about our present reality. Our diverse perspective gives us clues into what we may have missed in the past. As Brian Swimme and Tom Berry explain in *The Universe Story,* "At the heart of the universe is an outrageous bias for the novel, for the unfurling of surprise in prodigious dimensions throughout the vast range of existence....The universe comes to us, each being and each moment announcing its thrilling news: I am fresh. To understand the universe you must understand me."

Those that make you return,
for whatever reason,
to God's solitude,
be grateful to them.
Worry about the others, who give you
delicious comforts that keep you from prayer.
Friends are enemies sometimes,
And enemies friends.

— Jelaluddin Rumi

The battle is not to the strong alone; it is to
the vigilant, the active, the brave.

— Patrick Henry

Focus on appreciating each party's perspective and needs. In the case of our four friends at Diamond Construction, all involved need to appreciate Blaze's wishes for the company along with Gene's insight into the employees' needs. They need to discover what each founder knows about the current financial mess and to answer the question, What do they all most desire for the future?

Look for a long time at what pleases you, and longer still at what pains you.

— Colette

PRACTICAL TIPS

TIP 1: DEVELOP A CODE OF CONDUCT

Every spiritual tradition contains a code of conduct. Whether it is the Ten Commandments of the Jewish and Christian traditions, the ten virtues of Buddhism, or the *yamas* (abstinence from violence, lying, and greed) and *niyamas* (observance of purity, acceptance, and study) of Hindu yogic tradition, every religious system prescribes similar guidelines for working together. Gawain and Arthur were successful because they held fast to personal rules of engagement. The values spelled out in their story follow a standard code of ethics. As the story explains, *"both men and women"* should always:

1. Be respected.

2. Be kept safe and sound.

3. Have "sweet nothings" whispered in their ears.

4. Be able to get their own way.

The characters in the legend model a code of conduct. Gawain respects both Arthur and Lady Ragnell and demonstrates how to create safety in relationships. He appreciates all that Lady Ragnell is by whispering "sweet nothings" in her ear at the end of the story. It is only through Gawain's commitment to his rules of conduct that the evil spell over Lady Ragnell is ultimately broken.

We articulate our values and commitments in conflict through following *ground rules.* Ground rules are the basic agreements that are made when in conflict. Like going by a rulebook in sports, following ground rules is a great way to extend respect to all parties in a conflict, to define the playing field, and thus to make all parties feel safer. Although each conflict is unique and may require unique ground rules, here are a few guidelines to keep the conflict fire burning under control:

BE RESPECTFUL

- Never interrupt, engage in name-calling, or intimidate.

- Be willing to contribute and listen.

- Create an open forum so that all issues can be discussed. Treat everyone's opinion as valuable.

- Make all participation in discussion voluntary, respecting others' needs for privacy and space.

CREATE SAFETY

- Keep other parties not immediately involved in the conflict out of harm's way by not discussing it with them. All dealings, issues, and frustrations should be kept confidential.

- Agree to identify all the parties in the conflict. Players feel safest when they know with whom they are playing.

- Select a time that honors everyone's schedules. Are you a morning person? Is the end of the day a good time to settle in to talk? Jan, an observant business associate of mine, has mapped out her customers' "good" days and "bad" days and refuses to call them during less than optimal times.

- Create a safe location. Using neutral territory as the playing field can improve everyone's sense of safety. Select a space free of distractions to keep the conflict energy flowing. If you are battling with a child, as an adult, your height, weight, and position of power immediately put her into a less than safe position. Meeting with others in their territory and at their level can increase their sense of security and keep them interested in participating.

Exactitude in some small matters is the very soul of discipline.

— Joseph Conrad

Much of chanoyu [Japanese tea ceremony] involves training one to see the world around us.... To see, in chanoyu, is to let the distorting lens of social custom and valuation fall away, and to perceive and appreciate things for themselves.

— Kakuzo Okakura

WHISPER SWEET NOTHINGS

- Point out *what is going right and what you appreciate about the other parties.* Where do we all agree? What has each team member contributed? Who has displayed courage and integrity? Both men and women love to hear sincere positive statements "whispered in their ears."

STRIVE TO LET EVERYONE GET THEIR OWN WAY

- Commit to finding a solution that honors everyone's underlying wants and needs.

- Be willing to explore options and to let go of initial positions.

- See everyone as equal and valuable participants.

TO EXPLORE

What rules of conduct will you follow, regardless of others' approaches in conflict? Can you develop ground rules that foster team respect, safety, and appreciation? Begin every meeting with a review of or commitment to these ground rules. Post, model, and return to them as a discipline.

TIP 2: COUNT YOUR BLESSINGS

The greatest teachers throughout history have purposely created conflict to change and expand their students' perspectives. The strange King of the Forest acts as the elder of the story by asking, "What does woman want?" and creates a life-or-death dilemma. Many figures such as Jesus Christ, Buddha, Socrates, and Muhammad also posed difficult questions to their disciples and used those questions to turn the world on its ear. For thousands of years, Zen masters have presented paradoxical *koans*, translated as "problems," to enlighten their pupils. Students seek master teachers to be tested and transformed. In these traditions conflict is a spiritual discipline.

However, our initial response to conflict is most often fear or its emotional cohort, anger. We confront a natural aversion to change, and the potential loss it brings, and often we automatically move into a fear-based fight-or-flight response. It seems no coincidence that all the

Gratitude makes sense of our past, brings peace for today, and creates a vision for tomorrow.

— Unknown

Reflect upon your present blessings, of which every man has many — not on your past misfortunes, of which all men have some.

— Charles Dickens

traditions that use conflict as a spiritual discipline also use a daily practice of "counting blessings." We are advised to give thanks or to appreciate all that we have been given. As author John Updike once said, "Ancient religion and modern science agree, we are here to give praise. Or, to slightly tip the expression, to pay attention."

Neurology now proves what these traditions have known for centuries. Dr. Dan Baker, clinical psychiatrist and author of *What Happy People Know* explains that by completely focusing your mind on what you value and believe to be a blessing, "you have a shield from fear." Appreciation moves us into the neocortex, where creative and objective processing occurs.

When I was diagnosed with basal cell carcinoma on the tip of my nose, I was terrified by the words *cancer* and *surgery*. In my fear I was unwilling and unable to do the needed research to appreciate the risks, surgical options, and possible complications. I went to the same-day surgery center six weeks later unprepared. I was shocked by three painful surgeries, the size of the excision, and an eventual skin graft. Several surgical and pain management options would have been much to my benefit, but I wasn't aware of them.

In the weeks after my surgery I was terrified of the medical profession, the sun, and the future. I didn't want to go outside. My dread and misery worried my family. When I was lying in bed one morning, Dr. Baker's advice (coupled with what I had learned in my own spiritual training) ran through my head. I began, "Thank you for allowing me to be alive. Thank you for my children. Thank you for my husband." I felt better. I kept going, "Thank you for this day," and I pushed myself to list all that I valued and loved. After a few days, I amazed myself as I said, "Thank you for the carcinoma." I could actually begin to see how this conflict with my body and the sun contained opportunity and learning. Once I could appreciate my enemy, I began gathering valuable information about my continuing battle between light and skin.

TO EXPLORE

There are many ways to count your blessings, but Dr. Baker suggests the following few:

If the only prayer you say is thank you that will be enough.

— Meister Eckhart

The truth is, if you asked me to choose between winning the Tour de France and cancer, I would choose cancer. Odd as it sounds, I would rather have the title of cancer survivor than winner of the Tour, because of what it has done for me as a human being, a man, a husband, a son, and a father.

— Lance Armstrong

1. Spend three to five minutes, preferably three times a day, thinking about something you deeply appreciate, for example, friends, ice cream, your first kiss.

2. Construct a top-five list, such as top-five favorite foods or top-five things I love about my children.

3. Develop a list of the blessings of a crisis, that is, what you appreciate about a dispute or illness. Review this list every time fear arises when you confront the crisis.

TIP 3: IDENTIFY YOUR OPPONENT

Identifying exactly who or what we are fighting against is the first hurdle in conflict. Our opponent might be a person, an organization, or an entire community or culture. It may be within us, as a perspective that doesn't match our other perspectives. Our opponent might be an unchanging law like aging or death, or it could be a serious illness.

It isn't always easy to identify our enemy. Was Gawain's opponent the King of the Forest or was it *woman?* What happens when you stub your toe on a rock while engaged in a discussion? When you start yelling, doesn't it take a bit of sorting in the first few seconds to figure out if it is the rock, the person, or your clumsy feet that you want to throw across the street? Blaze may feel that Gene or Edina is his enemy, even though they are working on the common goal of saving the company.

To identify your true opponents begin within. Knowledgeable scientists always start with the discipline of discovering how they will affect an experiment. From understanding their preconceptions and biases, they work to gauge themselves and their influence on the situation at hand. Often our adversaries reside *within us,* telling us that it is not right to act a certain way or to possess some attribute, be it laziness or the ability to be successful. We thus attack anyone who proves us wrong. King Arthur's life was at great risk when Gawain initially saw Lady Ragnell. Gawain's preliminary disgust with her almost cost Arthur his life. However, as we saw in the legend, valuable information is often hidden in those who display despised traits. How can we look beyond what causes

Although the enemy is numerous, they can be kept from fighting . . .
And so prick them and know the pattern of their movement and stillness.
Form them and know the ground of death and life.
Appraise them and know the plans for gain and loss.
Probe them and know the places of surplus and insufficiency.

— Sun Tzu,
The Art of War

our bile to rise to identify and gather information about our opponents and the conflict?

Many traditions support the belief that others mirror our gifts, our faults, and our unknown facets for us to see. What we are unwilling to see in others is often what we are unwilling to recognize in ourselves. Those schooled in psychology would say that when someone gets under our skin we are *projecting* the unacknowledged or disliked parts of ourselves onto that person. When someone's impatience sends me through the roof, it is actually my own impatience being mirrored to me. When another teaches a class with perfection, it is actually my own potential I have seen. Although I may not inherently be a murderer, a liar, or lazy, I have the capacity to manifest all these characteristics and am choosing to ignore or repress this capacity. Because I have not yet made peace with the fact that I am all parts of this interconnected system, I may take out my blindness on another. Spiritual warrior Thich Nhat Hanh, who has committed his life to activism through nonviolence, explains our innate interconnectedness in his poem "Please Call Me by My True Names":

When a man's fight begins within himself, he is worth something.

— Robert Browning

> Do not say that I'll depart tomorrow
> because even today I still arrive.
>
> Look deeply: I arrive in every second
> to be a bud on a spring branch,
> to be a tiny bird, with wings still fragile,
> learning to sing in my new nest,
> to be a caterpillar in the heart of a flower,
> to be a jewel hiding itself in a stone.
>
> I still arrive, in order to laugh and to cry,
> in order to fear and to hope.
> The rhythm of my heart is the birth and
> death of all that are alive.
>
> I am the mayfly metamorphosing in the surface of the river,
> and I am the bird which, when spring comes, arrives in time
> to eat the mayfly.

I have had more trouble with myself than with any man I have ever met.

— Dwight Moody

I am the frog swimming happily in the clear water of a pond,
And I am also the grass-snake who, approaching in silence,
*   feeds itself on the frog.*

I am the child in Uganda, all skin and bones,
my legs as thin as bamboo sticks,
and I am the arms merchant, selling deadly weapons to
*   Uganda.*
I am the 12-year-old girl, refugee on a small boat,
who throws herself into the ocean after being raped by a sea
*   pirate,*
and I am the pirate, my heart not yet capable of seeing and
*   loving.*

I am a member of the politburo, with plenty of power in my
*   hands,*
and I am the man who has to pay his "debt of blood" to my
*   people,*
dying slowly in a forced-labor camp.

My joy is like spring, so warm it makes flowers bloom in all
*   walks of life.*
My pain is like a river of tears, so full it fills up the four oceans.

Please call me by my true names,
so I can hear all my cries and my laughs at once,
so I can see my joy and pain are one.

Please call me by my true names,
so I can wake up,
and so the door of my heart can be left open,
the door of compassion.

It is the mark of an educated mind to be able to entertain a thought without accepting it.

— Aristotle

Wilma Mankiller, the first female principal Cherokee Nation Chief, was asked why she wore a two-headed wolf pendant. Mankiller explained that the two-headed wolf represents who we are and what controls the daily choices we make. For each characteristic, there is a corresponding balancing energy, and both are critical for existence. With creation comes destruction. With patience comes impatience. With compassion we find indifference. We culturally place value judgments on particular traits. We say that it is "bad" to be impatient and "good" to be patient. However, if a two-year-old is about to run across the street, being impatient will save that child's life. Each trait is necessary and appropriate at certain times. As sage commanders, we need to know the complete potential of our internal armies and then choose when and where to use all these traits, turning them into strengths.

When we close our eyes to the traits we carry within us, we try to muzzle one head of the wolf. This head just grows angry, while we unconsciously use the unacknowledged trait in all types of unsavory ways. It is the mother slapping her children for being disrespectful. It is the daughter snickering to a friend about how judgmental and critical her mother is. The irony sometimes screams into our deaf ears. And sometimes it whispers.

Recognizing the two heads of the wolf within us provides us with great personal power. Arnold Mindell, in *Sitting in the Fire*, states, "If your friends tell you that you behave one way but you feel another way, you probably are repressing a part of yourself.... Or, if you claim to be open but secretly feel that you want to moralize and criticize others for their behavior, you may be confused when people become defensive around you. It's better to know yourself and state your views directly.... The point is not that you are whole and balanced, but that you are able to notice your one-sidedness and use it." Knowing we have a trait, we can then use it responsibly.

Look at everything as though you were seeing it either for the first or last time. Then your time on earth will be filled with glory.

— Betty Smith,
A Tree Grows in Brooklyn

Tell me what you pay attention to and I will tell you who you are.

— José Ortega y Gasset

TO EXPLORE

In this conflict, who is getting on your nerves? What attributes do you absolutely hate? In what package could a helpful guide appear in your conflict? Would you turn them away?

Make the assumption, just for today, that those repugnant people hold an important nugget of information for you. See what you find.

TIP 4: RESEARCH BEHIND ENEMY LINES

Just as Gawain rode throughout the kingdom asking his question, we too must fully conduct our research. This is not always an easy task, since we are always struggling against the *limits of our perception*. For example, as a woman raised in the Christian tradition in the United States, I have a limited understanding of what it is to be a Muslim male raised in Iraq. I need to gather information before rendering an opinion on the situation in the Middle East. Using the following four techniques will improve your information-gathering skills:

1. Change your point of view.

2. See the extraordinary.

3. Suspend assumptions.

4. Be a spy.

CHANGE YOUR POINT OF VIEW

By listening intently to the hideous Lady Ragnell, Gawain demonstrates the power of keeping an open mind. He traveled and continually changed his point of view as he tried to understand what it meant to be a woman.

We have the ability to expand our perspective and thus our appreciation by finding new ways to look for information that we might otherwise have missed. For example, we make assumptions about the size of things by where they sit in the sky. K. C. Cole, in *First You Build a Cloud*, says, "You can alter the size of the moon merely by changing your perspective. When you see the 'large' moon on the horizon, if you look at it upside down — say through your legs — so the perspective of the horizon disappears, it will suddenly appear 'small' again. Often we have to turn things upside down to see them in a proper perspective."

There are a multitude of ways to change your point of view. Make everyone switch seats halfway through a heated discussion. Pretend you are your opponent and describe the other's position until that other party says you've got it right. Ask your opponent to tell you about the conflict as though it were a myth or a fairytale. Stand on a chair, lie on

We die to each other daily. What we know of other people is only our memory of the moments during which we knew them. And they have changed since then. To pretend that they and we are the same is a useful and convenient social convention which must sometimes be broken. We must also remember that at every meeting we are meeting a stranger.

— T. S. Eliot, "The Cocktail Party"

Every hour of the day and night is an unspeakably perfect miracle.

— Walt Whitman, "Song of Myself"

the floor, go for a walk. Draw a picture of the conflict. Andy Warhol once said, "An art object can be looked at from three hundred and sixty different perspectives. I just forgot to do that with my own life." See everyone and everything in conflict as a fascinating stranger that can be explored from at least 360 viewpoints.

TO EXPLORE

We rely so much on our sight. One way to change your point of view is to remove it! Close your eyes when you are listening to someone. Have your team wear blindfolds for twenty to thirty minutes to discuss a selected topic. Talk to a friend in the dark. Notice how the conversation changes, where it feels different, what you learn, and what you hear that you might not have heard before.

SEE THE EXTRAORDINARY

When Lady Ragnell descends from the horse the elemental challenges of the Earth phase raise their wily heads. We see Gawain's *limits of perception* in his initial revulsion to Lady Ragnell. We also see how *inertia* has set in when he tells her quite proudly that he already has three perfectly wonderful answers to the question, "What does woman want?" However, through employing his initial ground rules or commitments, he demonstrates how to search for the extraordinary beyond what he thinks he knows.

One night, I watched a nature program on the camouflaging capabilities of animals. An octopus can move into a coral reef and transform its skin texture and color to exactly match its surroundings. It can mimic a sea snake, a plant, or a deadly eel to protect itself. I was moved to tears as I watched the awesome tricks and techniques of this sea creature. This experience struck me as an example of appreciation on two fronts. First, the octopus is a powerful natural example of appreciation. It understands its changing environment and adapts to it. It appreciates its enemy.

Second, I love to eat octopus. That is an ultimate conflict, the killing and eating of another. It was much easier not knowing about this beauty and intelligence as I ordered a plate of paella. My ease and

The universe is not a collection of objects, but a communion of subjects.

— Thomas Berry

Great Spirit…grant that I may not criticize my neighbor until I have walked a mile in his moccasins.

— Native American prayer

It's not enough to hate your enemy. You have to understand how the two of you bring each other to a deep completion.

— Don DeLillo

ability to exploit another is diminished whenever I develop more understanding of him or her. I may continue to enjoy octopus, but I hope it will be with greater reverence. Learning or remembering an opponent's story is a practice in appreciation.

Without appreciation, in some part of ourselves we can pretend that we are completely separate. We make it simple: you are evil, and I am good, so you must be destroyed. We go to sleep, or our mammalian brain goes to sleep, and the reptilian brain overrides it in its fear for survival. At an extreme, it makes it possible for an eleven-year-old boy in Sierra Leone to cut off the hands of another. When he was interviewed, he said, "It is not me, it is someone else that does these things. I feel so terrible that these things have happened." It is easier to hate another if I do not realize that she's had a terrible day, is afraid, insecure, or just seeing the situation from a completely different perspective. If I can close my eyes to your wonder and humanity, I can continue in my hate, anger, or evil.

Once upon a time a man whose ax was missing suspected his neighbor's son. The boy walked like a thief, looked like a thief, and spoke like a thief. But the man found the ax while digging in the valley, and the next time he saw his neighbor's son, the boy walked, looked, and spoke like any other child.

— Lao-tzu

TO EXPLORE

To remind myself how infinitely complex and awe-inspiring the people with whom I battle are, I reflect on some extraordinary facts listed in Matthew Fox's *Sins of the Spirit, Blessings of the Flesh*:

- "If the DNA in our bodies' cells were uncoiled and laid end to end, it would reach to the moon and back 100,000 times!

- Three million replacement cells are manufactured in bone marrow each minute.

- One human body contains a hundred times more cells than there are stars in the galaxy.

- The human eye can respond to light over a range of 1 trillion to 1, whereas the detectors we have made so far have a range of only 300 to 1."

We are extraordinary beings. Let yourself be amazed. List a dozen facts about your opponents that you find surprising. Can't list a dozen? Don't engage in conflict with that person or team until you can.

SUSPEND ASSUMPTIONS

As we read in the legend above, "That's a good answer, but it's incorrect," we learn about the danger of making assumptions. Gawain had jumped to the conclusion that he was ready to return to Arthur, assuming that he had the right answers. He was so convinced he almost didn't listen to Lady Ragnell. If Gawain had not been willing to suspend those assumptions, Arthur would have lost the forest and his life, and Gawain never would have married his beautiful bride.

Often we don't ask questions in conflict since we figure we already know the answer. Recognizing assumptions is a critical part of breaking through our limited perception and resistance to learn more about our enemy. Assumptions are our shortcuts to decisions. They help us get to action in a pinch, a process that has come in handy during our evolution as a species. Yet we often make long chains of assumptions, creating our own perspectives of reality. However, as K. C. Cole points out, "If even one of those assumptions is just a little bit wrong, our perceptual conclusion will be a great deal wrong."

Since we begin developing our assumptions as young children, it is not always clear when we jump to conclusions. In *Fifth Discipline Fieldbook*, Peter Senge advises us to *suspend* or unearth assumptions when we are in dialogue with others. By detecting our assumptions and just letting them hang out we can check if they are valid. Having assumptions isn't the issue; it is knowing what they are that is.

Gathering information takes practice. If we jump to the land of conclusions and false assumptions, we will miss valuable information and alternative perspectives, creating our own desolate island. Alternatively, *The Art of War* explains that, "[f]aced with chaos or conflict, the sage commander looks first to the largest reference point. No matter what ground he has been given, he always thinks bigger. Loosening his gaze on the immediate and short term, suspending his habitual view, he looks to the space around things. . . . He is careful not to fixate on a particular way they might manifest and thereby avoids insignificant skirmishes."

From a martial arts perspective, this quality is called "beginners' mind." When a student achieves a black belt it is acknowledged that she has now just *begun* to practice. Black-belt artists assume they know

That life is worth living is the most necessary of assumptions, and were it not assumed, the most impossible of conclusions.

— George Santayana

"Now will you tell me where we are?" asked Tock as he looked around at the desolate island.
"To be sure," said Canby; "you're on the Island of Conclusions. Make yourself at home. You're apt to be here for some time."
"But how did we get here?" asked Milo, who was still a bit puzzled at being there at all.
"You jumped, of course," explained Canby. "That's the way most everyone gets here. It's really quite simple: every time you decide something without having a good reason, you jump to Conclusions whether you like it or not. It's such an easy trip to make that I've been here hundreds of times."

— Norton Juster,
The Phantom Tollbooth

115

nothing and must begin again as though they were new students. They make no assumptions.

TO EXPLORE

To practice suspending assumptions, answer the following questions: If I told you I was a middle-aged father of four, what assumptions would you make? What car do I drive? What do I look like? What are my politics? What is important to me? What are my passions, fears, and hopes? How old am I, for that matter? If I started to raise my voice in conflict, what assumptions would you make? Extend this practice to listening to another player speaking. List all the assumptions you are making about him and the issue he is discussing.

WALK A MILE IN YOUR ENEMY'S SHOES: BE A SPY

Lady Ragnell is the consummate spy. She understands the enemy, be it her brother or "woman" in general. And just like any spy worth her salt, she must strike a deal in order to provide any information.

To know your enemy, be your enemy. In addition to asking questions to understand the other's position, you can take other actions to understand your adversaries. Be or employ a "spy" and slip into the other's world. For example, you are battling with your son over his teenaged choices. Drop intelligently and humanely into his life and suspend your adult assumptions. With a subtle touch, listen to his favorite music and the conversations in the back of your car between his friends after school.

You don't have to be sneaky, just to ask sincere questions. My wise and articulate teenaged son Cameron is usually happy to explain what I am missing. I asked him one day, when wondering what his future career would hold, what he loved and was passionate about. He smiled and said, "Mom, I'm a fourteen-year-old boy. All I think about is sleeping, food, and girls."

The practice of spying not only provides you with benefits; it compliments and values the other. We all want to feel important, interesting, and worth another's investigation. Your *sincere* willingness to understand creates goodwill and, in turn, willingness in your opponent to understand you.

The Soul unto itself
Is an imperial friend, —
Or the most agonizing spy
An enemy could send.

— Emily Dickinson,
"Life, The Soul Unto Itself"

From infancy on, we are all
spies; the shame is not this but
that the secrets to be
discovered are so paltry
and few.

— John Updike

It is critical that you be honest about your intentions when spying. What deal are you entering into? Are you willing not to use the information provided to discipline your son? If not, the results can be disastrous for you and the relationship. How often have you been asked a question and felt your heart seize up? A voice inside screams, "The data you are about to give may be used against you: *stop!* Say nothing of importance." Gathering information about another requires:

1. Employing the ground rules of respect and safety for all players, including spies.

2. A clear contract: What are you asking for and why? Is it to destroy or to take your enemy whole?

3. An understanding that the opponent is also spying on you.

Since we can only control our own actions, it is critical to check your intentions. A good self-check before any interchange is to ask, "Why am I having this conversation? What do I want?" We need to be honest about our assumptions about both our opponents and ourselves.

It is knowledge that ultimately gives salvation.

— Mahatma Gandhi

TO EXPLORE

Look for spies. Information sources such as magazines, websites, conferences, and books can provide a wealth of information gathered from behind enemy lines. Look to those who watch the rhythms and patterns of the players in question. For example, advertisers can tell you a lot about the desires and fears of teenagers, mothers, and baby boomers. It is the job of many organizations like trend research firms, hate-crime watch groups, and lobbyists to gather just the information you might need.

ART OF CONFLICT: CREATE A PORTRAIT

A biographer or a painter knows how to appreciate a subject. The artist searches every nook and cranny to understand the nuances and inner workings of their model. This is what turns a simple description of another's attributes into a work of art. Van Gogh's portraits of one mailman painted over multiple decades and his many self-portraits show more than a command of painting; they display a command of the person.

PAINTING THE PORTRAIT

I suggest completing all three parts of the following exercise, but even doing part A should yield some interesting results.

I don't paint things.
I only paint the difference
between things.

— Henri Matisse

PART A

1. Select a subject from a current conflict.

2. Pretend, if only for this exercise, that you are fascinated with your subject.

3. Write down everything that you know about your subject without stopping for as long as you can, in four sections: physical qualities, emotional qualities, history, and beliefs.

4. Write the answers to the following questions. What are the subject's:

    • Dominant physical characteristics?

    • Health issues?

    • Sources of stress?

    • Most important relationships?

    • Family members? (who are they? where are they?)

    • Greatest accomplishments?

    • Particular talents and gifts?

    • Greatest passions, fears, threats, or edges?

    • Overriding beliefs?

5. Circle any paradoxes or complexities you find.

6. Gather other points of view while appreciating your subject. Ask only, What do you know about this subject? If a response is, "Why do you ask?" only answer, "Because she fascinates me."

7. Note where you are lacking information.

8. Remembering that you are pretending to be fascinated with this person, try to gather the missing information without divulging your conflict.

PART B

1. Read through all the information that you have gathered.

2. Close your eyes and let all the information seep in.

3. On a sheet of paper, create your subject. The image you create doesn't even need to look like the subject. Crayon, craypas, paint, or pencil work well. You can make a magazine collage. Create as complete of a picture as possible.

Or:
Write a brief biography using the gathered information.

PART C

1. Write in your journal about this exercise and your experience doing it.

AN ELEMENTAL ROLE MODEL: MARIA MONTESSORI

Appreciation is a life skill. Maria Montessori, inventor of the Montessori school philosophy, is a real-world example of how mastering the capabilities of an appreciative warrior can globally revolutionize our treatment of children and their education.

Born August 31, 1870, in Chiaravalle, Italy, Montessori did not shine academically as a child but was known more for her strong will and commitment to service. At ten, when she was very ill, she told her mother, "Do not worry...I cannot die; I have too much to do."

The greatest of all gifts which [Montessori teachers] will bestow on [the children] is the gift of themselves.

— Maria Montessori

119

To pay attention, this is our
endless and proper work.

— Mary Oliver

Montessori went against the social norms of the day by choosing at sixteen to enter a technical college to study engineering. In 1892 she was the first woman in Italy to enter medical school. She adamantly refused to be a teacher, one of the few accepted female professions in Europe. Montessori gained national attention not only for being the first woman awarded a medical degree from the University of Rome but also for her calm, reasoned public speeches regarding the franchise of women.

Her vocation as an innovator of education began in 1897, when she was asked to work with mentally retarded children. By 1899 she became the director of a new school for mentally retarded children in Rome that she built on the radical idea that these children could be taught basic skills such as reading and mathematics.

Two years later, she returned to academics to study teaching. She was horrified as she observed classrooms of "normal" students. Witnessing rote chanting of the teacher's words, straight desks, and dull methods, Montessori discovered that poor teaching rather than poor students was the prevailing problem in Italy's education system.

How could children be effectively and respectfully taught? To answer this question, she opened the first Montessori school, Casa dei Bambini, outside Rome in 1907. Her goal was to create a safe and nurturing environment that respected the innate worth of all her pupils. She said, "I have come to appreciate the fact that children have a deep sense of personal dignity. Adults, as a rule, have no concept of how easily they are wounded and oppressed."

Montessori became fascinated with her subjects. She honored and respected the young children as she created pleasing and interesting teaching materials. She allowed them to "have their own way" by making all the materials accessible to the students to use when *they* were ready. She would then sit back and watch to see which materials were actually used, gathering information as she listened to the children's feedback.

She proved that children want to be independent, responsible participants. If given the right materials and respect, they will. Montessori once wrote, "When a child is given a little leeway, he will at once shout, 'I want to do it!' But in our schools, which have an environment adapted to children's needs, they say, 'Help me to do it alone.' And these words reveal their inner needs."

She found that children go through periods of sensitivity to different subjects between the ages of two and a half and six years. "During this time, their minds were open to learning in a different way than they were during any other age." Every Montessori instructor must appreciate the child and know which materials are appropriate to introduce during each sensitive period. Nothing is forced. Montessori believed that the child is the leader and that the teacher should observe the child and guide the flowering of the child's natural gifts.

Understanding how our drastic assumptions can cloud our thinking, she said, "We must be humble and root out the prejudices lurking in our hearts. We must not suppress those traits which can help us in our teaching, but we must check those inner attitudes characteristic of adults that can hinder our understanding of a child." As a result, Montessori's innate appreciation has transformed hundreds of thousands of souls into engaged, lifelong learners and participating members of society. By 1913 there were over a hundred Montessori schools throughout the world, and today more than four thousand can be found in the United States alone.

SUMMARY: EARTH — DISRUPTION

ATTRIBUTES	We land in the *Earth phase* when we: • Recognize there is conflict. • Work with what exists today. • Focus on convincing the other parties that we are right. • Confront anger or stubbornness.
TASK	The goal of this phase is to objectively *gather as much information as possible* about the conflict and its parties.
CHALLENGES AND ELEMENTAL PRINCIPLE	To overcome the challenges of *inertia* and *limited perception,* we practice the principle of *appreciation.* *Appreciation* is described by the spiritual traditions as *awareness with gratitude.*

TIPS AND TECHNIQUES	To improve our appreciation skills and breeze through the Earth phase it is helpful to:
	1. Develop and follow a *code of conduct,* remembering to:
	    • Honor and respect.
	    • Create safety.
	    • Whisper sweet nothings.
	    • Strive to allow everyone to get their own way.
	2. *Count your blessings.*
	3. *Identify all opponents in the conflict.*
	4. *Research* behind enemy lines by:
	    • Expanding your point of view.
	    • Looking for the extraordinary.
	    • Suspending assumptions.
	    • Being a spy.

VOCATION AND DISCIPLINE	Lasting cultural traditions have long used *warrior* training to develop mastery of the Earth phase. The warrior is expected to be *observant, mindful, honorable,* and *respectful* of everyone. The daily discipline of *physical centering* is advised for moving through this phase.
ELEMENTAL GIFT	During the Earth phase engage all parties in working toward a solution by *asking open and sincere questions.*
ART OF CONFLICT	*Creating a portrait* fosters appreciation skills and expands understanding.
ELEMENTAL ROLE MODEL	*Maria Montessori*

CHAPTER 11

Phase 2

Water — Chaos

- **TASK:** Relax
- **ELEMENTAL PRINCIPLE:** Separate
- **CHALLENGES:** Attachments and emotions of grief
- **BEST ELEMENTAL GIFT:** Humor and humility

Know the male,
Hold the female;
Become the world's stream.
By being the world's stream,
The Power will never leave.

— Tao Te Ching

This is a story from long ago; we attribute its earliest form to Aesop, the great Greek
fabulist of the sixth century B.C.E. There once was a tree, a great oak tree rooted on a
bank of a river. Next to this tree grew a little weed. It was not much of a thing, skinny
and green, rather silly looking next to this impressive tree. One day the tree looked
down and noticed this modest weed. He said, "You are a strange and ugly thing. Too
bad you are not like me, so beautiful and grand. I am rooted deep into the earth, and
my branches reach broadly to the sky. Too bad you are so meek and straggly." The weed
demurred to these pronouncements, not sure what was true but impressed by the weight
and girth of this huge form. "I am sure you are right," she said, "but I'm sure happy
not to be just a seed. I can go nowhere, so please pardon my presence."

One day the river swelled way beyond its banks. It swept up and over the weed. She bowed her head to the earth and let the water flow over her. She waited quietly in the stillness under the current until the river subsided. When she was able to lift her head once again, she looked around and found that the grand oak was gone. She asked, "Oh, great tree, where have you gone?" And she heard a fading reply, "I was torn from the bank and am now floating down the river. Oh, I should have been as supple and humble as you. Now I will die."

We must be willing to let go of the life we have planned so as to have the life that is waiting for us.

— E. M. Forster

INTRODUCTION

The situation appears to turn for the worse for the Diamond Construction team as Blaze, Gene, Amy, and Edina now dive into a chaotic phase whose watery depths can be dark and confusing.

As Blaze and the other owners of Diamond Construction sat around their paper-cluttered conference room, it was clear that firing thirty employees was not the answer to their crisis, nor was waiting for another contract to come their way.

Gene was adamant that if they fired thirty employees he would leave and they would need to buy him out, which would effectively end the company. No amount of intimidation from Blaze would change his mind.

"Where I come from," Gene added, "when a dog outlives his usefulness, we don't take him out back and shoot him. Our mission says we serve our customers and our employees," said Gene. "That's why I work here."

"We started out so strong, won every contract we bid on, and were voted the city's best working environment," Edina reflected. "What a terrible year, and with construction down and Ace winning every major bid in the past six months, I don't see a way out. I haven't slept in days; you know Blaze and I have everything riding on this business."

"I love what we've created together," Blaze added sadly. "I can't imagine working anywhere else."

Discouraged and miserable, the four sat in silence.

Cross-culturally, stories about water are often sobering, as is the Water phase. Water tales traditionally send protagonists to the depths of a river or sea to crawl along its bottom. Stories abound about the Water of Life, in which one sip of this elixir gives health and immortality, but to find it, one must travel far and usually lose much along the way.

During the Earth phase, we surveyed the landscape trying to understand the wants, needs, and limitations of each person's argument. We rolled up our sleeves and jumped in to "fix the problem." But sometimes, as can be seen in the story of Diamond Construction, the proposed solutions are not feasible. When there appears to be no solution, you have plunged into Water. We move from advocating for a solution to fearing that resolution is completely impossible. In this bewildering phase nothing is clear. It may last just moments as we shift gears or, unfortunately, it may drag on for months as we wrestle with the potential repercussions of letting go of our initial positions.

The Water phase is often the most difficult, since it feels as though you are at the bottom of a muddy well at midnight with no escape in sight. Depending on the issue, we may feel frustrated and depressed, wanting this phase to stop now! The fight-or-flight reflex really starts kicking in if we feel boxed into a corner. However, believe it or not, this is the richest and most potent time in conflict. In water tales, the humble and flexible are rewarded handsomely. All water must be allowed to flow freely, and when it is repressed in these tales, it ends up destroying even the innocent without discretion. We must relax into this chaos and flow with its current to move beyond what is to the grander what is possible.

If you try to save your life you will lose it. If you are willing to lose it, you will be saved.

— Mark 8:35

The ancient Taoist yin/yang symbol laid over our conflict mandala can provide us with additional insight into conflict's characteristics. The yin/yang icon shown in the figure on the following page represents our reality as comprising perceived opposites, such as female/male, chaos/stability, action/rest, and earth/heaven. Taoism believes that what we perceive as opposites are actually partial views of a greater whole represented as the circle.

The black and white also represent two different types of power. The black part, or yin, of the Taoist symbol is associated with the night, the land of emotions, dreams, and the "nonrational" or right-brain response. It is considered receptive, feminine, or magnetizing. The white part, or yang, of the symbol is associated with the day, that which we can see and touch, the action-oriented part of us. It is our rational, logical, and left-brain response.

The first phase of conflict, Earth, is an action-oriented time when we gather data by asking questions and doing research. We were working with what is available and visible. Then we move to the black of the Water phase. Things get murky, and we can't see where we need to go next. This is a receptive and emotional stage of conflict. We have to wait and just let things be as they are.

Our lives will be changed. Both our beliefs and our actions will become responsive.... But this will only happen as we allow ourselves to be engulfed by contradictions.... With Jonah, we will be delivered. But first, we will be swallowed into darkness.

— Parker J. Palmer

Conflict's lifecycle and the Taoist symbol

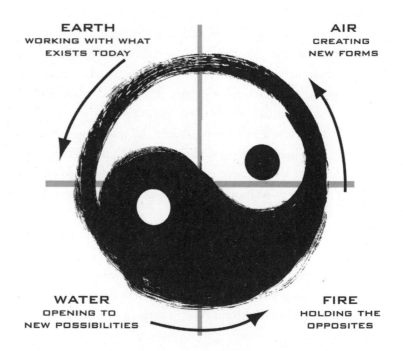

EARTH
WORKING WITH WHAT
EXISTS TODAY

AIR
CREATING
NEW FORMS

WATER
OPENING TO
NEW POSSIBILITIES

FIRE
HOLDING THE
OPPOSITES

Yet note that within the nucleus of all systems in chaos there are organizing principles and an innate order, represented by the white dot at the center of the dark. In Water we return to our core values and separate them from outdated approaches and beliefs. As Tom Watson Jr., former president of IBM, once said, "If an organization is to meet the challenges of a changing world, it must be prepared to change everything about itself except [its basic] beliefs." Blaze and his friends must now determine what is fundamentally important and open themselves to new possibilities as Gene steers the team toward addressing if "serving our customers and our employees" is such a core value.

From a sports perspective, this is the time when we "hit the wall." We may train harder, push our team to try that same play yet one more time, and remain stymied by our outdated approach. At the beginning of his career, for example, André Agassi practiced sporadically and was prone to outbursts. His style yielded mixed results, and he was not able to consistently win matches. Later he developed new strategies and training techniques and became the top-ranked player in the world. To win, we first separate from the old and assess what is possible. Once accomplished, we, like Agassi, can reemerge as top players wielding a new playing strategy and perspective.

Conflict asks us to let go of outdated beliefs and to evolve our perspectives. We are asked to change, which innately we know is a good thing. Yet change often triggers our hard-wired fear of death. It is not that we will die if we change, but some perceptions or old habits might need to go. When we let die who we are today so that our situation can improve, we must overcome the fear of loss, death, and pain. Being flexible to loss and rebirth is the task of the Water phase.

Water has long been associated with the obscure and turbulent river of our emotions, the unknown, and the ability to flow. It is the greater potential, the void from which all forms arise; just as all the plants, animals, and continents arose from the seas. In the Western tradition, it smacks of loss of control and depression, and we'd like to stay away from that dim pit for all we are worth. We are much more comfortable with the known and action-oriented rational "day" of conflict. Blaze and his friends do not know what to do, and they are justifiably miserable. As fear of failure and loss seeps into their minds, they suffer.

Thus it is in this confusing and often painful phase that conflicts begin to escalate into "wars," not just on an international level but also

There are so many little dyings every day, it doesn't matter which one of them is death.

— Kenneth Patchen

on the personal. Author Arnold Mindell defines a conflict as a "war" when the parties feel despair and begin to see their opponents as their enemies. It appears there is nothing more to learn, so parties may seek more power by considering some form of violence. We must watch for this type of escalation, since this is when wanton destruction occurs.

The "yin" phases of conflict are recognized throughout the world as a critical component of conflict resolution and of life. It is a time of letting go of outdated assumptions and beliefs. In the space created by this flexibility, new ideas and possibilities rush in. By reclaiming this phase and being willing to play through it, we will open ourselves to a wealth of creative solutions. We surrender our fixed positions. This is the phase of loss, and in order not to suffer, paradoxically, we must let go. Flexible, we become willing to look at the situation in new ways. Blaze and his friends might ask, Must we fire employees to keep the company afloat? Must the problem be completely resolved by the end of the month? Does the company need to continue? We now stretch beyond old boundaries toward what is possible.

ELEMENTAL PRINCIPLE: SEPARATE

There are several ways to conceive of this notion of being flexible. Imagine that our mind is like a fist. When we love something dearly, we want to hang on to it tightly, protect it, and never lose it. We make a fist and hold on tight. We will do the same when we deeply believe in something. True appreciation, the elemental principle of the first phase, creates this sensation. We take snapshots in our minds of perfect moments or ideals and want it to be like this forever. We become proud and possessive of what we have. And yet holding too tightly stifles growth and causes suffering. Like the great oak in our story, we become weak when we sink in our roots too deeply. Our children must be allowed to grow up, our construction companies to change, and our worlds to evolve. We have to let them go.

We can also think of appreciation and separation, the elemental principles of the Earth and Water phases, as the two parts of a breath. Think of appreciation as the dynamic action of inhaling, the making of a fist. In conflict separating is the natural receptive response of exhaling,

I have died so little today friend, forgive me.

— Thomas Lux

What is soundless, touchless, formless, imperishable, Likewise tasteless, constant, odourless, Without beginning, without end, higher than the great, Stable —
By discerning That, one is liberated from the mouth of death.

— Katha Upanishad 3.15

or opening the fist. Inhale, and fall in love with some idea, form, or person as they appear today, and hold them tightly, just as the four friends above love their company. Now exhale, letting them go to be as they are and as they need to become. There is constant creative tension between these two elemental principles of conflict. It is a dance between engaging, or falling in love with life, and recognizing that everything is impermanent and must change. We need a balance of both love and detachment. If I don't show up, I suffer. If I don't separate, I suffer. As a Zen koan teaches, *I must hold tightly with an open hand.*

The willingness to stand apart or to *detach* is taught in most spiritual traditions, from Christianity to indigenous cultures around the globe. We Westerners get stuck on the word *detachment,* since we often equate it with divorcing our emotions from a situation or no longer caring. Yet *detachment is the ability to let things be as they are without a need to control or change them.* In conflict, this is a critical skill to finding a solution that supports everyone as they are. *The Art of War* counsels us to strive to be *formless.* To be formless is not to take a fixed stand or to have absolutes. We learn to be comfortable in chaotic times of random change in which the next stage is not predictable. Comfort with change and chaos brings a conflict player many more options for resolution.

We are counseled to "ride the wave" of change and chaos that connects us all and leave behind all that we were sure of. In the spiritual traditions, this is the *way of the pilgrim* embodied in those brave souls who leave everything behind in search of ultimate truth. This is the way of St. Francis of Assisi, Muslim pilgrims to Mecca, and the New Scientists like Einstein who search beyond current beliefs and comforts to find unifying principles to serve humankind. These pilgrims:

1. are humble and have a good sense of humor.
2. are relaxed and able to stretch beyond their boundaries.
3. let go of attachments, except for a few core values.
4. create space for themselves and others.

We might think that following this way of the pilgrim makes us vulnerable, but in actuality when you are formless you are protected

BIRDWINGS

*Your grief for what you've lost lifts a mirror
Up to where you're bravely working*

*Expecting the worst, you look, and instead,
Here's the joyful face you've been wanting to see.*

*Your hand opens and closes and opens and closes.
If it were always a fist or always stretched open,
You would be paralyzed.*

Your deepest presence is in every small contracting

*And expanding,
The two as beautifully balanced and coordinated
As birdwings.*

— Jelaluddin Rumi

If you begin to understand what you are without trying to change it, then what you are undergoes a transformation.

— Krishnamurti

from your enemies. Your adversaries don't know how to find you to attack since you have no set configuration. They don't know any of the weaknesses of your fixed positions, because you have none. When you are formless you are flexible enough to select the most powerful and strategic form in the moment of action.

In *Built to Last,* Collins and Porras found that visionary and lasting companies are extremely supple and tenacious in resolving conflict. They are always prepared to kill, revise, or evolve an idea but do not give up on the organization. Even though each successful company that they studied held to certain unchanging core principles, everything else was up for grabs, be it their products, their organizational structure, or the market segments they served. Just as in nature, in which the longest-surviving species is the most flexible, those systems that are the most adaptable last the longest. "And who was there at the very beginning of multicelled life? You guessed it — the jellyfish.... They have outlasted animals with more bulk and brains. Their strategy for survival has been spectacularly successful: keep it simple and go with the flow."

PRACTICAL TIPS

TIP 1: LET EMOTIONS FLOW

The Water phase follows Nietzsche's saying "that which doesn't kill us makes us strong." In this phase you may be awash in dismay and depression or contending with those feelings in others. Try to stop these feelings, and you will find suffering or destruction close behind. Nor is this the time to give unsolicited advice or to tell another to "snap out of it."

The weed knew, when the water came, that it is best just to relax and bend your face toward the earth or be humble. Masters around the world tell us when we move into the dark, negative, gray-clouded, or watery path, we fare best when we are flexible and thus are able to let go of outdated beliefs. Ana Perez Chisti, a Sufi lineage holder, counsels that fighting against this phase and its emotional content only exacts more angst. She says only when we *relax* will we find our answers.

I invite you to think of the Water stage as gestation. During the Earth phase, you selected some land (the conflict at hand), gathered a

Faced with a reality which lies beyond opposite concepts, physicists and mystics have to adopt a special way of thinking, where the mind is not fixed in the rigid framework of classical logic, but keeps moving and changing.

— Fritjof Capra

Everything flows.

— Lao-tzu

bunch of seeds (information about yourself and your enemy), and planted those seeds. This is the time of letting that information mix with and be transformed by the conflict. Things will transform if we let the gestation process occur. Allow things to be as they are. Let everyone feel just what they need to feel. If we relax into this current of emotion the water will feed the planted seeds, and we will birth new plants in the Fire phase.

TO EXPLORE

Practice relaxation. Think of yourself as the weed. The raging water of this phase will pass; you just need to wait. Meditation, as described in part 2, can support this relaxation process. Find ways to go with the flow for a time. Give yourself and others permission to be discouraged and depressed. Fighting against emotions will only make them more pronounced.

TIP 2: LET IT BE A STORY

During the past decade I have collected folktales and told them monthly to my children's classmates. Year after year I tell stories of King Arthur, of dogs with eyes the size of windmills, and of talking animals. Month after month, at the end of the stories, at least one child in every classroom under the age of nine will ask me, "Is that story true?" In mediation after mediation as each side would describe what had happened and I heard multiple conflicting stories, I used to ask myself that same question.

Teachers from the beginning of time have used stories to teach. The story of the tree and the weed has been used for thousands of years to instruct about flexibility and humility. This is a powerful tool because we use stories to structure how we view the world. The tree's belief system lay in the story he told about being the most valuable and important plant around. Was this story true? Whether or not it was, it structured the oak's reality. The most powerful structuring forces are our creation stories. These stories describe where we came from and who we are in relation to the rest of the world. They tell if I am a wanted, supported, loved part of the world. They describe who is good and who is evil. Your belief in the world as either a good or a bad place is dictated

Space is the breath of art.

— Frank Lloyd Wright

by your creation stories. And these extremely important stories structure how you confront conflict. My belief that you are out to cheat me or there to support me is birthed from it.

For example, notice how often you hear the following story structures used to describe a conflict:

Something we cannot see, touch or get our hands around is out there, influencing life. Information seems to be managing us.

— Margaret Wheatley

- Once upon a time, everything was good.

- Then someone wrecked it by introducing something bad.

- Now we are separated from that perfect state and are not able to return.

- We are waiting for a powerful figure to come set things right again.

This story framework, derived from the dominant Western creation story of Adam and Eve, is continuously used to describe most conflicts, from our environmental situation to family issues and community ills. And yet it is not the only available "true" story. The new scientific description of the evolution of our universe tells a very different tale:

- *Conflict is necessary.* A stable system carries within it disorder. A chaotic system carries within it stability. All healthy systems must move back and forth between states of stability and chaos as they evolve.

- *Good and evil are relative.* It is impossible to fully quantify and judge overall good and evil when everything is complexly interconnected.

- *Both creation and destruction support survival.* The Universe is expanding in a continuing narrative, with destruction and creation playing equally important roles.

Joseph Campbell said that we should not underestimate the power of story. In fact, stories actually have a life of their own; it could be that *the stories* are using us to make themselves real. Professor of Religion at New York University James Carse says, "We do not go out searching for stories for ourselves; it is rather the stories that have found us for themselves.... Whole civilizations rise from stories — and can rise from nothing else.... The Torah is not the story of the Jews; it is what makes Judaism a story.... Myths told for their own sake are not stories that have meanings, but stories that give meanings."

Do animals really talk, as in my folktales? Did your dog really bite the neighbor, as heard at the mediation table? Is the witch truly "wicked"? The "truth" doesn't matter as much as the answer to the question, "Does this story serve me?" I have found that some stories can lead us directly into self-destruction. The cultural story entitled "To be happy I must buy lots of stuff" appears to have Americans by the throat and in grave conflict with our environment.

We can also hold too tightly to our belief in the singular *truth* of our stories and seek to destroy those who disagree. This dynamic sparks holy wars in all their guises and is a recurring theme throughout civilization. Galileo looked at the universe from a vastly new perspective and wrote a new story about the earth's place in the cosmos. He was branded a heretic and was lucky to live out his days as an expatriate. In modern times, think of the child in the dysfunctional family whose story does not jibe with those of the others and who dares to speak it anyway. I have mediated cases of corporate whistle-blowers, marveling at the anger and abuse directed toward those who relate a different version of reality. As George Bernard Shaw once said, "All great truths begin as blasphemies."

When I separate myself from my beliefs and see them as a story I use to understand reality, I am empowered to investigate and change my vision. Quantum physics proves "that there can be many points of view, or many faces of truth, some even mutually contradictory, and yet all equally real in potential sense." The story can control me, or I can control the story. I am not suggesting that we should be in denial or become deluded by writing a fantasy story about our lives; rather, I am proposing that we must recognize that our limited perception makes it impossible to understand the full "truth" in any situation. By recognizing that we continue to create stories to explain how the world works, just as we have since human beings could first speak, we are able to move beyond worrying about whether something is "true" to finding a new or greater

No finitely describable system, or finite language, can prove all truths. Truth cannot fully be caught in a finite net.

— Kurt Gödel

story that will serve our community. Listening in this way helps me to stay open to hearing more of the other person's perspective and to get clues about the story hiding behind what she is saying.

As Walter Truett Anderson explains in *Reality Isn't What it Used to Be*, "[L]ife is a matter of telling ourselves stories about life, and of savoring stories about life told by others, and of living our lives according to such stories, and of creating ever-new and more complex stories about stories — and that this story making is not just about human life but is human life."

Clinging is never kept within bounds,
It is sure to go the wrong way;
Quit it and things follow their own courses,
While the Essence neither departs or abides.

— D. T. Suzuki

TO EXPLORE

Look at your current conflict as a story. Tell it to yourself as a "once upon a time" tale. Who are the good guys, and who are the bad? Does your story follow the format of the Adam and Eve story, the one described by New Science, or another creation story? What tests are laid out in this story? What tasks are you asked to complete? See if you can describe your opponent's story. What is your creation story? What is your opponent's creation story, and how might these stories be influencing this conflict? In the next phase we will work to create a story that includes all versions of a situation.

TIP 3: DETACH

WHERE DO YOUR ATTACHMENTS LIE?

The weed took herself lightly and was able to survive and thrive. What are we holding onto with tight fists? Angeles Arrien provides a great rule of thumb on attachment: "If I cannot tease you, you are overly attached." Laughter separates us from our fixed beliefs and ideals. It allows us to suspend our assumptions out in front of our noses and see how we are structuring our world. It creates space for us to grow in.

What Women Want:
To be loved, to be listened to,
to be desired, to be respected,
to be needed, to be trusted, and
sometimes, just to be held.
What Men Want:
Tickets for the World Series.

— Dave Barry

In a conflict, make a list of all your beliefs. Phrases like "The sky is blue," "I am a great tennis player," or "He hates me" might show up on your list. Notice which ones you would not feel comfortable being teased about. Notice which beliefs have not been tested and thus are part of your underlying assumptions. Practice flexibility by finding a counterexample to each of those assumptions. For example, "It is important for children to get good grades" might be a good rule of thumb but not necessarily true. Einstein and Edison, who were brilliant, influential men and notoriously terrible students, dispel that truth.

TO EXPLORE

Poke holes in your story. What assumptions are you making? Can I tease you about them? The more you can put under the microscope, the more flexible you become and the more solutions you make available to this conflict.

CHOOSE YOUR CORE VALUES AND LET GO OF THE REST

As they grow and transform, systems contain some *self-referencing information* that is used to tell these systems into what form they should evolve. This is the information or assumption that a system holds as "law" and around which it organizes itself when undergoing change or evolution. Using the metaphor from our fable of the weed and the tree, this information is our roots.

In the system of the human body our DNA provides these structuring laws. As we age, our DNA tells our physical system as it changes to create our eyes, ears, and bone structure in a certain manner. Since our complete body system regenerates over a one-to-twelve-month period, Deepak Chopra describes a human being as more of a river than as anything frozen in time and space. We appear fairly stable because of the organizing *information* of our DNA. Within a corporation, certain core values will be used to determine how the business will grow and expand. In a family setting, we all have undying beliefs that determine how we spend our time and money.

I also structure my decisions around certain internal rules. For example, I might hold the ideal or core principle that my family is my highest priority. When in conflict I will "reference" that belief and make decisions about my future evolution based on it. During the Water phase we evaluate what beliefs should be "laws" or core values. The more we are willing to question and modify our beliefs, the more possible solutions to the conflict we will find.

Can one die, psychologically, to all one's past, to all the attachments, fears, to the anxiety, vanity, and pride, so completely that tomorrow you wake up a fresh human being?

— Krishnamurti

There is creative tension to be found between flexibility and standing by some fundamental structuring principles. We search for balance between being too attached or too adaptable. On the one hand, if I have too many governing rules about proper conduct and how the world should work, I become inflexible; think of someone you know whose entire belief system is non-negotiable. On the other, if I have no internal rules to guide me, I will be adrift in the seas of the Universe and unable to accomplish or commit to anything of value.

Most often we turn too many of our beliefs into "core values" and become rigid. For example, in our family the children play instruments because of research showing that practicing an instrument nurtures the development of a child's brain. Cody, one of our offspring, after playing the violin for five years, wanted to play the baritone instead. I balked, saying that this was not possible. I hesitated because I had the following unconscious fixed beliefs:

1. This child should continue to play the violin since he has expertise and shouldn't start over.

2. We have spent enough money on instruments.

3. I don't have time to switch him over to a new instrument or to find him a new teacher.

By poking at all our assumptions and paring down core values, we open ourselves to more solutions. Learning from Cody, who when confronted with a new idea will often say, "Let me think about it," I stopped and had to ask myself, Why can't he start over with a new instrument? It would not affect the influence on his brain development. Why couldn't we trade the violin in for a baritone? And, Why couldn't we set a feasible time schedule for this switch? A bit of openness on my part invoked a similar response in my son as we stretched beyond these self-imposed boundaries and searched for new possibilities together.

As with most conflicts, a final resolution could not be seen from the outset. Cody decided to play both the violin and a used baritone, taking lessons for the first and playing the second at school. I am bothered

On a personal level, the principle of harmony implies a spirit of reverence and humility. There can be no genuine acknowledgement of others unless one is able to discard the self-attachments that dominate life in society. Indeed, the failure to perceive the deepest humanity of others is one of the greatest causes of strife in the world.

— Kakuzo Okakura

now to realize that my initial closed-mindedness might have kept him from a continuing love of music.

TO EXPLORE

List your personal core values just as an organization documents a set of guiding principles. What are the guiding beliefs of each system with which you are involved? How do they affect your decisions? Can you be teased about your core values? These values, although critical to the health of the system, must never be beyond reproach. List your top priorities in a current conflict. Are they core values?

RELEASE PROJECTIONS: TAP INTO ALL AVAILABLE POWER

When we create assumptions and use them to judge another we often project unwanted aspects of ourselves. "I hate her. She is so selfish. He thinks he is so smart. What a bimbo," we might say with disdain or disgust. The tree projected its fears of weakness and ugliness on the weed. As we saw, this was a clear projection since the tree was the weaker of the two. As noted previously, others mirror traits present in us that we may not wish to recognize. When we don't recognize these attributes we lose access to the information they carry and to their ability to save our lives or help us resolve a conflict.

Many authors on conflict resolution suggest that we separate people issues ("You are a creep") from our differing perspectives or assumptions about the actions or events ("I think I owe you $500, you think I owe you $750"). If I can detach and make peace with my enemy's attributes, I can work on the external issues or the problem with more clarity and effectiveness. As William Ury, author of *Getting to Yes*, advises, "be tough on the problem, not on the person."

When we are able to let go of projecting our unowned traits onto others and focus on the problem at hand, we open ourselves to incredible power. When we own the possibilities of which we are capable, we move quickly through the Water stage. We flow and become strong. Translating the well-known biblical phrase "love your enemies" directly from Aramaic, Jesus' spoken language, Neil Douglas Klotz interprets these words not as a nicety but as advice about projection:

So quite often, the easiest way to get rid of a Minus is to change it to a Plus. Sometimes you will find that characteristics you try hard to eliminate eventually come back, anyway.... And sometimes those very tendencies that you dislike the most can show up in the right way at the right time to save your life, somehow.

— Benjamin Hoff,
The Tao of Pooh

From a hidden place,
unite with your enemies from the inside,
fill the inner void that makes them swell outwardly and fall
out of rhythm: instead of progressing, step by step,
they stop and start harshly,
out of time with you.

Bring yourself back into rhythm within.
Find the movement that mates with theirs —
like two lovers creating life from dust.
Do this work in secret, so they don't know.
This kind of love creates, it doesn't emote. (Luke 6:26)

Looking at Jesus' words through this lens, we note that our external enemies may only be mirrors of disowned parts of ourselves. The enemy in the phrase "love your enemies" refers to those who make our skin crawl. We are counseled not to confront the external enemy but to go within. As Hoff explains in the sidebar on the previous page, each trait that might be seen as a minus can always be turned into a plus and used to our benefit if we are willing to stop, go within, and own it.

Debbie Ford, who writes about the topic of projection in *The Dark Side of the Light Chasers,* tells a story of her great aversion to racism and her continued work to eradicate discrimination. In her vigor she disavowed the presence of racism in her own heart and simply hated anyone "racist," thus becoming a different variety of chauvinist. When confronted with the possibility that she was a bigot, her answer was to look in the mirror and tell herself that she was racist for hours until it no longer mattered. She suspended the assumption that to be racist was "bad" for a moment and noticed that her focus on race as an issue had involved her in helping disadvantaged African Americans. Once she was comfortable with her own capacity to separate from others because of their race and to choose when to use this trait, her perspective and her relationships were transformed.

Buddhist teacher Pema Chödrön teaches another approach to overcoming projection and putting ourselves in the driver's seat. Using the

If we could read the secret history of our enemies, we would find in each man's life a sorrow and a suffering enough to disarm all hostility.

— Henry Wadsworth
Longfellow

Buddhist practice of *tong len,* when we see the mother screaming at her child in the check-out line, we are to inhale saying "impatience" and exhale saying "love" or "peace." We then might inhale saying "cruelty" and exhale saying "compassion." We bring in and own the hated behavior and respond by sending out an understanding of wholeness and of the truth that we control our own responses.

TO EXPLORE

What traits do you most hate? For each one, find one example of how it may be used for good. For example, not only can the act of killing be perceived as an evil act, but it is also what we use to create food (we kill animals and plants). Notice which traits you are unwilling even to discuss.

LET GO OF THE PAST: FIND FORGIVENESS

Forgiveness is the ultimate form of letting go or detachment. We allow an action to move into the past. It does not mean that you are condoning an action or that you will allow it to happen again. If we are able to absolve we open ourselves to new possibilities and structures by separating ourselves from the old ones. When we refuse to pardon an action we become stuck in and controlled by an old story. When we don't forgive, we act as jailers holding another in prison. Neither the prisoners nor the jailers are free to move on. When we forgive we reap great benefits since we no longer limit our solutions to exacting revenge. This is the wisdom of every spiritual tradition I have encountered.

The weed showed no anger or resentment toward the tree or toward the overwhelming water. In this state of fluidity she was able to move with the changing environment and remain unharmed. When we refuse to let go of the past, we ultimately make ourselves weaker and more brittle.

TO EXPLORE

Gail Straub, author of *Empowerment,* counsels that forgiveness can happen in degrees. If a team member has caused you significant harm and it seems impossible to let this go, try forgiving that person just 1 percent. Pick just one action or part of an action you are ready to let go. Notice

> *The curious paradox is that when I accept myself just as I am, then I can change.*
>
> — Carl Rogers

> *I am worn out with groaning, Every night I drench my pillow And soak my bed with tears; My eye is wasted with grief, I have grown old with enemies all around me.*
>
> — Psalms 6:6–7

Grief drives men to serious reflection, sharpens the understanding, and softens the heart.

— John Adams

Accept the world as it is. If you accept the world, The Tao will be luminous inside you And you will return to your primal self.

— Tao Te Ching

the resulting flexibility and well-being. Using this feedback as a guide, then forgive a bit more when you feel ready. Follow this model until the hurt is removed and the team is back on track.

TIP 4: CREATE SPACE

To master flexibility is to understand Water's power. In the Taoist tradition, this is the practice of Wu Wei, or effortless action. Wu Wei allows the nature of things to be as they are without the need to force or change them. In Wu Wei, students meditate hour after hour on a stream to learn water's attributes and thus its formlessness. Water knows how to change form instantly and get to where it ultimately wants to go, using all sorts of creative avenues. Cup your hands under a faucet and watch how water finds its way back to the earth. Its strength lies in its consistency. Water accepts how things are. In acceptance there is great power: look at the weed's ability to become like the water and survive a torrential flood without harm.

Water causes great destruction when it is not given the space it needs. The flood will come eventually. We learn from water about the importance of giving others space and an ability to determine their own future.

If we can love and accept ourselves when we are mean, impatient, fat (a good Western choice), depressed, or lazy, we can do the same for others. When we can accept our friends even when they are cruel, our children even when they are spoiled and selfish, and our neighbors when they are too boisterous, we create a space in which they know they are safe. When people know they are safe as they are, they are more apt to work on any disputes and on your relationship. *The Art of War* reminds us that when we let go and create space we diminish aggression and paradoxically bring the situation under our control.

Harrison Owen, once an Episcopal priest and now a corporate consultant, has spent years studying what makes healthy human systems. He has found that groups of people will naturally move to a place of order and resolution *if they are given the ability to move and flow.* He calls this belief system "Open Space Technology." Employing what he calls the "Four principles and one law," meetings are organized by the following:

Four Principles of Open Space:

1. Whoever appears are the right people.

2. Whatever happens is the only thing that could have happened.

3. Whenever it starts is the right time.

4. When it's over, it's over.

The Law of Two Feet: If you find yourself in a situation where you are neither learning nor contributing, use your two feet and move to a more desirable place. Responsibility for attendance resides with the individual.

Using the tenets of Open Space Technology people are able to relax and accept that a meeting is just as it is supposed to be with the right people and at the right time. They relax knowing that they can come and go as they see fit. Meetings are convened with no agenda. The participants are free to bring forward whatever topics should be discussed, for example, "new products," "renaming the organization," or "financial stability." Topic champions then volunteer and create a meeting spot and time to discuss the topic further. If I am interested in the topic, I will show up at that meeting. I may stay for five minutes or two hours; I decide. I might speak or just listen; again, I decide. Then when I am ready, I might go to another subgroup, create a new subgroup, or choose not to participate. It is an organic process as people move from place to place, groups grow and shrink, and work gets done. Participants are often amazed at how quickly major tasks are completed using this philosophy. Owen's precepts have successfully and expediently supported large groups of intensely conflicted parties from Boston to South Africa to develop solutions without any intermediary or formal conflict resolution procedures.

Creating space by accepting everyone's free will and choices actually makes it easier to stick with the conflict and with one another until completion. One client who was considering divorce asked me, when I told her to stick with the conflict, "Are you saying that I must stay in this marriage?" "Absolutely not," I replied. "I am suggesting that you continue to engage with your spouse, in your own time, to determine a workable relationship for all parties. Only you know if you need to stay

Put down your opinion, your condition, your situation, then you will not be stuck. Always stay open. . . . Zen means put everything down. Then you can control any situation or condition.

— Seung Sahn

Something we were withholding made us weak until we found it was ourselves.

— Robert Frost

or leave the relationship." As we hold the *intention* to find a solution and
to create space, people can come and go as they choose. According to
Owen's tenets, the perfect solution will present itself at the right time,
with the right people, if given the room to appear. To believe in detachment, the spiritual practice of the Water phase, is to know that a solution will present itself if we just allow everyone space to be as they are
and accept that chaos will naturally return to stability.

Silence and meditation also help us to create space. They relax us
into a place of formlessness. Matthew Fox counsels that if we can be at
ease and go deep enough using meditation and silence, we will move
beyond projection, create some space, and experience an underlying
interconnecting wave or oneness. In this state, we let go of the old ways
of seeing and open ourselves to new, inclusive solutions.

The practice of meditation is found in all the spiritual traditions. The
Eastern traditions, especially Buddhism and Taoism, which focus on
the importance of formlessness as a principle, have much to teach us about
meditation. Such a seemingly easy exercise is considered by many to be
the most difficult of spiritual disciplines. Simply, meditation is quieting the
mind in silence. Meditation can be done sitting or lying down. I included
a centering technique in part 2 to get you started; there are also lots of great
books on meditation that will help you to practice creating space.

The medieval Christian mystic Meister Eckhart sends us to our
internal landscape when he states, "Enter into your own ground and
work there and these works which you work there will all be living." But,
you say, what am I to do when I am in the heat of battle? I can't stop
and take twenty minutes to meditate. Here is where taking a break or
using silence comes into your playbook. It is a Western belief that we
must keep forging ahead, regardless of where we are. This is not the case
in many other parts of the world.

For example, traditional Native American negotiations include a
great deal of silence and introspection. Sister Jose Hobday, Franciscan
nun and Native American activist, tells the story of a typical powwow-
planning meeting. At one Montana meeting, representatives from all
over the state gathered. Who will provide and maintain the latrines is
always an issue. Sister Jose describes eloquently how long periods of

silence during this meeting were punctuated with sentences like "The Rocky Boy tribe will bring the food." Or "We know what a great job Wolf Point does with the latrines." The negotiation effectively occurred not only through words but also through quiet.

Just stop talking. Or ask for some time to think. Add the "Law of Two Feet" to your ground rules. Ask to return another time. Give yourself some space to become formless and let all the information sink in.

TO EXPLORE

To improve our ability to stay engaged in conflict and to cope with the emotional roller-coaster of this phase, Janette Rainwater, in *You're in Charge: A Guide to Becoming Your Own Therapist*, provides a useful exercise to use during stressful moments. When you find yourself drifting or squirming, give yourself some space by asking yourself the following questions:

1. What is happening right now?

    • What am I doing right now?

    • What am I feeling right now?

    • What am I thinking right now?

2. What do I want right now? (Check your intention.)

3. What am I doing right now that will prevent me from getting what I want? What would I like to choose instead? (Rainwater states all you need to then do is say to yourself, "I choose...")

4. Breathe, let go, and move on.

ART OF CONFLICT: DESTROY TO CREATE

Great artists know that to make a work of art, the artist must be detached from it so the painting or sculpture can evolve into its highest and best form. This is the lesson that the weed in our story teaches as it evolves, and it is what we will practice in the following exercise. This exercise will warm up our creativity, the skill we will foster in the next phase.

Be open to the outcome, not attached to the outcome.

— Angeles Arrien

For this exercise you can use a photograph, book, painting, or piece of pottery. Choose what will work best for you. If you choose pottery, you will need mosaic materials that can be bought at any craft store. For paper-based art, you will also need glue and a large sheet of paper.

- Select a piece of pottery or painting you have created or a favorite photo or book of photographs.

- When and if you can stand it...if you have chosen a piece of pottery, break it into small pieces (please take proper precautions). If you're using a paper object, tear it into pieces.

- Sit with what you have in silence until you are ready to create, noticing the beauty of the broken pieces, the shapes they make, the colors.

- Notice your internal landscape. Was it easy or hard to let go of the original form? What object would you refuse to pick to do this exercise?

- Use what you have to create something new.

The art of breaking or using broken pottery or china to create mosaic is commonly called *pique assiette,* a folk art found around the world. Popular into the early twentieth century, the practice was probably borrowed from an African American tradition of decorating grave sites with jugs and objects owned by the deceased. A variation of the craft incorporates other small objects such as jewelry and photographs and is called "what not" or "memory jugs." Using this art form as a metaphor is especially relevant in this phase of conflict. In the Water phase, we are called on to let go of the current beloved forms, break them apart, and see what hides within. From these pieces we can then create a more lasting whole.

Pique assiette translates from French into "stolen from plate" and is a reference to the modern father of this craft, Raymond Edouard Isidore. In 1938 Isidore began to collect glass and pottery shards in the fields near his home in Chartres, France, to escape from boredom. It is said that he became obsessed with the craft and covered every surface, both inside and

All the arts we practice are apprenticeship.
The big art is our life.

— M. C. Richards

outside, of his house and garden with mosaic patterns. Only the white sheets of his bed went uncovered.

AN ELEMENTAL ROLE MODEL: MAHATMA GANDHI

No man in recent history has exhibited the extraordinary power hidden in flexibility and detachment more than India's Mahatma Gandhi. Humble and uncomplicated like our kind weed in the parable, Gandhi was stronger and more resilient than the mighty ruling governments of his time.

Mohandas Karamchand Gandhi was born in 1869 in Porbandar, India. He was married at thirteen to Kasturbai, to whom he would stay married until her death in 1944. Educated in law in England, Gandhi moved to South Africa in 1893 after a few years of practicing law unsuccessfully in India. Within a month in South Africa, Gandhi committed himself to fight the serious racial prejudice that pervaded that country. Subsequently, Gandhi moved between India and South Africa, finally returning to India in 1914. Gandhi devoted his life to social activism. He championed many causes, including the rights of miners in South Africa, removing the class of the untouchables in India, and developing religious tolerance between Hindus and Muslims throughout Asia. Gandhi's best-known successful campaign was to establish home rule in India.

Although a very flexible and reflective individual, Gandhi had two beliefs around which he organized his life, truth and *ahimsa*, or non-violence. He said, "I hope I have no policy in me save the policy of Truth and *ahimsa*. I will not sacrifice Truth and *ahimsa* even for the deliverance of my country or religion." In 1909 Gandhi declared a disinterest in material possessions and took a vow of poverty and celibacy to support the pursuit of these principles. It was around these core values that he also organized his campaigns for justice. Gandhi creatively used civil disobedience to establish India's sovereignty.

Gandhi was very clear that to follow *ahimsa* and to fight against injustice one must separate the man from the deed. He said, "This *ahimsa* is the basis of the search for truth. I am realizing every day that the search is in vain unless it is founded on *ahimsa* as the basis. It is quite proper to resist and attack a system, but to resist and attack its author is tantamount to resisting and attacking oneself." Gandhi always worked to take the enemy whole.

Devoutly following the practices of the Water phase, Gandhi honored both the admirable and the difficult: "My imperfections and failures are as much a blessing from God as my successes and talents, and I lay them both at His feet." His devotion to humility was simply stated as, "Truth is not to be found by anybody who has not got an abundant sense of humility." Gandhi also understood the power of humor. "If I had no sense of humor, I should long ago have committed suicide." He knew that to find creative ideas, one must forge through the confusion of this watery phase. He said, "A votary of truth is often obliged to grope in the dark."

Gandhi's actions belied the practice and power of formlessness. First, he would meditate and bring each conflicting perspective, religion, and political party into his being. Then he would act with resolve and reverence in striking and creative ways. Then he would return to prayer. The British never had any idea what Gandhi was going to do next. He did much of his work in secret, in prayer and quiet contemplation intermingled with powerful, love-filled acts. Commenting on the power found within these practices he said, "God demands nothing less than complete self-surrender as the price for the only real freedom that is worth having. And when a man thus loses himself he immediately finds himself in the service of all that lives. It becomes his delight and his recreation. He is a new man, never weary of spending himself in the service of God's creation."

Gandhi understood that to take the enemy whole one must separate impermanent forms from their underlying essence, or in this case, the person from the action.

Gandhi would often move beyond his own faith to quote the Prophet Muhammad and Jesus on the importance of unconditional love and peace. For example, Gandhi was noted as paraphrasing the Muslim Koran, saying that the only demons live within our own hearts and it is there that all battles should be fought. By letting go of projections, he was able to love without conditions and see the situation with greater clarity. This power of holding all within us can be immense. Gandhi would say, "I am a Christian, a Hindu, a Buddhist, a Jew." With this attitude he was able to unite a nation and nonviolently overpower an imperialist government.

Gandhi was assassinated in 1948 on his way to evening prayers.

SUMMARY: WATER — CHAOS

ATTRIBUTES	We flow into the *Water phase* when we: • Feel discouragement, deep frustration, or despair. • Can't see a solution within current parameters. • Are aware that new ways must emerge.
TASK	The goal of this phase is to *relax* into the overall chaos and wait.
CHALLENGES AND ELEMENTAL PRINCIPLE	To overcome the challenges of *grief* and *holding too tightly,* we practice the principle of *detachment.* Separation or *letting go* is described as holding tightly with an open hand or caring objectively.

TIPS AND TECHNIQUES	To improve our flexibility skills and move through the Water phase it is helpful to:
	1. *Let emotions flow* freely.
	2. See *reality as a unique story* we tell ourselves.
	3. *Let go of attachments* by:
	    • Laughing at yourself.
	    • Carefully preserving core values and letting go of all else.
	    • Recognizing your projections on others.
	    • Forgiving others and yourself.
	4. *Give everyone space* to move by employing Owen's Four Principles and One Law of Detachment:
	    • Whoever appears are the right people.
	    • Whatever happens is the only thing that could have happened.
	    • Whenever it starts is the right time.
	    • When it's over, it's over.
	    • Responsibility for attendance resides with the individual.

VOCATION AND DISCIPLINE	Pilgrims drift effortlessly through the Water phase. These wanderers are *humble, flexible, and still despite external chaos.* The daily discipline of *meditation* is advised for moving through this phase.
ELEMENTAL GIFT	During the Water phase engage all parties in working toward a solution by *practicing humility and humor.*
ART OF CONFLICT	The artistic practice of *destroying to create* fosters flexibility and detachment skills and opens us to creativity.
ELEMENTAL ROLE MODEL	*Mahatma Gandhi*

CHAPTER 12

Phase 3

Fire — Creativity

- **TASK:** Capture new ideas
- **ELEMENTAL PRINCIPLE:** Contemplate
- **CHALLENGES:** Oppression and anxiety
- **BEST ELEMENTAL GIFT:** Acknowledgment

*I have no special revelation of God's will. My firm belief is that
He reveals Himself daily to every human being, but we shut our ears
to the "still small voice." We shut our eyes to the "pillar of fire" in front of us.*

— Gandhi

Once upon a time, in Russia, a beautiful young girl stood at her mother's deathbed. Her mother called to her and said, "Vasilisa, when I die you will be blessed, but before I go I have a gift for you." She handed her child a doll. Just like Vasilisa, she wore a white shirt, a black skirt, and a red embroidered apron. Her mother said, "Take this doll and keep her safe with you in your pocket always. Feed her and then listen to her. Don't tell anyone of her existence." And then she died.

Vasilisa followed her mother's advice. She cared for the doll, and the doll cared for her. As it usually goes in fairy tales, after a time, her father remarried a woman who was as cruel as her mother was kind. She brought to the marriage two wicked step-sisters. Vasilisa grew more beautiful and supple each day as these women became more brittle, spiteful, and crooked. After a time the father died, and Vasilisa was left to serve as maid to these awful women.

One day the stepmother and sisters conspired to kill Vasilisa. They said, "Let us extinguish our fire. We will make Vasilisa go into the forest, to the house of Baba Yaga to bring fire home. She will surely be killed by wolves or by that wicked witch." The stepmother came to Vasilisa and said, "Our fire has gone out. You must go into the woods to the house of Baba Yaga and get us fire. I am too old, and my daughters are too afraid." Vasilisa consulted the doll, who said quietly that this was a task that Vasilisa could do. The beautiful young maiden walked out into the forest with the doll in her pocket.

At each fork in the path to Baba Yaga's house, the doll would say, "Go left" or, "Go right." Vasilisa followed the doll's instructions. She fed the doll and thanked it for its help. As she walked down the path, suddenly a black rider on a black horse galloped across the path. Night fell immediately. A while later, a rider dressed in red on a red horse rode across the path in front of Vasilisa, and the sun rose. A white rider with a white horse soon followed. It was at this moment that Vasilisa arrived at the house of Baba Yaga.

Resting on dancing legs that reminded Vasilisa of those of a chicken, the house lunged and swirled. Its fence was made of human bones and skulls. Its knocker was a roaring pig's snout. Vasilisa asked the doll, "Is this the house we seek?" The doll nodded.

Above the house in a large cauldron, Baba Yaga flew. She used a large pestle to steer her pot as she flew down to the ground to meet Vasilisa. Oh, what a frightening sight Baba Yaga was. She had iron teeth and a long, greasy goatee.

"I know you," Baba Yaga said. "Your stupid family has let the fire go out and you have come to me to save you. Why should I do such a thing?" Vasilisa consulted the doll and said, "Because I ask, Auntie." "What a wise answer," said Baba Yaga. "But you know, too much knowledge too soon can age one very quickly." "Come in, child, we shall see if I will give you fire."

Vasilisa went into the dancing, terrifying house with Baba Yaga. She watched as the old woman devoured food for forty men served to her by three sets of hands extended in mid-air. She left Vasilisa a morsel of bread and a thimble of soup. She said as she pointed to a large pile behind her, "I am going out. Take this corn and separate the mildewed kernels from the fresh. Then clean my house and make my food. When I return all this must be done," her eyes glowed red, "or you will not live to see the dawn." And she left into the night with the skulls of the fence glowing with green fire.

Vasilisa began to cry to the doll, "How will all this be possible? How will I ever be able to complete all these chores in time?"

"Eat a little, sleep a little, all will be well," the doll replied.

Vasilisa drank the soup, fed the doll, and fell asleep. When she awoke, there were two perfect piles of corn in the corner of a clean house. All Vasilisa needed to do was to make the meal.

Baba Yaga returned greatly disappointed to find all the chores completed and soup simmering on the stove. She sighed and clapped her hands three times, and the suspended hands reappeared. They filled the room with the yellow chaff as they ground the fresh corn into meal. Clapping again, the hands disappeared.

After eating all the food except for a small end of bread and a bit of soup Baba Yaga said, "See this pile of dirt behind the door? Separate the dirt from the poppyseeds within it. Clean the barn, make my food, or you will not see another dawn." And the old woman stepped into the night.

Again Vasilisa cried to the doll. "Eat a little, sleep a little, and all will be well," said the doll. Vasilisa ate, fed the doll, and curled up on the floor, exhausted. She again awoke to a clean room and two piles, one of poppyseeds and another of dirt. Baba Yaga burst through the door as Vasilisa was finishing the meal, foiled again.

After the three hands were summoned to press the oil from the poppyseeds and after they disappeared again, Baba Yaga asked, "So child, do you have any questions?"

She consulted the doll and said, "Who was the black horseman?"

"He is my night," Baba Yaga replied.

"The red?"

"My dawn," she said. "And the white is my day. Any more questions?" she asked menacingly.

How she wanted to ask about the hands, but the doll began jumping up and down in her pocket. "No more questions. As you have said, too much knowledge too soon can age one very quickly."

"Where have you become so wise, child?"

"By the blessings of my mother," Vasilisa replied.

"Blessings? BLESSINGS! We'll have no blessings here. Out with you!" screamed Baba Yaga.

Baba Yaga grabbed the young woman by the arm and shoved her out the door. "Take this," Baba Yaga said briskly as she grabbed a skull from the fence, magically filled it with fire, and stuck the skull on a bone. Vasilisa began to thank her but the doll stopped her before the words rose from her chest. "Run!" said the doll. Vasilisa ran down the path with the skull eyes glowing red. Back through the forest she ran, following the instructions of the doll as she heard, "Go left," or "Go right" at each fork, nearing her home at dusk.

The three horrid women huddled in the house, freezing, for, you see, they were not able to restart the fire that they had extinguished. Terrified of the skull and amazed she had survived, they cowered as Vasilisa opened the door.

The skull spoke: "Vasilisa, do not be afraid. Let me burn through the night on the mantle; all will be well."

The skull's eyes followed the evil stepsisters and mother, watching their every move from their mantle perch, and by morning all that remained of the wretched women were cinders.

INTRODUCTION

The Diamond Construction management team, after sitting in silence and discouragement, wades through the Water phase to continue their conversation...

It takes a golden ear to empty enough of itself to hear clearly.

— M. C. Richards

"Payroll is due Friday, which will almost max out our line of credit," Blaze observed. "We need a plan fast."

Edina suggested, "Why don't we meet tomorrow? Can we make a decision then? I need a little time to think."

Amy agreed, "That should work."

"Maybe it is time to cut and run," Amy thought. "Perhaps Ace Construction is the better horse to be betting on."

At noon, the four returned to their offices. Blaze decided to eat lunch alone and read his newspaper. Amy walked to the local sandwich shop, where she often found Marty Phelps, Ace's CFO. Edina and Gene went out for lunch to talk.

Amy found Marty and joined him to eat. Amy held her cards close to her chest by simply asking, "How are you?"

Blaze loved the classified section of the paper. He used to read it daily as a kid, searching for secret clues to an imagined treasure hunt. To console himself, he went to the want ads.

Long-time friends, Edina and Gene sat down to eat, drained and contemplative. She finally said, "Gene, I'm with you; we started the company to make a difference, and that was a reason I could stand behind. But I'm not sure I know what 'serving' even means anymore. All I know is I love Blaze, this company, and my friendship with you. I'm terrified we are going to lose everything. I don't want to fire anyone either, but Gene, what do we do now?"

"Dee," as Gene liked to call Edina, "I want to kick myself. I shouldn't have hired the staff for the Gerber contract before we had it in the bag. Ace wins the contract, and the irony is we've now got some of the best talent in the city. I love this company too, and I don't want to leave, but someone needs to stand up for the employees, and that's always been my job."

"Well, that is not something you should do alone, and I'm sorry that I have stuck you in that box. We made a commitment to care for our employees. How can we do that, even if we go out of business?" Edina replied.

The next day, Blaze walked into their meeting excitedly carrying an envelope of newspaper clippings. When the others sat down, Amy began, "I need to get something off my chest before we continue. I was ready to bail out on you and this mess yesterday. So I went to find Marty Phelps at Ace. I'm really sorry. But I have to tell you, you're stuck with me and you've got to hear what I learned from Marty..."

Marty, assuming Amy to be a loyal partner to Edina and the other founders, didn't suspect that Amy might be willing to change employment. Instead, he began to explain that all the success Ace was experiencing was creating great challenges for the company in terms of infrastructure, hiring, and project management. Marty tried to paint a good picture, but he hoped Amy might be able to steer him to some answers. "They need help," Amy added, "and I think they are desperate enough to pay for it. We staffed for the Gerber job, and they didn't."

"Competitors as customers," Edina replied. "Never thought of it that way."

"How about engineering firms as customers, road departments, hospitals, and IT companies?" added Blaze. "You know how I love the classifieds. Well, I found ten ads for project managers yesterday and thought, well, they should talk to us. I bet they don't have a clue, and meanwhile, we've got excellent project managers. Heck, all four of us were project managers once, and everyone says we've got the best training in the industry."

"What are you saying?" Gene replied.

"I'm saying we are a construction company, but maybe we are also a project management company," Blaze continued.

"Edina and I also spent yesterday thinking about the company and its mission," Gene said. "I've realized that I hate layoffs because we made a commitment *to care for these employees. Edina asked me if there is a way we can care for an employee even if we have to do layoffs. Edina and I think we can."*

New ideas streamed forward as they discussed their insights.

Nearly all men can stand adversity, but if you want to test a man's character, give him power.

— Abraham Lincoln

Around the world, fire stories teach about transformation. These folktales caution us about fire's destructive power and show us how to harness it for gain. The heroes know how to pay careful attention to their surroundings and not to discount creative sparks from even the smallest creature. Wisdom can hide in every crevice. The ancient story above is told throughout central Europe and highlights the power of harnessing fire.

We become a little battle weary after the Water phase and thus are willing to let go of what at first might have seemed non-negotiable, as we see when a tired Edina and Gene meet for a more open-minded lunch. The situation is still fuzzy and we may feel overwhelmed, wondering how all the conflicting perspectives could possibly coalesce into a solution. Beliefs and constraints push against one another, and the battle really heats up. We move to the time before dawn that feels the darkest. Yet it is now that the sun will come up; there is a solution cooking, we just need to wait for it. That is the secret of the creative process.

As discussed in chapter 11, the natural conflict between the Earth and Water phases centers around *love*. We fall in love with something as it is in the Earth phase, and in the Water phase we must learn to love it unconditionally and let it go so it may transform. The Earth and Water phases teach us how to love both conditionally and unconditionally, how to hold tightly with an open hand.

In the Fire and Air phases, we learn about power. Fire is the element most associated with creativity or spirit. It represents enthusiasm, wild ideas, and passion. Fire is considered a transformative power, and through its heat we have edible food, boiling water, and warm homes. The fire of this phase can burn away all but our most important core values and cook up a creative new solution. Controlling fire allowed us to create civilization.

To move through conflict and through life, we must create a balance between love and power. When we are all love without power, we allow ourselves to be battered and stepped on. When we're all power without love, we create horrific dictators such as Mao and Franco. Amy first aligns only with power as she sneaks off to an undisclosed lunch meeting, forgetting her commitment to her associates. However, when she balances her innate love of and respect for her friends with the powerful information she gathered, ultimately her integrity creates a clear path to a creative solution.

THE PLAY BETWEEN LOVE AND POWER IN THE MANDALA

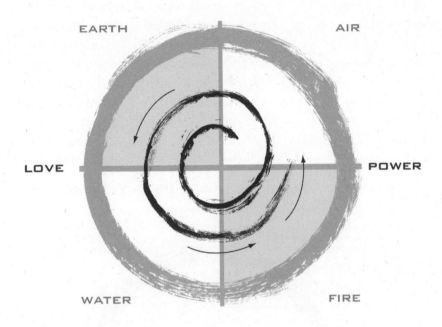

Parenting is a constant tough balancing act between love and power, a continued dance of adoring your children while setting firm boundaries to protect their health and welfare. At one extreme, some parents love their children yet shy away from the powerful activities of setting curfews, supporting homework habits, and administering discipline. At the other end of the spectrum some parents have their children well trained and polite with little thought to the emotional impact of their powerful actions. I find it is a never-ending process of learning about how to clearly exert my power as a loving parent.

In sports, here coaches turn up the heat to improve play. Good trainers introduce a new way of approaching the game and then push the player to relinquish old habits and create new ones. For the player it can feel relentless as the trainer admonishes them to try one more time. With love, they powerfully wear the players down, taking them to their edge again and again. They get the players to "play their hearts out" during the heat of the battle. *Heat* and *heart* are important themes of the Fire phase.

This fire does not exist alone. It needs earth and air (form and expression) to survive. Water can contain or can arrest it. So to take advantage of the fire or creative sparks arising within us, we need to use *all* that we've gathered in the Earth phase to fuel it and we need to express (Air) our new fiery ideas. We must also be constantly aware of and use the emotional landscape that we encountered in the Water phase. During the Fire phase we must try to let as much of the conflicting information as possible be "true" for a moment to find the creative solution. We will feel creative tension as the opposites continue to fight within us, and it can be overwhelming.

Conflict's lifecycle through the Taoist symbol

EARTH
WORKING WITH WHAT
EXISTS TODAY

AIR
CREATING
NEW FORMS

WATER
OPENING WHILE
HOLDING CORE VALUES
AT THE CENTER

FIRE
HOLDING THE
OPPOSITES

The holding of the opposites, in which the Fire phase contains equal amounts of the perceived opposites of light and dark, is symbolized above in the yin/yang symbol. When we are open to all the seemingly conflicting pieces of information, the bigger picture magically appears. Open to possibilities, Blaze looks in the newspaper as he did when he was an imaginative child. When Amy has an unusual lunch date, she finds some valuable clues to their future solution. We don't have to go out and search for an answer that incorporates all the perspectives. If we are paying attention, the answer will materialize and can be translated into action in the final Air phase.

The Fire phase is a time of *contemplation,* or the practice of the mystic, also called the contemplative. We sit back and listen to the voice that speaks within our hearts, that part of us that can see the greater picture through the conflicting perspectives. The root of the word *contemplate* is "space in the heavens marked off for augural observations." An augur was an ancient Roman official charged with observing and interpreting omens to guide the country's leaders. To contemplate is to pay attention and look for the signs. In the Western world, we would call this "listening to our intuition." We might notice coincidences and synchronistic events. Some may use their dreams or ideas that appear upon waking to find a unifying resolution. To *contemplate* is to search for a unifying solution that takes everyone whole.

The story of Vasilisa reminds us that we do not need to force the creative process; rather, we need to pay attention. From systems theory we know that "[c]reativity is nothing else but the unfolding of evolution." This is the phase when a system evolves as it restructures around all the information it has gathered and disintegrates any old strategies that no longer apply.

ELEMENTAL PRINCIPLE: CONTEMPLATE

An attentive scientist watches nature and translates burrs sticking to his socks into Velcro. A garbage can lid and newspaper are transformed into musical instruments, and the hit musical *Stomp* is born. After the gestation of Water, it is here that new forms and new ways can be birthed.

Out of clutter, find simplicity.

— Albert Einstein

All mysticism is characterized by a passion for unity. To the mystic, true Being and Ultimate Reality are One.... This Reality contains, yet transcends all there is. It is the One in whom all is lost and all is found.

— Ursula King, *Christian Mystics*

Blaze reads the newspaper and redefines his company's mission. Our internal fire or creativity speaks, like Moses' burning bush or Vasilisa's doll and fiery skull. And like Moses, we aren't always excited to hear what it has to say. Yet it is what drives our life purpose and dreams.

Throughout his writings the poet Rumi incorporated the theme of listening intently to the fire within. The following poem captures the essence of this inner fire and of how it should be used to seek solutions in conflict:

One must live in the middle of contradiction because if all contradiction were eliminated at once life would collapse. There are simply no answers to some of the great pressing questions. You continue to live them out, making your life a worthy expression of a leaning into the light.

— Barry Lopez,
Arctic Dreams

LOOK FOR PASSION, PASSION, PASSION, PASSION

Passion burns down every branch of exhaustion.
Passion is the supreme elixir and renews all things.
No one can grow exhausted when passion is born.
Don't sigh heavily your brow bleak with boredom.
Look for passion, passion, passion, passion.

Futile solutions deceive the force of passion.
They are bandits who extort money through lies.
Marshy and stagnant waters are no cure for thirst however
limpid and delicious it might look.
It will only trap you and stop you looking for fresh rivers
that could feed and make flourish a hundred gardens just as
each piece of false gold prevents from recognizing
real gold and where to find it.

False gold will only cut your feet and bind your wings saying,
"I will remove your difficulties" when in fact it is only dregs and
defeat in the robes of victory.

Run, my friend, run from all false solutions.
Let divine passion triumph and rebirth you in yourself.

We should not succumb to fear and grab the first available solution. The Fire phase brings an inherent fight against time, which turns up the heat. However, if we can be vigilant and hold the creative tension of the disparate structures or stories fighting within us, we will ultimately birth a superior and longer-lasting solution in which both you and I are right. We remember that throughout the Universe a foundational breakthrough will create a multiplicity of options. Creativity explodes and provides "an abundance of novelties, many of which do not survive." There are thousands of options. However, the task is to listen intently to uncover the right one.

For example, some solutions will demand a lot of work. They will "cut our feet and bind our wings," as Rumi says. When an employer wishes to increase an employee's productivity, her first solution might be to baby-sit that worker, watching his every move like a hawk. After a week of following the staff member around, the manager is exhausted and frustrated that she hasn't been able to get any of her own work done. This approach might get the employee on track, but it is not a sustainable solution.

In our folktale the doll shows Vasilisa that there is always an elegant solution hidden in the myriad of options. Elegant solutions carry their own energy; they flow. In *The Art of War* elegant solutions carry a special type of power called *shih*. As in chess, though there may be many possible moves, there is often one that is the most potent, while being simple and beautiful. This dynamic is based partially on the position of the pieces, their relative power, their relationships to the opposing pieces, and timing. The sage commander knows how to cultivate *shih* by collating the information gathered (Earth) and listening to the greater flow of forces (Water). He lets go of all he knows and opens himself to new possibilities. This is the development of inner knowing, or "knowing the unknowable." The *shih* within a solution is temporary. Therefore, a fixed solution to resolve a reoccurring problem is not possible because the forces of the Universe are always shifting and changing. The solution just "feels" right. Its *shih* is palatable.

In his book *The Tipping Point: How Little Things Can Make a Big Difference* Malcolm Gladwell describes how elegant solutions operate. Gladwell depicts ideas or solutions that carry extraordinary influence or change, even though in themselves they are minor shifts. Elegant solutions act like epidemics in that with very little effort they have sweeping effects across a community. The Internet as a solution to our communication

If I were to wish for anything, I should not wish for wealth and power, but for the passionate sense of the potential, for the eye which, ever young and ardent, sees the possible. Pleasure disappoints, possibility never.

— Søren Kierkegaard,
Either/Or

challenges is a good example of such a contagious idea. These solutions instantly capture our attention; they use the unseen connections or relationships of a community, and they appear at the right time. They are full of *shih*.

To find the elegant solution we must follow Vasilisa's lead and cook up a solution by following the three steps:

1. *Stop:* In this phase we pause and assess what we have learned thus far. We get our bearings through *acknowledgment*. We throw all we have gathered into the pot and turn up the heat.

2. *Look:* Then we look to our intuition or to what's cooking by being attentive to ideas, dreams, and synchronicities.

3. *Listen:* We listen carefully for creative insights and their applicability. There will be many possibilities, so we will also test some ideas and cast them away.

These same three stages can be found in the practice of mysticism, or of listening to the heart's fire, and are described by such Christian contemplatives as Teresa of Avila, St. John of the Cross, and Dom Marmion. Effective wilderness trackers and medical doctors also follow these steps as they use both the rational and the nonrational, integrating both learning and intuition to determine their location and where they need to go next. They know that by acknowledging all the information they have gathered, getting quiet, and then listening intently they make better decisions under tense, life-threatening situations.

PRACTICAL TIPS

TIP 1: STOP

To effectively find a solution, we first stand still so that we can see and hear more clearly. When we halt briefly we can focus on the world around us. Remember how Vasilisa stopped at each fork of the road and asked the doll where to go next. Before any action, she pauses, takes in her situation, and listens to her intuition (symbolized in the story by the

Do not pray for tasks equal to your powers; pray for powers equal to your tasks.

— Phillips Brooks

To listen well is as powerful a means of communication and influence as to talk well.

— Chief Justice John Marshall

doll). An old Native American teaching story on stopping to listen has been translated into the following poem by David Wagoner:

LOST

Stand still. The trees ahead and the bushes beside you
are not lost. Wherever you are is called Here,
and you must treat it as a powerful stranger,
must ask permission to know it and be known.
The forest breathes. Listen. It answers,
I have made this place around you,
if you leave it you may come back again, saying Here.

No two trees are the same to Raven.
No two branches are the same to Wren.
If what a tree or a bush does is lost on you,
you are surely lost. Stand still. The forest knows
where you are. You must let it find you.

When we stand still for a bit, as Blaze, Amy, Gene, and Edina did when they took a break and went to lunch, we can see the forest through the trees. We can recognize where in the woods we stand. Like Vasilisa we can then hear the voices that support our well-being. How often do we feel lost, not understanding where we are in a relationship, in a dispute, in our career, or in our life's journey? If we are able to rest and fully acknowledge our current position, from there we can map out our next steps.

My husband, Bruce, was raised on a guest ranch in southwestern Montana. From the time he could walk, he rode horses and entertained guests from all over the world. Each summer, he would guide groups of city folk through thickets and over mountain trails in the brilliance of the Rocky Mountains. And along with them he would get lost. When I asked him how he would get home again, he said, "I realized that I just needed to get really quiet. I'd tell the dudes to get off their horses, that we were taking a break, and I would buy myself some time. I'd just sit and listen. Then I would know which way to go next. It was never

Misfortune! Good fortune
supports it.
Good fortune! Misfortune hides
within.
Who knows where it ends?
Is there no order?

— I Ching

You have to stare the world in
the face although the world
may look at you with blood-
shot eyes. Do not fear. Trust
that little thing in you which
resides in the heart.

— Mahatma Gandhi

obvious and sometimes looked like the worst direction of all to proceed in. But it always led us home if I trusted it. The answer was already there — I just needed to listen."

OPEN THE HEA(R)T

As we take in our surroundings, how can we most effectively tune ourselves to hear the wisdom we need to resolve this conflict?

A mother of a client had a very painful childhood. She lost both parents and the maternal grandparents who had cared for her by the time she was an adolescent. After a breakdown as a young adult and a failed marriage, she rarely spoke about her past. As one of her six children, her daughter Ellen had asked her mother a hundred different ways about her life and the world that haunted both of them. Yet her mother chose to hold her silence.

Then late one night, Ellen called her mother to say she had just seen a movie from 1948 that she thought her mother must have seen and enjoyed. That night at midnight, her mother's stories from 1948 and earlier began to pour forth, tales of her childhood, her parents, and the family dog. These were the stories Ellen had wished for but had given up hope of ever hearing. Ellen said, "I have never felt so connected to my mother in my entire life. When I said, 'I love you' at the end of the call, I really meant it from a deep place inside myself."

When I asked what was different that night, Ellen said that she had not called her mother for any other reason than to tell her about the movie. It was late and quiet at both homes. Both women were tired, and all the internal thinking, worrying, and strategizing voices were asleep. Their hearts were open, truth spoke, and it was heard.

Scientists and mystics agree that the human heart is a powerful source of radiant information. A seminal study by Professors Gary Schwartz and Linda Russek of the University of Arizona shows that an electromagnetic field (EMF) emanates around our bodies, primarily from our hearts. In fact, the field emitted from the heart region is five thousand times more powerful than that from the brain. With focused attention on the heart through relaxation techniques such as Chi-Gong, meditation, and noncontact therapeutic healing, brain and heart waves of

You can only hope to find a lasting solution to a conflict if you have learned to see the other objectively, but, at the same time, to experience their difficulties subjectively.

*— Dag Hammarskjöld,
Markings*

the EMF synchronize within us and promote health. Most religious traditions call this energy "fire" and believe it is the source of wisdom. In Christianity, Sufism, Judaism, and other traditions, within this "spark of the soul" or fire in our hearts God resides in us.

We also have neural receptors in our hearts. Studies show that our hearts actually tell our minds what to think. You verify this when you listen to the slick executive or politician who says all the right things but you walk away knowing that something isn't quite right. The information received at the heart level does not match the information exchanged through words. A University of California, Berkeley, study showed that if we "unlearn" crossing our arms and legs, we both feel and are perceived as more open and approachable. When we combine this research with the EMF studies of the University of Arizona, it seems reasonable that removing any barriers to our heart's EMF would allow us to listen more directly and openly to any information given.

The hardest part of this conflict phase to grasp is a willingness to listen. I find that sometimes I do not want to hear what is being said. Fear surrounds us all. When a friend speaks of her pain or fear, I don't always want to know about it. I am afraid I will lose her, our relationship, and my view of the world as a happy and safe place. It is why we turn away from the picture of the starving child and, depending on our worldview, from the picture of the happy family eating a holiday meal.

Listening insists that we enter into the world of the unknown without fear. Listening demands courage or a strong heart. When we strip away all that we know and suspend it in front of us, even for a moment, magic occurs. Madeleine L'Engle, after losing her forty-seven-year-old son, provided this perspective: "Creativity comes from accepting that you're not safe, from being absolutely aware, and from letting go of control. It's a matter of seeing everything — even when you want to shut your eyes." By acknowledging fear and consciously working to keep our hearts open we will hear the answers.

We are compassionate when we connect to another's heart or "passion" and contemplate their wounds and their joys. I can use contemplation to transform the "wavelength" I'm on and come into rhythm with another. As a woman, I must understand the challenges and hopes of men. As an adult, I must contemplate the heartfelt joy and struggle of

It is only with the heart that one can see rightly. What is essential is invisible to the eye.

— Antoine de Saint-Exupéry

The friend who can be silent with us in a moment of despair or confusion, who can stay with us in an hour of grief and bereavement, who can tolerate not knowing, not curing, not healing, and face us with the reality of our powerlessness, that is the friend who cares.

— Henri Nouwen

today's children. As a parent with a devoted spouse, I must spend time understanding the work and life of a single parent. By entering another's suffering and passions we open our hearts and develop an expanded perspective.

TO EXPLORE

In conflict, *stop* and assess your location. Take some time to observe where you stand. Make no decisions; just be an observer. Who is with you? What is their status? What is yours? Create stillness around you so you may see where you are and hone your heart to hear where you should go next. Don't do anything until the next step is clear.

LIST WHAT YOU KNOW ABOUT YOUR LOCATION

Be compassionate as your Creator is compassionate.

— Luke 6:36

The main challenges of this phase are anxiety and frustration or oppression. Time becomes our enemy. We see these characteristics in Vasilisa as she faces the huge tasks of sorting the corn and poppyseeds, the other chores, a short time frame, and the risk of death. We can see the first step to overcoming these challenges and moving through the Fire phase when she first *lists what is overwhelming her.*

The elemental gift of acknowledgment described in part 1 helps strengthen our hearts and keeps the fire burning under control. Acknowledgment is the powerful act of consciously noticing something, and it helps keep everyone involved. As painter and critic John Ruskin said, "The greatest thing the human soul does in this world is to see something, and to tell what it saw."

The test of a first-rate intelligence is the ability to hold two opposed ideas in mind at the same time and still retain the ability to function.

— F. Scott Fitzgerald

Internal acknowledgment consists of reciting everything you know about a problem, whether or not you agree with it. As we read when Edina described their current situation at lunch with Gene, acknowledging our beliefs and fears can act as a pressure valve that relieves oppressive anxiety. External acknowledgment is even more powerful, since you are able to let another know that you see them and understand their argument. It relieves their concern, and as a result they are more willing to see you. When we acknowledge all the opposing views it strengthens us and allows the larger picture to emerge.

Through acknowledgment we can consciously collect the fuel and feed the fire. We are then able to weather the internal storm and emerge not only to rewrite the way we perceive the world but also to redefine our cultural stories. In the last one hundred years in the United States we have seen African Americans and women of all races creatively expand their stories and respond to the struggles of racism and sexism. By acknowledging the warring stories through discussions on human rights, societal roles, and equality, they have changed the larger cultural belief system. In just one hundred years, the expanded African American's and woman's story can now include the phrases, "I vote, I participate in the highest branches of government, I am wealthy and powerful. I now *write* rules for my society."

A moment's insight is sometimes worth a lifetime's experience.

— Oliver Wendell Holmes

TO EXPLORE

List everything you know about a conflict. What do you believe? What do your opponents believe? What is clashing? What are the constraints? What is causing you and others anxiety? Just as writing a to-do list when the workload becomes overwhelming eases the stress, pulling together what you now know about a situation helps move you toward resolution and away from exploding!

TIP 2: LOOK

We can use many information resources to help us answer the question posed by a conflict. Vasilisa's doll, symbolizing intuition or our inner voice, demonstrates the power of also looking to nontraditional sources. Some consider these "signs from the heavens" that will give us clues about where to proceed in this conflict. Open your inner and outer "eyes," and you may see the solution.

Dreams come when the connection between the body and soul is broken.

— Chinese proverb

LOOK TO YOUR DREAMS: CALLS FROM THE PILLOW

Dreams are regarded as a valuable and accepted source of insight, inspiration, and guidance by virtually every cultural tradition in the world. Tibetans spend their lives watching and working with dreams. The Aborigines of Australia see their dreams as the most powerful aspect of their time on this earth. The Old and New Testaments speak of powerful waking dreams, visions, and sleeping dreams that changed history. Jungian and other psychological philosophies look to our dreams to decipher internal conflict and to gauge our mental health.

Since conflict as a state asks for an expanded or shifted perspective, listening to our dreams can provide great insight as our minds reprocess gathered information in novel ways. Just like our conversations, not all our dreams will yield tremendous, conflict-transforming insights. Author Kelly Buckeley states that cross-culturally dreams are watched warily since misinterpretation has caused great strife and conflict throughout history. Some dreams are classified as "true, meaningful and/or spiritually valuable, and other dreams as false, meaningless and/or spiritually insignificant." However, we can often feel when a dream is ripe with information.

There are many methods for interpreting these important dreams, although my personal favorite is what Jeremy Taylor calls "If it were my dream." In this method, I tell others my dream, and the other parties pretend to be me as they interpret it. This method incorporates the premise that I can only provide you ideas based on my own limited perspective. As Jeremy says, "Any interpretation will be a shameless projection." Yet this projection or perspective can hold great insight.

The rules of "If it were my dream" are as follows:

1. I share my dream in complete confidence.

2. Others in the group ask questions to fill out the picture of the dream I have created. Typical questions might be, How did the dream end, What colors were present, When and where did it occur, and How did you feel?

3. If another feels moved, she provides an interpretation of the dream *as if the person speaking were the dreamer.* One begins, "If it were my dream, I…" and continues the entire interpretation in the first person. This allows the dreamer to remember that he is not being analyzed or judged and that the interpretation belongs only to the one speaking.

4. Only the dreamer knows, by the feeling of "Aha, that's it!" if the interpretation holds truth in his experience.

The function of dreams is to teach the waking mind how to forget what it thinks it knows but doesn't.

— William R. Stimson

5. There are always multiple layers of a dream. Physical, emotional, and spiritual planes are simultaneously represented within a single dream image.

TO EXPLORE

Write down your dreams while in conflict. Look for reoccurring symbols. Ask your partner or a friend to play "If it were my dream."

LOOK TO THE SIGNS

Most traditions use some type of oracular practice as a tool to determine the next step in a difficult situation. Through the ages, inspiration and guidance were found by opening a favorite book or religious text randomly and selecting a passage with closed eyes. In the Christian tradition, this is a form of contemplation, called *Lectio Divina*. The text that "jumps out of the book" holds the answer to the question; the mind is quieted to understand it. The randomly selected text is read multiple times or repeated during meditation. The contemplative then quiets the mind to understand an expanded meaning of the message. Medieval priest St. John of the Cross described this process in four stages: read, empty the mind, pray or ask a question, then contemplate or listen.

The Taoist tradition calls on the *I Ching*, or *Book of Changes*, both as an illuminating text on the sixty-four states of change and conflict and as an oracular tool. To use the *I Ching*, one asks a question and throws three coins or sticks six times. The landing position of the coins or sticks is used to build a six-line symbol or hexagram that translates into one of the sixty-four states of change described in the *I Ching*. The reader then contemplates the advice given for that particular phase of change. In shamanic and Buddhist traditions one asks a question and then contemplates the answer by listening to a fast, constant drumbeat or to a series of bells or gongs. It has been proven that these sounds temporarily alter brain wave rhythms, which opens us up to new insights and images. In shamanism this process is called "journeying" to find an answer.

Jungian psychology also takes advantage of the ancient power of symbol to help us hear the inner voice. "The psychological mechanism for transforming energy is the symbol," explained C. G. Jung. The

There is something in the soul which is only God and the masters say it is nameless, having no proper name of its own.

— Meister Eckhart

A rock pile ceases to be a rock pile the moment a single man contemplates it, bearing within him the image of a cathedral.

— Antoine de Saint-Exupéry

Tarot, a card deck containing eighty-four themes, provides such a symbolic system to describe the human journey and its surrounding challenges and resources. Like the *I Ching*, the Tarot can be used to ask for guidance or can be seen as a symbolic guide to follow.

Watching for synchronistic or coincidental events is yet another listening device found throughout the spiritual traditions. For example, say I am trying to figure out the right approach to use with a difficult co-worker. Suddenly, a book on a friend's coffee table containing information on just that subject catches my eye. I overhear a conversation about effective communication while riding the subway. A class on co-worker relations is being offered at the community center just down the street.

We only find what we are looking for. By bringing a conflict into focus in our minds with a *willingness to hear*, we can then begin to look for the solution. All the ideas swirl around us — we just need to catch them. The Tarot, the *I Ching*, journeys, random text selections, and synchronistic events all provide information that we just have to choose to hear. Just as with dreams, only the recipient knows if the information or an interpretation of it is valuable or "true." Also, just as with dreams, the masters say that we must weigh this information with all the other data we receive before knowing what our heart's fire is trying to tell us.

TO EXPLORE

Open a book to a random spot. What does it tell you? Silly as they may seem, the above oracular tools may be just what you need to change your limited perspective on a situation.

LOOK TO OTHERS

The character of Baba Yaga in our folktale reminds us that solutions to our problems often come in strange packages. What would happen if in every conversation we believed that we were speaking with the teacher who holds all the answers in every conflict? What if we believed that the perfect answer could be found by listening to the grocery store clerk or to the ramblings of a six-year-old? Wouldn't we pay attention?

---

*Events make known
the will of God.*

— Sister Therese Couderc

---

*According to the Kabbalah, at
some point in the beginning of
things, the Holy was broken up
into countless sparks, which
were scattered throughout the
universe. There is a god spark
in everyone and in everything,
a sort of diaspora of goodness . . .
the Holy may speak to you
from its hidden places at any
time. The world may whisper
in your ear, or the spark of
God may whisper in
your heart.*

— Rachel Naomi Remen

In the Earth phase we addressed listening to others, even the ugly and smelly Lady Ragnell of our King Arthur legend, to gather information on the situation as it exists today. We return to this practice in the Fire phase as we seek not just information but also innovative solutions. Here we attempt seeing another not only as a source of information but also as a source of great wisdom.

We have the opportunity to learn more by believing that each of us holds a god spark, or extraordinary insight. When I am listening to another, can I hear this essence speaking? What is it saying? I will feel like I see glimmers of this spark, this common connection, at different points when someone converses, and then it will be gone. Perhaps it is because at that moment I see and hear clearly as my filters and veils of judgment drop. Perhaps, it is often hidden and hard to discern, but our bodies react with a "yes" when we hear it.

Be not forgetful to entertain strangers: for thereby some have entertained angels unawares.

— Hebrews 13:2

TO EXPLORE

Apply the above dream-deciphering method to conflict interpretation. Try to remember that just as with dream interpretation, any perspective I might provide you with is just a "shameless projection" of my own experience. Yet you might see and understand elements of an issue that I have missed. If you are asked to listen to another person's conflict, first refer to the code of conduct described in the Earth chapter:

Act with courage and dignity; stick to the ideals that give meaning to life.

— Jawaharlal Nehru

1. Hold all you hear in complete confidence.

2. Ask questions in order to gain as complete a picture as possible.

3. To offer your perspective, begin with, "If it were my conflict, I..." speaking in the first person throughout your interpretation.

4. Remember that only the person in the conflict will know what is true in her situation.

5. Also remember that each conflict contains multiple layers. A dispute with a co-worker may be more closely related to a conflict from twenty years ago than to the current issue. Each

conflict holds rich materials for understanding our physical, emotional, and spiritual aspects.

Trust thyself, every heart vibrates to that iron string. Accept the place the divine providence has found for you, the society of your contemporaries, the connection of events. Great men have always done so.

— Ralph Waldo Emerson

LOOK WITHIN

Just like another may hold great wisdom, so do we. To listen within, sometimes it helps to move a conflict outside of you to capture creative ideas. That is perhaps why in the folktale the doll was selected as the story's symbol. It shows how much easier it is to hear our inner wisdom when it is standing in front of us. The following exercise can serve as a method to move what is spoken within to a place where we might hear it better. This exercise was adapted from *The Fifth Discipline Fieldbook* by Peter Senge, who credits Clif Barry with its development.

THE PROJECTOR AND SCREENS

Find two partners to participate. You will be the "movie projector" or speaker, and your two friends will act as "screens" or listeners. First, the projector selects a conflict, preferably an internal one. The projector then describes one side of this conflict to the first screen and the other side to the second screen. If I am trying to decide where to go on vacation, one friend might represent the argument to go to Mexico and the other to go to Florida. The screens must listen very carefully, since they will take on the perspective given to each of them by the projector as though it was their own. They will only be able to use the information you as the projector provide them, for example, "I want to go to Mexico because it's fun to speak Spanish, I love the food..."

Next your screen friends turn to one another and, as though they were the parties in a conflict, they present their sides to each other. The projector may jump in at any time to clarify the positions, and the screens may ask questions to further clarify the positions you have given them. After five to ten minutes of discussion, the three participants share their experiences.

Participants in this exercise often report that just hearing a personal conflict as an outside observer provokes new creative solutions and perspectives. It is also a great listening exercise as a "screen," knowing you must defend a position and thus carefully gather information about your position.

TO EXPLORE

Use the projector and screens with your team to solve your current conflict. Each team member brings his or her own questions to the conflict. I might ask, "Should I leave the organization?" I might think out loud using this exercise to try on different possible resolutions: "Should we move to New Mexico?"

LOOK FOR THE SPARKS: BRAINSTORM

What if we don't have time to quietly contemplate and watch for the signs? What if we are in the heat of the battle at a negotiation table? To tune our minds and hearts to the optimal wavelength, add a brainstorming session to every discussion in conflict. When a meeting is called in advance to discuss a conflict or difficult situation, add an invitation to brainstorm to the meeting notice. Also add written ground rules to the meeting invitation informing others that solutions that arise during the brainstorming phase of the meeting will not be criticized. If participants feel that their jobs or relationships are at risk in communicating new ideas, have an impartial third party gather and collate potential solutions.

When we move into brainstorming mode, we see everyone at the table as containing a unique and creative perspective. There are no bad ideas. We suspend judgment of ideas and people. Ideas flow from the listening stage into the world. The more information participants are willing to share, the better the solution will be. Simply write down what is shared without judgment or discussion.

Ask each participant to be prepared to bring their most creative and audacious solutions to the problem at hand. Those who internally process information, or introverts, will often prepare before the meeting, whereas you will find the extroverts digging up and processing solutions during the meeting itself. If there is time, writing in a journal can be a great internal brainstorming tool. The key to writing as brainstorming is to keep going, even if there appears nothing to say. Write freely for five to ten minutes on each of the following questions. Doing this allows any answers that

Everyone should carefully observe which way his heart draws him, and then choose that way with all his strength.

— Hasidic saying

If you want to make peace, you don't talk to your friends. You talk to your enemies.

— Moshe Dayan

might lie within you to creep from your right brain (the creative part) to your left brain (your rational part) and on down to the paper.

TO EXPLORE

Pose the following questions either in a brainstorming session or in your journal to open the channels of communication:

1. What would the "best of all possible worlds" solution look like?

2. Where am I flexible, and where am I rigid with this problem?

3. Where can I take responsibility for my role in this conflict?

4. What can I acknowledge about others or myself in the conflict?

5. What are ten possible answers to the conflict?

6. Which solution pushes me the farthest, and which is the most plausible?

It takes a lot of courage to release the familiar and seemingly secure, to embrace the new. But there is no real security in what is no longer meaningful. There is more security in the adventurous and exciting, for in movement there is life, and in change there is power.

— Alan Cohen

These questions touch on the mental, emotional, and spiritual aspects of the conflict. Once you've dialogued with yourself about the conflict, writing readies you to return to your adversaries with some potential solutions. Remember, in the natural world, with each breakthrough that arises a multitude of options present themselves, many of which do not survive. Don't get attached to your solutions, since lots of them won't work; rather, see them as starting points and ways to understand the conflict, your comfort zone, and your growing edges.

TIP 3: LISTEN

We must now decipher which solutions carry *shih*. In the folktale the doll looked just like Vasilisa, which tells us that to know if an answer is correct, we must return to ourselves. Our own bodies are actually our best tools for divining the next step in conflict.

LISTEN TO YOUR BODY

Our bodies respond to information and can guide us to the best solution. Learning what "yes" and "no" feel like in your body and trusting this wisdom can be a useful method in conflict. For example, let's notice what your body does when things are not going well. Imagine the following scenario: It is 5 o'clock, and you are in the grocery store. You are hungry and can't find the pasta sauce. If you have children, add them to your shopping experience. They are hungry and letting you know all about it. Suddenly down the aisle comes the one person you do not want to see, seeking you out to talk about the one thing you don't want to discuss. Your back is against the cereal boxes, and this person is laying out their case point by point. Your kids are tugging at your clothing. You are still hungry and looking for an escape. Is your heart constricted? Jaw tense? Stomach in knots? Are your eyes darting? Does your head hurt? Is your throat aching? Are your shoulders up around your ears? Would you be ready to run or attack? Here your body is saying "no" in one way or another to the current imagined situation.

In comparison, picture yourself in your favorite place on earth under the best of conditions. Perhaps it is in the mountains or on a beach with afternoon sun and a gentle breeze. How does your body feel now? Under these conditions I feel relaxed, right with the world. In this state I can find what "yes" feels like physically as my entire being agrees with the world around me.

When I become tense, my physical responses can hold clues:

1. Much of the information we take in comes in through our head. A tight forehead or headache might be telling us that we are unwilling to absorb some piece of information.

2. The shoulders, the throat, and jaw all support our communication. Constriction in these areas can mean we have something we want to say but are not expressing it.

3. The heart is our center of courage. Sudden tightness in our chest often signals some type of fear.

4. The gut and stomach hold clues to our emotional core. Our self-esteem or emotional health is being affected when our stomach is tied in knots.

When one is pretending, the entire body revolts.

— Anaïs Nin

The heart outstrips the clumsy senses, and sees — perhaps for an instant, perhaps for long periods of bliss — an undistorted and more veritable world.

— Evelyn Underhill

Our body can tell us what step to take next. For example, a tight throat can signal the internal question, "What do I want to say but am unwilling?" Or it might allow us to respond, "I need time to think about what you've said. I want to respond but I am not ready."

We listen for a solution. Our body can also tell us if a solution feels right or not. An idea appears but my heart constricts. Using my body wisdom, I can then ask myself, "What scares me about this solution?" "Is this a valid fear?" From here I can work on the fear or recognize that this is not yet the right solution and continue to listen or revise.

WHAT IS TRUE?

You cannot truly listen to anyone and do anything else at the same time.

— M. Scott Peck

Truth equates to what feels deeply, surely right. When truth is elusive, the following exercise, adapted from Zen and Hindu practices, can be very helpful. Do this exercise in a spirit of curiosity and playfulness. Have a partner ask you the question, "What is true for you in this conflict?" or, "What is true for you at this moment?" depending on which question makes the most sense.

Please note that the role of the partner in this exercise can be demanding in that as you search in your internal nooks and crannies to find the truth your partner may sense your discomfort and wish to relieve you of these feelings. He might want to lighten the situation with laughter or advice or try to move away from the uncomfortable subject. This will only stop your search, and his intervention should be avoided. Tell him he needs to be relentless in his questioning and to stop only when you are willing to. Your partner should not provide any feedback until the process is complete. He should just ask the question and then stay completely present to the experience. This is an exercise for the partner in "witness listening," that is, being a witness to another without rescuing, judging, or offering advice.

Answer the question. When you begin to slow down or stumble, your partner should return to the question. Reply. Again, as you slow, your partner returns to the question. At each pause, the partner asks. Continue in this way for at least fifteen to twenty minutes or until you feel that you have hit on a "truth." Truth possesses an inherent energy. Your body will feel open and will say "yes" when you find it. You and your partner will feel it.

TO EXPLORE

Watch what happens in your body when something doesn't feel right. What body signals alert you that you are ready to flee or fight? What signals tell you that all is well with the world? How do you feel physically when you lie?

Isn't this what poetry is, letting what is there be there, radiantly, all of it? When we become involved with "all of it" we are likely to get tuned in on hidden matters. We are likely to begin to hear things.

— M. C. Richards

ART OF CONFLICT: POETRY

In this phase of conflict, we are trying to hold within us everything we have heard. When we do this effectively, it is as though all the pieces of information are the ingredients, and the energy of creative tension mixes and cooks those ingredients to make a fantastic meal — if we can stand the heat! In our folktale Vasilisa was advised just to listen and take all the contradictory information within her. She then was told to sleep, or to awaken her subconscious creativity, and a solution would birth itself.

Poets know how to stay centered and sane through this fiery phase. Their art is to hold and love all seeming opposites, uniting them through their subconscious creativity. Harkening back to the fiery practice of acknowledgment discussed in part 1, poetry is an extraordinary form of this elemental gift and can center us while we are holding disparate views and priorities.

Writing poetry can feel like a daunting process. However, anyone can do it. Here's an exercise to help you write a poem about a conflict:

1. Find a quiet place, pen, paper, and twenty to thirty minutes of time alone.

2. Think about a current conflict. Picture the players, the emotions, the issues.

3. Begin listing everything that comes to mind about the conflict. Include colors, feelings, positions, players, and images, no matter

how strange. Write for at least five minutes. For example, if I were to list information about a neighborhood conflict over recycling cardboard boxes I might write:

- She's got time to garden while boxes fall out of her garbage cans.

- The dumpster is downtown.

- Garbage holds keys to our past; it is good, I am told.

- My green friends, how do I protect you and save my children's future?

- Does it really matter who's right?

- Too busy; there's not enough money for curbside.

- I see the blue sky, green trees, growing homes, and families.

- I feel hope and frustration, sprinkled with hopeless judgment.

- Is this the way to save the world or to pit men in battle?

Mix and match the above, and you can create poetry. It doesn't need to rival Robert Frost, but look what happens when the list is rearranged and includes all the opposites:

Boxes falling out of cans, abandoned
she sits in a neat garden
Keys to our past or to
my children's future.
Who's right?
Sky, homes, babies all neighbors to
my green friends, do I save you?
What justification for judgment
my garbage is good and yours is bad
Too busy, will there be enough time
hope and frustration sprinkled with hopeless judgment
does it really matter?

M. C. Richards, a master poet and teacher, summarized the connection between listening, poetry, and resolution when she wrote, "Perception if it is true is direct: inclusive: poetic."

When power leads man towards arrogance, poetry reminds him of his limitations. When power narrows the area of man's concern, poetry reminds him of the richness and diversity of existence. When power corrupts, poetry cleanses.

— John F. Kennedy

AN ELEMENTAL ROLE MODEL: HILDEGARD OF BINGEN

Our fiery heroine Vasilisa mirrored the true mystic. The mystic's gift, symbolized in the doll, is an honest and direct connection to the common consciousness that some call the Divine, Truth, or Mystery. One of the most prolific Christian mystics, Hildegard of Bingen modeled how mysticism can bring about technological invention, great compassion, and art.

Hildegard of Bingen was born in 1098 in Germany as the tenth of ten children. As was customary in those days, Hildegard was tithed to the Church and at the age of eight was sent to live in a Benedictine monastery. By eighteen, she had taken the vows of a nun. Hildegard had visions and premonitions from a very young age. In her early forties, not long after she had taken over leadership of a female Benedictine monastic community, Hildegard experienced a strong vision in which she was told to write about her constant communications with God. At first, she refused and, as a result, she became gravely ill. Lying in bed she decided that only through surrendering to God's request would she be healed. Hildegard writes, "Once I did this, a deep and profound exposition of books came over me. I received the strength to rise up from my sick bed, and under that power I continued to carry out the work to the end, using all of ten years to do it." The result was *Scivias*, or *Know the Ways*, which includes written and painted description of her visions.

Hildegard was a nun in service of others, and one of her organizing principles was to *heal creatively* in every form possible. She wrote the herbalist classic *Physica* that detailed the healing powers of native plants. She has been credited for inventing indoor plumbing in her region to reduce wintertime illnesses and to prevent the nuns from bloodying their hands from daily breaking through ice on the well. She also created extraordinary music, which possesses soothing, healing qualities.

As a mystic, Hildegard focused on seeking unity and interconnection to create resolution. She wrote, "God has arranged all things in the world in consideration of everything else ... O Holy Spirit, you are the mighty way in which every thing that is in the heavens, on the earth,

Wisdom resides in all creative works. Every artist ... at every act of birth has tasted of the cosmic terror that precedes creativity.

— Hildegard of Bingen

and under the earth, is penetrated with connectedness, penetrated with relatedness."

Through the undying faith in her visions and commitment to the heart Hildegard counseled and admonished the pope and other clerical leaders. She broke with tradition and built her own successful monasteries in Rupertsberg and Eibingen. She traveled widely, preaching to clergy, church officials, and laity.

To inspire us to contemplate the possibilities and search for a solution to conflict, Hildegard offered the following words:

> *Truly, the Holy Spirit is an unquenchable fire.*
> *He bestows all excellence,*
> > *sparks all worth,*
> > *awakes all goodness,*
> > *ignites speech,*
> > *enflames humankind.*
> *Yet in this radiance is a restorative stillness.*
> *It is the stillness that is similarly in the will to good.*
> *It spreads to all sides.*
>
> *The Holy Spirit then, through one's fervent longings,*
> *pours juice of contrition*
> *into the hardened human heart.*

SUMMARY: FIRE — CREATIVITY

ATTRIBUTES	We ignite the *Fire phase* when we: • Feel overwhelmed by conflicting ideas and options. • Notice the dispute heating up, feel anxiety and pressure mount. • Focus on creativity, innovation, and new paradigms.
TASK	The goal of this phase is to *capture new ideas.*
CHALLENGES AND ELEMENTAL PRINCIPLE	To overcome the challenges of *oppression* and *anxiety,* we practice the principle of *contemplation.* *Contemplation* involves assessing what we know and opening to hear our next step.

TIPS AND TECHNIQUES	To enhance listening skills it is helpful to:
	1. *Stop* and:
	   • Quiet your mind.
	   • Open your heart.
	   • Assess your present location.
	2. *Look* for all the creative information available through:
	   • Dreams and intuition
	   • Oracular tools
	   • Other people
	3. *Listen for* a solution full of *shih,* or innate power.

VOCATION AND DISCIPLINE	*Mystics* across the world know how to feel the fire within and around them. The traits of a mystic include an open and passionate heart, a quiet mind, and supreme trust in the greater consciousness. The daily discipline of *movement* is prescribed.
ELEMENTAL GIFT	During the Fire phase keep all parties from burning out *by acknowledging their gifts, contributions, needs, and perspectives.*
ART OF CONFLICT	The artistic practice of *poetry* fuels creativity and expanded consciousness.
ELEMENTAL ROLE MODEL	*Hildegard of Bingen*

Phase 4

Air — Stability

- **TASK:** Implement win-win solution and find areas of common ground
- **ELEMENTAL PRINCIPLE:** Communicate
- **CHALLENGES:** Fear of abandonment, self-doubt, and confusion
- **BEST ELEMENTAL GIFT:** Honesty

There is the grain of the prophet in the recesses of every human existence.

— Rabbi Heschel

*If you want to make peace, you don't talk to your friends.
You talk to your enemies.*

— Moshe Dayan

Before now, in a small village in China, there lived a widow with her three sons. The middle-aged mother was known throughout the region as the creator of the most beautiful and sought-after brocades. Because of her sewing, her family had modest means and were fed and sheltered.

One day after selling her latest brocade in the first half hour of market, she wandered happily among the stalls. Her eyes caught sight of a small painting of a white house with a red roof. Rich fields full of animals and crops surrounded this home. A small pond was filled with red fish. Birds called to her from this work of art that she had never seen before. This painting described perfectly the world in which she longed to live.

She fell in love with this picture and came home to tell her sons what she had seen. After she described the painting, her first son said, "You will never see that world in this life." Her second son agreed, calling her longing a folly. But her third son said, "Mother, why don't you buy that painting and make it into a brocade? It will be almost as good as living within it."

She was thrilled by this idea and ran to the market to buy the painting and the needed materials. And she began to work. She worked tirelessly day and night, burning pine boughs for light. The smoke brought tears to her eyes, and she sewed these tears into the pond and its neighboring stream. After a year, her two older sons came to her complaining, "All you do is work on your beloved brocade. We are tired of having to cut wood in the forest. Sell something so we do not have to work so hard." Her youngest son replied, "Don't worry, Mother. I will go to the forest each day and make enough money so that we may eat."

She continued to work. After two years, her eyes grew tired, and as she worked at night to the burning boughs her tears would fall upon the brocade, red with blood. These tears she sewed into the red roof and the sun and the small fish in the pond.

After three years, the widow finally completed the brocade. She called to her sons, and together they went outside to look at the completed work in the sun. But just as she unfurled the brocade for all to see, a strong wind came from the West and blew the brocade from the woman's arms. The gust lifted the fabric, and within seconds it was gone. The widow collapsed in a faint.

Her sons took her inside and laid her upon the bed. When she awoke she begged her eldest son to go East and recover her brocade. "It means more to me than my life," she cried.

So the eldest son set out. He walked for four months until he came to a small stone house in the mountains. In front of the house was a stone horse, mouth open and fixed, ready to eat some berries off a quaint bush. Out of the house came an old woman. He told her he was looking for his mother's brocade. "Oh, I know of this. It was the fairies who wanted this beautiful jewel. They have taken it to their castle so they may make one of their own. To get there, now, that is the problem," she explained. "First you will need to knock out your two front teeth, which I will place in the mouth of this horse. As I do this, he will come to life and will eat ten red berries from this bush. He will then carry you to the castle. You will need to travel East through the Ice Sea. If you even shudder or recoil from the cold both you and the horse will drown." She continued, "Then you will need to ride over Fire Mountain. The flames will lap at your legs, and the heat will be terrible. If you pull back from this fire, you and the horse will be burned alive. If you survive these trials, you will find the castle. It is on this path you must return."

She noticed his ashen face and laughed. The old woman scurried inside and brought out a wooden box. Handing him the box, she said, "There is enough gold in this box to keep your family comfortable till the end of your days. Take it and return home."

Well, the man looked at the gold as he walked West and said, "Gold for one goes much farther than gold for four." He went to the city, never to return to his mother again.

When the mother could wait no longer she called to her second son to go find the brocade, again saying, "It means more to me than my life." She was now ill and unable to rise from bed.

Her second son set off, traveling four months to the house in the mountains. He too heard of the trials that awaited him to reclaim the brocade. He too grew ashen at what he heard. The old woman laughed again and rewarded the second son with a box of gold. The young man walked West as did his older brother and said, "Gold for one is better than gold for three." He never returned to his mother again.

The widow became blind with grief. After four months, her last son begged her to let him go recover the brocade. She finally released him with hopes of his success.

Now, the youngest son took just two months to arrive at the stone house. The old woman emerged, shaking her head with amusement. She told him of the terrible journey that lay ahead and stood ready to provide him a box just as she had his brothers. Instead, the young man looked the old woman squarely in the eyes and knocked out his two front teeth. She bowed, took the bloody teeth, and placed them in the horse's mouth. A dashing stallion now stomped the ground in the stone horse's place. The horse ate the fruit, and the young man jumped upon his back.

To the East they rode. Through Ice Sea without as much as a shiver they rode. Over Fire Mountain with flames around their legs and torsos they rode without flinching. And there in front of the young man stood the fairies' castle.

Dismounting, he knocked at the door. A beautiful young fairy dressed in red answered the door saying, "We have been expecting you. We are just about done." As he entered the great hall he saw hundreds of fairies bent over two brocades. Upon one they sewed feverishly. Over another, they looked intently. This was his mother's.

The fairies brought the young man food and drink and showed him to goosedown pillows where he might sit and watch them work. When night fell, they hung a massive pearl above the brocades to light their work. He fell asleep. Late in the night, the fairies finished their copied brocade.

As the young fairy dressed in red passed by the widow's brocade one last time, she could barely stand the grief of saying good-bye to its beauty. After all had gone to rest, she sewed a small red fairy into the widow's brocade, sitting by the pond.

When the young man awoke before dawn, he was alone. He grabbed his mother's brocade, folded it into his coat, and ran out to the horse. He rode West over Fire Mountain and Ice Sea with steely resolve. He rode West to the stone house.

There he was met by the smiling woman who removed the front teeth from the horse and placed them unharmed in the young man's mouth. The horse became stone, poised once again to eat the fruit. She told him to wait, that she had a gift for him.

She emerged from the house holding deer-hide moccasins. "Place these on your feet, and you will be home before you know it," she said. Thanking her, he did, and soon he was home.

The young man ran into the house and carried his mother into the sunlight. With a strong grasp, they each held the edges of the brocade to admire it once more. As the widow touched the brocade, her sight was restored.

The brocade began to shimmer and shift in the sunlight. It began to expand and breathe. It grew larger and grander until it was the landscape itself. The widow's beloved scene became the world in front of her. There stood her house, rolling fields full of livestock. The rare birds flew overhead. And down by the stream, there sat the lovely young fairy dressed in red.

And, as these stories go, the widow shared this bounty with her neighbors so that they all lived in happiness and abundance the rest of their days. And, as these stories go, the young man married the fairy and lived most happily.

One day, two beggars walked in front of the gate. They saw an old woman and a handsome couple sitting by the pond and thought they should ask for some food. In surprise, they recognized their mother and youngest brother and slunk away in shame.

It is not knowing that is difficult, but the doing.

— Shu King,
The Huntsman

INTRODUCTION

It is time to test the new ideas that Blaze, Gene, Edina, and Amy have developed. Creating a three-pronged approach to tackle their current crisis...

Amy would speak with Marty at Ace Construction about subcontracting immediately.

Blaze would call each of the companies advertising project manager positions to make a presentation on their new division, Diamond Consulting. Blaze was energized: "I had never thought of building things outside of construction."

Within ten days, they would present their current situation and action plan to their employees. A common goal was set not to lay off any employees. In the effort to care for their employees they decided to offer unpaid leave and job-search counseling if they could not secure ample work for the company. And they would continue to meet weekly until the company was stable once more.

"I can live with being honest with the employees and trying to support them as best we can," said Gene. "I don't know how better we could serve them or ourselves."

The next day, Amy met with Marty. She was nervous about speaking of subcontracting, as she would be admitting to Diamond's current business challenges. And yet she knew that being direct would be a relief. Diamond Construction was a qualified team, and Ace would be lucky to work with them. Her honesty paid off as Marty then openly shared Ace's cost and time overruns. By the end of the meeting, Amy and Marty had tentative plans to partner on the large Gerber project, using Diamond's strong management skills.

Despite the tight finances, all four friends felt the best they had in months. The team felt solid and directed as they moved forward.

If you know these things, blessed are you if you do them.

— John 8:17

We are returning to where things make sense and where we find increased order and stability. We can feel the wind and see the light coming from the end of the tunnel that we were feeling our way through during the second and third phases of conflict. We have some creative ideas about how to move toward a resolution and perhaps a few beliefs that have been expanded or reassessed. We have learned about our opponents and ourselves. It's now time to act.

Air stories, like "The Magic Brocade," speak to the result of bringing creative ideas into concrete form. Air is often associated with action or communication, and air stories teach us how best to communicate or effect change. The Chinese story reminds us that if we effectively communicate as the widow did through her brocade, we can transform reality.

The element of Air is associated with communication and mental activities. Air is connected with breath, our constant action or communication with the world. Air is everywhere and though invisible is very potent if used effectively. Air makes new forms, from desert dunes to ocean waves and forest fires.

When we communicate, either through words or through actions such as works of art, we use the power of air. We can "blow someone over" or "blow smoke," or we can "inspire," which comes from the Latin word for breath and spirit. When we communicate we connect and *commune* with the greater *community* to which we belong. We create the "winds of change." Using the energy of air, we make our mark.

Masters from around the globe advise us not only to "know" but to act on our ideas without fear or doubt. For example, you realize you need to apologize to someone; now it is time to muster the courage and do it. In the case of Diamond Construction's founders, it is now time to make phone calls and meet with prospective customers. As in the natural world, acting is the logical extension of life. When the time is right, a pine tree drops a cone. The pumpkin plant releases its blossoms. The cat gives birth and nurtures her young. Systems return to *stability* through action.

Communication is the corresponding "exhale" to the "inhale" of listening that takes place in the Fire phase. We learn something, and then we respond. We notice that something is true, and we express it and complete the cycle. All our actions are a form of communication. We communicate through words, through art, and through building new structures. Communication is easy if we have truly listened to head, gut, and heart and now have the courage to act.

ELEMENTAL PRINCIPLE: COMMUNICATE

Powerful communication does not consist of a slick speech or a written essay. It may just be an honest description of our emotional landscape. "I am unclear about what to do next," "I have been furious with you," or "I'm exhausted and need to sleep," may be all we need to say. It is honesty about our intention and how we communicate this intention that will drive the ultimate results. Amy's integrity and clear intention to support her company and look for a collaborative solution with Ace Construction demonstrates the power of honest, direct communication.

Sincere words are not embellished;
Embellished words are not sincere.
Those who are good are not defensive;
those who are defensive are not good.
Those who know are not erudite;
Those who are erudite do not know....

The Tao of Nature
Is to serve without spoiling.
The Tao of Evolved Individuals
Is to act without contending.

— Tao Te Ching

Returning to the four phases mapped on the yin/yang, we are now predominantly in a phase of the known and the action-oriented, or in the white of the Taoist symbol. We are moving out of night into day, or from the irrational into the rational. We roll up our sleeves and get to work. We are defining the who, what, where, when, and how of our newly developed ideas.

Yet when mapping this stage onto the yin/yang symbol, you will note that the black dot captures our eye. The black dot is the underlying motivation or the *essence* of our communication. At the center lies my basic intention, or why I am communicating in the first place.

A dog is not considered a good dog because he is a good barker. A man is not considered a good man because he is a good talker.

— Chuang-tzu

THE WAY OF CONFLICT AND THE TAOIST SYMBOL

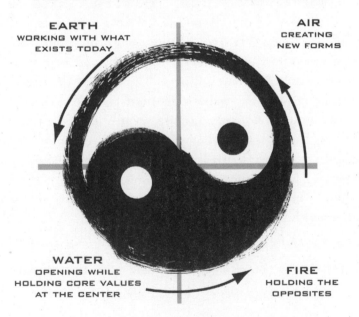

EARTH
WORKING WITH WHAT
EXISTS TODAY

AIR
CREATING
NEW FORMS

WATER
OPENING WHILE
HOLDING CORE VALUES
AT THE CENTER

FIRE
HOLDING THE
OPPOSITES

Those who powerfully communicate have a clear and often broadly inclusive motivation. Gandhi held countrywide peace, equality, and self-rule as his intentions in all pursuits. Hitler knew he wanted to conquer the world. The intention might be creative or destructive. Regardless, if it is clear and aligned with words and actions an innate force always comes through. Because of the clarity and broad appeal of these motivations, they both carried great energy.

My motivation may be to resolve a conflict. However, it could also be to teach another a lesson or to exact revenge. The motivation will be clearly communicated, whether we like it or not. We communicate our intention through visual and other sensory clues, and, if you are seeking to destroy your opponent, she will sense that something is amiss. If you are sincerely seeking to protect your opponent's interests and your own, he will eventually sense your sincerity. If I am clear about my motivation, I am rarely surprised by the results of a conversation. This is the power of honesty.

The impact of my communication derives largely from its under-lying motivation. As Gandhi once said, "True art takes note not merely of form but also of what lies behind. There is an art that kills and an art that gives life. True art must be evidence of happiness, contentment and purity of its authors." However, often we unwittingly hide our under-lying motivation from ourselves. Fear, self-doubt, and confusion are the Air phase's most common challenges. Thinking of the black dot at the center of the yin/yang symbol as the heart, try to keep the heart pres-ent and to trust it. Strive to place a unifying intention at the heart of each action to implement a win-win solution.

Four ideals create effective action, which I call the *principles of centered communication.* These are the values of a prophet:

1. *Act from truth:* Be honest.

2. *Act without a why:* Be detached from reward or punishment.

3. *Act from the largest possible perspective:* Include rather than separate.

4. *Act with acceptance and curiosity:* Cultivate courage.

John the Baptist, Albert Einstein, Susan B. Anthony, and Nelson Mandela are just a few examples of centered communicators or prophets who followed these guidelines. Rumi describes one who acts from this centered state in his poem "Ali in Battle":

Learn from Ali how to fight
without your ego participating

A promise is a cloud;
fulfillment is rain.

— Arabian proverb

The most exhausting thing in
my life is being insincere.

— Anne Morrow
Lindbergh

God's lion did nothing
that didn't originate from his deep center.

Once in battle he got the best of a certain knight
And quickly drew his sword. The man,
Helpless on the ground, spat
in Ali's face. Ali dropped his sword,
relaxed and helped the man to his feet.

"Why have you spared me?
How has lightning contracted back
into its cloud? Speak, my prince,
So that my soul can begin to stir
in me like an embryo."

Thought is the blossom;
language the bud; action
the fruit behind it.

— Ralph Waldo Emerson

Ali was quiet and then finally answered,
"I am God's Lion, not the lion of passion.
The sun is my lord. I have no longing
except for the One.
When a wind of personal reaction comes,
I do not go along with it.

There are many winds full of anger,
and lust and greed. They move the rubbish
around, but the solid mountain of our true nature
stays where it's always been.

The political campaign
won't tire me, for I have an
advantage. I can be myself.

— John F. Kennedy

There's nothing now
except the divine qualities.
Come through the opening into me.

Your impudence was better than any reverence,
because in this moment I am you and you are me.
I give you this opened heart as God gives gifts:
The poison of your spit has become the honey of friendship."

Powerful communicators often appear peculiar yet confident. Abraham Maslow described similar traits when asked about self-actualized people. He said, "These individuals are less inhibited, less constricted, less bound, in a word, less enculturated." Prophets by definition are not enculturated. They do not get caught in the power of cultural stories but instead bring forth new narratives.

The prophets, the centered communicators like Susan B. Anthony, did not buy into cultural stories about God, the Universe, and the roles of women and people of color. They didn't constrict and hide from the old accounts but instead responded with courage to the world with trust in the guidance they embodied. And through their bold action, their ideas took form and substance. They understood that they controlled the stories and their fear. They confronted the old myths and described new possibilities.

We may perceive prophets to be activists or those who are fighting against injustice. I believe we act as prophets whenever we honestly and inclusively communicate, bringing together perceived opposites. Prophets are compelling when they tell stories or describe truths that unify and create new possibilities. They sometimes make implicit sense, or they open new doors and appear crazy. Regardless, we are prophets when we discover what is deeply and completely right for us and then communicate it in all that we say and do.

Don't judge his actions by what you would do. You are not living completely within truth as he is.

— Jelaluddin Rumi

PRACTICAL TIPS

TIP 1: ACT FROM TRUTH

Your body will signal when you have found a truth. If you are not clear, your lack of *integration* will come through. As dancer Gabrielle Roth reminds us, "We can't run from the body, and the body is the one part of us that can't lie. I can sit here and tell you a lie, but my body will tell you the truth....Someone tells us one thing but we pick up different vibrations. If we want the truth, we need to enter into our own physical universe and experience what is there." As we discussed in the previous chapter, if your throat, heart, or any other body part feels constricted, you have not arrived at a truth you can stand behind. The truth might elicit fear, but you will feel an "aha" when you have found it.

Meditate. Live purely. Be quiet. Do your work with mastery. Like the moon, come out from behind the clouds! Shine.

— Buddha

Angeles Arrien states that clear communication occurs when your words, actions, and tone are in alignment. A friend whom I regard as a very intuitive listener describes unaligned people as "fuzzy." She says that she sometimes finds herself squinting to try to bring them into focus. It is this lack of alignment that causes us to walk away confused from a smooth-talking executive or a slippery politician. The words sound good, but nothing else seems to match.

All conflict poses a question, and in this final phase we answer it. Sometimes it is a simple answer that does not greatly affect our lives. Other times we are presented with a question, and our responses determine our life paths. Martin Luther King Jr. was asked to lead the Montgomery bus boycott. In his affirmative answer, his life and ours were transformed as he led America farther out of segregation and discrimination than anyone else had in the twentieth century.

In the beginning of the movie *Jerry McGuire*, the smooth sports agent played by Tom Cruise is asked if there could be another more ethical and fulfilling way to treat his clients. The question is posed, and conflict begins (Earth). We watch as he struggles through despair and disgust as he realizes the adverse effect of his current slick-talking approach (Water). During a sleepless night in a hotel room, we see the protagonist sweat through the Fire phase and become inspired. Air takes hold as he writes a memo that describes a creative new way to work in his industry and then circulates it to everyone in his company. That memo changes his life in all kinds of uncomfortable yet transformative ways.

Many times throughout the movie he wishes that he had never created the mission statement. He is fired. He loses all his clients. His fiancée literally knocks him flat with a well-placed punch as she dumps him. He tries to downgrade his manifesto, repeatedly saying, "It was just a mission statement." And yet the mission statement holds true. It is what inspires his beautiful young business partner to stick with him through thick and thin. And it allows the protagonist to discover his core values and to chart an inspiring new course in his life and in the lives of those who surround him.

I wonder how often Martin Luther King Jr. wondered what his life might have been like if he had not led the bus boycott. No death threats and more time with his family. Less stress and strain. And yet his

When I hear a man discoursing of wisdom...I compare the man and his words, and note the harmony and correspondence of them.

— Plato

willingness to communicate changed a nation and inspires people throughout the world to this day.

Sometimes Air can be a very difficult stage as the "rubber meets the road." Truth is revealing and thus can be terrifying. When we know what must be said, we often wish we could forget. But we must act. Truth has a way of getting out. For example, I realize that I am unhappy in a job and really want to quit. That truth, as much as I might want to ignore it, has a life of its own and a power that finds its way through. Since we all communicate nonverbally, others will notice something but might not be able to fully interpret the truth. Even though I may be able to consciously ignore my feelings, you will still pick something up. I might be consistently late for meetings or slow to return my manager's phone calls. I might avoid eye contact or forget to turn in a critical report. And those who are part of the system in conflict, such as my employer, might act on this information. We've all seen this happen. The world responds to my nonverbal communication, and I am surprised that I have been fired. And yet these actions are ultimately responses to the power of my underlying communication, even if it is never clearly articulated.

Internally, a truth will eventually dog us until we give voice to it. It creates sleepless nights. It catches us off guard as it flies out of our mouths when we are angry or tired. Unfortunately, because of the inner conflict it might have to maneuver around, it can often come out garbled and subject to misinterpretation. When we consciously own and communicate the truth, it causes less damage and carries much more power. Sometimes it is difficult to communicate. When I facilitate discussions I always expect a subset of people to find me afterward to tell me "just one thing." This is the truth that has to be said. Acknowledging how powerful and critical this need is can often help us to overcome our initial fear and speak our truth.

Truth is not static, it is simply what we deeply know today. It is a partial and hopefully growing picture of reality that is being asked to be shared. I have found that to describe what I believe to be true, it is best to begin with "I." "I" statements are verbal recognition that I hold only one of many possible perspectives of reality. Instead of saying "the

A person's true wealth is the good he or she does in the world.

— Muhammad

The truth is more important than the facts.

— Frank Lloyd Wright

property line is here" or "you are mean," we open the door with, "In my experience, I believe the the property line to be here" or, "I perceive you as mean." Sometimes quite subtle, the discipline of reframing with "I" statements gently reminds us to leave room for another's views and for an expanded perspective that serves everyone.

TO EXPLORE

Practice the first step in centered communication by following the three guidelines:

1. *Trust your heart* and stand by it.

2. *Be direct:* Speak openly and directly with the person with whom you are in conflict. We have more of an impact when we communicate directly to the proper party or parties.

3. *Take control of where and when you speak:* Use what you have learned about right timing and location during the setting of ground rules in the Earth phase of conflict. Your communication can carry more *shih* if you consciously choose when, where, and with whom you share it.

TIP 2: ACT WITHOUT A WHY

One communication trap is expecting a certain outcome. Masters throughout time have advised us to speak our hearts and let the results be what they may. The youngest son in the Chinese tale did not focus on an ultimate reward. He knew what he had to do, and he did it. Amy models this detachment as well in her conversation with Marty.

Christian mystic Meister Eckhart constantly advised, "Work without a why." Mindful action without thought of reaction forms the foundation of most traditions. This is the tenet of detachment or letting go as described during the Water phase. We are letting go of our expectations about the outcome of our communication.

The action/reaction trap is commonly found in the simple statement, "I'm sorry." Sometimes I might say I am sorry not because I am but because I want you to like me again. Or I might have the expectation that

But such is the irresistible nature of truth, that all it asks, and all it wants, is the liberty of appearing.

— Thomas Paine

The wise man acts without expectation of reward and completes his task without claiming merit.

— Lao-tzu

an apology will get you to leave me alone. A *sincere* apology is the highest form of acknowledgment, but a *manipulative* apology usually leaves everyone resentful and angry. I am resentful if you do not accept my apology. You will be resentful because you sense that I am trying to manipulate you.

Great players do not play to win; they win by playing well. Their underlying motivation is not the outcome, but the process. A beautiful example of centered communication without expectations is the Japanese tea ceremony, or *chanoyu.* With careful preparation, the host selects flowers, art, tea, and decor. Each action reflects the host's motivation to serve and honor the guest. Each detail holds a wealth of information conveyed without words. Sen Rikyu (1522–1591) established the foundations of this ritual as it is known today. Rikyu advised that we must have no designs on others and that we must not try to impress or compete. He said, "It is good for the spirits of guest and host to be in mutual accord. But to want to be in accord is harmful. If both guest and host have attained a grasp of the way, a sense of harmony will arise spontaneously."

Without the need to control the outcome, we will more quickly reach resolution and stability. Scientifically, freedom from the outcome has been shown to more quickly create harmony and order within a system. As Margaret Wheatley describes in *Leadership and the New Science,* "The two forces we have placed in opposition to one another — freedom and order — turn out to be partners in generating healthy, well-ordered systems." Let people be as they are, and give yourself the freedom to be true to yourself.

TO EXPLORE

To tie together the first two principles, trusting your heart and being detached, using the following rules of thumb can be helpful before communicating:

*   Internally ask yourself, *"Is this true?"* Listen to your body response. This question slows us down enough to be aware of the content of our statement and to practice centering ourselves. We commit to act if our body responds with a clear "yes."

A man who seeks truth and loves it must be reckoned precious to any human society.

— Epictetus

All my life I have struggled to make one authentic gesture.

— Isadora Duncan

- Then ask, *"Will this still be true if everyone here disagrees or responds negatively to what I express?"* Check your body response. Are you focused on a particular outcome? Is it for group or boss approval? If you are focused on an outcome, then you have not arrived at the truth and it is not the time to act, but to reflect.

- Finally, ask, *"Will I feel incomplete if I don't say this? Will I need to say this to someone else later?"* The last question reminds us that certain information must be shared and that we must act when called to do so.

TIP 3: ACT FROM THE LARGEST POSSIBLE PERSPECTIVE

If you are focused only on your personal interests, from a military perspective, you have an army of one. If you are sincerely focused on the interests of a larger group, you can receive their energy and enthusiasm as well. In turn, if you incorporate the wants and needs of both you and your opponent, the full energy of the co-created relationship becomes available to you. Here solutions that enable you to take your enemy whole are quite powerful. We see this in the inclusive example of the youngest son in our folktale, since all his actions are focused on the well-being of his family, or the larger whole.

First, include as many perspectives in your solution as possible. To M. C. Richards, centered communication is a "bringing in...rather than leaving out." The more you seek to integrate multiple potential solutions, whether rational or wild, the stronger your solution will become. Integrating all the parties' wants and ideas into the final solution will have everyone contributing to its success. Include emotional, physical, intuitive, and mental information to create powerful statements. Inclusion creates momentum.

For example, in the book *Difficult Conversations* members of the Harvard Negotiation Project describe three different conversations occurring in every communication: "content" conversations, "feelings" conversations, and "identity" conversations. This concept acknowledges that in every communication we are focused on what is happening, how it affects our relationships, and how it affects our self-esteem. To effectively communicate is to recognize and to achieve a balance between the task at hand, the

The first rule of intelligent tinkering is to keep all the pieces.

— Aldo Leopold

The great seal of truth is simplicity.

— Herman Boerhaave

relationships, and our identities. Say I ask you to help me plant a garden. If I focus solely on the task and forget about our relationship and our personal identities by briskly saying, "Plant three rows over there right now," our friendship and your self-esteem may suffer. If I focus solely on our relationship or on making you feel valued we might not complete our task. To expand our scope we need to acknowledge and include information about the task, the relationship, and our self-esteem in all our communication. One way to incorporate the task, emotions, and identity is to *reframe* the information you have gathered. To reframe we restate all the data we have collected with objective statements. The use of the word *and* supports this union. I might say, "I really appreciate your help *and* am glad we get to spend the day together. I need to get the garden planted today *and* worry that we will run out of time because it is supposed to rain this afternoon. What do you think we should attack first?"

When we acknowledge the others' positions, emotions, and interests, they are more apt to support the planning process. Using the elemental gift of acknowledgment in reframing I am able to garner your energy and support in creating a solution. For example, if I am late picking up my husband at work, I might say, "You needed me to be here on time and I was late. I could have called you and didn't. You seem frustrated. I'm sorry — you deserved a call. I too am frustrated because I hit terrible traffic and have so much on my plate right now. I shouldn't have taken my frustration out on you."

Another way to focus on inclusion is to "watch your language," not for expletives, but for the assumptions and filters hidden within your words. Our unique perspectives on reality are developed through family, cultural background, education, generation, and other developmental influences. Often we use them to make assumptions. Assumptions influence every conversation. What *good* means to me may be different from what it means to you. My assumptions direct my subsequent actions when I hear you call me a "good friend." The same could be said of the terms *hard worker, polite child*, or *loyal employee*. Checking out assumptions surrounding key words pivotal to a solution helps to ensure that everyone signs up for the same resolution.

Sometimes our language does not easily incorporate the new. Einstein described this struggle when he said, "We have great difficulty in representing the world of experience to ourselves without the spectacles of

The harder the conflict, the more glorious the triumph. What we obtain too cheap, we esteem too lightly; it is dearness only that gives everything its value. I love the man that can smile in trouble, that can gather strength from distress and grow brave by reflection. 'Tis the business of little minds to shrink; but he whose heart is firm, and whose conscience approves his conduct, will pursue his principles unto death.

— Thomas Paine

It's a strange world of language in which skating on thin ice can get you into hot water.

— Franklin P. Jones

the old, established conceptual interpretation. There is further difficulty that our language is compelled to work with words which are inseparably connected with those primitive concepts." Sometimes new language and new metaphors must be invented to resolve conflict.

Jerry White, director of the Landmine Survivor's Network, describes the conflict with words inherent in translating the name of his organization into the languages of its six network countries. The word *network* in many of their countries is associated with underground intelligence and thus inspires fear and distrust. Because of the discrimination against those with disabilities in some countries, *landmine survivor* is commonly translated as "mutilated" and even "garbage." Jerry's testing of assumptions and search for appropriate language in each country that fully respects and empowers landmine survivors has been a difficult yet critical task.

And so knowing victory is fivefold —
Knowing when one can and cannot do battle is victory.
Knowing the use of the many and the few is victory.
Superior and inferior desiring the same is victory.
Being prepared and awaiting the unprepared is victory.
The general being capable and the ruler not interfering is victory.

— Sun Tzu,
The Art of War

TO EXPLORE

Some words — *God, spirit, enemy, religion, work, good, bad, evil, dark, white, black, shadow, feminine, masculine, love,* and *creativity* — contain hooks. Words evoke images and emotions. Sometimes these words are critical components of a solution. To make sure a solution is inclusive and lasting, strive to understand what those images and emotions are for each individual. Watch for words that seem sticky, loaded, or bothersome to the other parties. If I say you are "unethical," ask me to define what "unethical" means. What does it mean to be a "hard worker" or a "loyal friend"? What does it mean to "love" someone?

TIP 4: ACT WITH ACCEPTANCE AND CURIOSITY

The youngest son in the Chinese folktale reminds us that conflict can involve pain. He rides through Ice Sea, reminding us of the Water phase's potential for emotional suffering. He gallops over the Fire Mountain, enduring the intensity and ripping apart of the third phase of conflict. He models that we should confront the pain, hold true our core values, and cultivate courage.

So how do we stay out of fear and be courageous in our communication? How do we play to the end? We can return to practices that help us feel safe. Before and while communicating, practice centering, using any of the exercises provided in part 2: movement, meditation, creative expression, and grounding. Use the elemental gifts of questions, humor and humility, acknowledgment and honesty.

Prophets from around the world add prayer as a practice for confronting pain and gathering courage. *Prayer* can be a loaded, image- and emotion-evoking word. To describe the physiological state that opens the heart and gives us courage, or "prayerfulness," author and physician Larry Dossey writes,

> Prayer tends to follow instructions laid down by religious traditions; prayerfulness does not. It is a feeling of unity with the All, rather than with specific leaders, traditions or holy books. Intercessory prayer has a tendency to ask for definite outcomes, to structure the future, to "tell God what to do," such as taking the cancer away. Prayerfulness, on the other hand, is accepting without being passive, is grateful without giving up. It is more willing to stand in the mystery, to tolerate ambiguity and the unknown. It honors the rightness of whatever happens.

Prayerfulness is the attitude of acceptance that gives the prophet the courage to seek and speak truth. It is adopting the curiosity of a child. Thomas Crum, in *The Magic of Conflict*, calls this the attitude of discovery: "Discovery is a place that doesn't know, doesn't evaluate, and is willing to see what is.... Discovery enables us to let go of the filters of our past and the blinders of our expectations."

Personally, to embrace this attitude, I pretend that I am in a laboratory and that the conflict at hand is an interesting experiment that I am conducting. Like a kid dissecting a frog, I try to look in all the nooks and crannies to see what I can find. When I don't like what I find within or without, I try to practice the elemental gift of humor and humility by reminding myself that there is no perfectly right way to feel or to be. This faith in myself and in the Universe empowers my actions.

TO EXPLORE

Practice prayerfulness before communicating by silently reciting a phrase, poem, or chant. I offer two centering meditations from a great prayerfulness resource, *Prayers for Healing:*

You have to accept whatever comes, and the only important thing is that you meet it with courage and with the best that you have to give.

— Eleanor Roosevelt

Hold on to what is good
    Even if it is a handful of earth
Hold on to what you believe
    Even if it is a tree that stands by itself
Hold on to what you must do
    Even if it is a long way from here
Hold on to life
    Even if it is easier to let go
Hold on to my hand
    Even if I have gone away from you
                  — Pueblo blessing

All shall be well
and all shall be well
and all manner of things shall be well.
           — Blessed Julian of Norwich

ART OF CONFLICT: WRITING A NEW STORY

Centered communicators write their own stories. The widow of our folktale demonstrated the power of developing a new vision of the future through her brocade, which symbolized how action can create new realities. In the twentieth century, Martin Luther King Jr. demonstrated how to effectively create a new story for our nation and for the world. He taught us this method through his famous speech "I Have a Dream":

I have a dream my four little children will one day live in a nation where they will not be judged by the color of their skin but by the content of their character....I have a dream today!

When we become discouraged with the way things are, we must remember that we have the power to effect change by becoming prophets for the way that they could be. Having a dream of the future that holds the ideals of the prophet can transform the conflict. Our new vision of the future must be inspiring to as large a group as possible. In the following exercise we will use Dr. King's refrain of "I have a dream" to document what we have envisioned in the Fire phase so it may become real in the Air phase of conflict.

I HAVE A DREAM

Begin with an eight-and-a-half-by-eleven sheet of paper, a journal, a pen, a box of new crayons (they are always inspiring), and a quiet space.

Sit quietly, close your eyes, and ask yourself, "What would I like to see happen in the future?" For a moment, suspend all limits; assume that you have enough time, energy, resources, and relationships to make anything possible.

Picture this in your mind. Who is there? What is happening? How do you feel? Where are you? What inspires you? What will inspire others? Be in this future.

Now, open your eyes and draw this future in symbols, words, or pictures. Write in your journal all that you can remember as you answer the questions above.

Last, translate this future into the following format as taken from King's speech: "I have a dream that..." Let your picture and vision turn you into a prophet in your home, community, or organization.

AN ELEMENTAL ROLE MODEL: MARTIN LUTHER KING JR.

Difficulties are meant to rouse, not discourage. The human spirit is to grow strong by conflict.

— William Ellery Channing

Brave and true, prophets often seem otherworldly, or they demonstrate a seemingly unattainable code of conduct. However, we need look no further than fifty years ago to the American South to find a real-world prophet who changed the world through his voice and heart.

Deemed a prophet of and for the people, Martin Luther King Jr. stands as one of the most influential U.S. figures of the twentieth century. Born on January 15, 1929, in Atlanta, Georgia, King was raised in a Baptist household by parents Reverend Martin

Luther King and Alberta Williams King. By the age of eighteen King was licensed to preach in his father's church and was ordained a year later.

King graduated from Morehouse College that same year and continued his studies, earning a bachelor of divinity degree from Crozer Theological Seminary and a doctorate of systematic theology from Boston University by 1955.

King was installed as pastor of Dexter Avenue Baptist, a prestigious church in Montgomery, Alabama, with his young wife, Coretta, at his side. Two events were to shape the rest of his life. The first was Mrs. Rosa Parks, a respected forty-two-year-old black seamstress, refusing to sit in the back of the bus on December 1, 1955. The second was the question posed by local community members: Would he be the spokesperson for the 383-day nonviolent public bus boycott? King, who called on Christ for the spirit and on Gandhi for the method, led a successful boycott that elevated him to the national stage as a promoter of racial equality and desegregation. As President Lyndon Johnson said in 1965, "And who among us can say we would have made the same progress were it not for [King's] persistent bravery and his faith in American democracy." With millions of supporters and a strong activist church movement behind him, King was able to raise the world's consciousness. He received the Nobel Peace Prize in 1964. In 1968, Martin Luther King Jr. was assassinated.

As a centered communicator and prophet King offered the following inspiration:

1. *Act from truth:* "After discovering what one is made for, they should surrender all of their being to the achievement of this. They should seek to do it well, that nobody could do it better. They should do it as if God Almighty called them at this particular moment in history for this particular reason. And that, is what a person's life is."

2. *Act without a why:* "[The] means must be as pure as the ends.... In other words, we cannot believe, or cannot go with the idea that the end justifies the means because the end is preexistent in the means."

3.   *Act from the largest possible perspective:* "Now let me suggest first that if we are to have peace on earth, our loyalties must be ecumenical rather than sectional. Our loyalties must transcend our race, our tribe, our class and our nation; and this means we must develop a world perspective."

4.   *Act with acceptance and curiosity:* "So the nonviolent approach does not immediately change the heart of the oppressor. It first does something to the hearts and souls of those committed to it. It gives them new self-respect; it calls up resources of strength and courage that they did not know they had. Finally, it reaches the opponent and so stirs his conscience that reconciliation becomes a reality."

SUMMARY: AIR — STABILITY

ATTRIBUTES	We breeze into the *Air phase* when we: • Begin to *test and implement* the creative ideas found in the last phase. • Become anxious or controlling. • *See stability and balance returning* to relationships and reality.
TASK	The goal of this phase is to *create a win-win solution* or to find areas of common ground before proceeding back to the Earth phase.
CHALLENGES AND ELEMENTAL PRINCIPLE	To overcome the challenges of *fear* and *self-doubt*, we practice the principle of *telling the truth.* *Centering communication in truth, detachment, acceptance, curiosity, and the greatest vision possible* marks the actions of a prophet. It acknowledges that each interpretation of reality is unique and valid.
TIPS AND TECHNIQUES	To become a *centered communicator:* 1. Act from truth. 2. Act without a why. 3. Act from the largest possible perspective. 4. Act from acceptance and curiosity.
VOCATION AND DISCIPLINE	Our *prophets* across the world practice the daily discipline of *song or story* to enhance truth telling and courageous solutions.
ELEMENTAL GIFT	During the Air phase, keep all parties from blowing up or away. *Be honest.*
ART OF CONFLICT	The artistic practice of *story writing* fuels confidence and faith in the future.
ELEMENTAL ROLE MODEL	*Martin Luther King Jr.*

PART 4

IMPROVE YOUR CONDITIONING

*We become most
what we think about all day long.*
— Ralph Waldo Emerson

CHAPTER 14

The Mental Game

The transmigration of life takes place in one's mind.
Let one therefore keep the mind pure,
for what a man thinks, so he becomes.

— Upanishads

Sports gurus from around the world know that it is the mental game that rules performance. As Yogi Berra is quoted as saying, "Half this game is ninety percent mental." Now that we understand what we want to have occur in conflict, we can use the same mental conditioning that successful athletes and entrepreneurs use to achieve their goals.

So often we find ourselves in a rut when it comes to conflict patterns. We might say, "OK, this time I am going to stay engaged, not scream at my husband or run away. We are going to work together and find a solution." Needless to say, often we don't work together and find ourselves yelling instead.

Rupert Sheldrake describes nature as governed by habits. Clearly our constant patterns of behavior, from relating to others to making breakfast, are habits. He believes we will continue to repeat our habits until they no longer work. It may be an old habit to use intimidation when someone confronts you. This may have become a habit because it effectively got others to leave you alone. However, you may now realize that you have little intimacy or trust in relationships because of this habitual reaction.

To transform conflict it is critical not only to read about the conflict practices described within this book but also to turn them into new habits. For example, after reading, you may want to become skilled at appreciating your opponents or to pause before responding in a heated argument. The Hindu sacred text the Bhagavad Gita reminds us that no one attains their goal without action. Change takes practice. However, if I consistently tell myself that I am terrible at conflict or have poor appreciation skills while I am trying to learn new skills, these internal battles will hinder progress. The following exercises will assist us in creating *mental attitudes* that support developing new habits.

AFFIRMATIONS:
THE MIND TALKS AND THE BODY WALKS

> *The idea is like a blueprint, it creates an image of the form, which then magnetizes and guides the physical energy to flow into that form and eventually manifests it on the physical plane.*
>
> — Shakti Gawain

We can talk and visualize ourselves into new habits. Our internal conversations or "mind talk" are powerful determinants of our behavior. Olympic sports consultants now spend hours training the athlete's brain as well as her body. Studies show that if athletes believe that they will win, they often do. In the 2000 Summer Olympic Games Marion Jones would not be dissuaded from her belief that she would win five gold medals. When she left with three gold and two bronze on her chest, I'd say that she was not far from the reality that she had visualized for herself.

The tenets of creative visualization are readily found within the spiritual traditions of daily interrogatory prayer and chanting. Christianity provides us with the wisdom that if we ask for something and have the faith of a mustard seed, we will receive it. Of course, we can tell ourselves that we want to be thin, rich, beautiful, and a Zen master of conflict until the cows come home, and still nothing seems to change. And we can pray for something that never comes true. Experts in creative visualization offer the following guidelines for turning your conflict dreams into reality:

To create a new reality, first begin by finding a quiet place and allow yourself at least thirty minutes to do the following exercise. This exercise focuses on developing a new way of approaching interpersonal conflict, but it can be modified to create affirmations in almost any situation.

STEP ONE: SEE YOUR GOAL

In their book *Empowerment* David Gershon and Gail Straub suggest that to create a new reality you begin by becoming quiet and walking in your mind into the situation as you wish it to be, without any constraints. In the best of all possible worlds, how would you like a situation, a relationship, or yourself to look?

Close your eyes, take a few deep breaths, and center yourself. Spend a few minutes clearing your mind of all thoughts, letting them pass through. Now imagine yourself walking into a garden. Color it with flowers and trees of your favorite variety. Create the perfect weather and comfort zone for yourself. When you are ready, invite a person with whom you are struggling (imagine him in his best possible state) into your garden. Allow him to sit down and talk with you in this place. *Do not limit your vision* by saying, "He would never do that" or, "He won't listen to me." Imagine the best possible situation just for a few moments.

Now visualize how your best conversation would go. What would you like to be able to say? How would you like to be acknowledged? What would you like to hear? How would you like to respond? After you have spoken, how would you like to leave that person and return home? Again, in this vision, there are no "shoulds," "can'ts," or "won'ts."

When the conversation has ended, return home and spend a few moments recording the internal garden and your conversation in a journal. Include colors, sensations, emotions, and images since these can hold symbolic clues about what needs to be included in the resulting affirmation. Say I have just seen my brother enter the garden and we have spoken about how important our relationship is to each other. We have apologized for past wrongs and made a commitment to develop a deep and nurturing friendship. I would write down the details of our conversation, what my brother and I were wearing, my feeling of peace and gratitude, and how I could hear birds singing in the trees.

STEP TWO: DIG UP THE OLD BELIEF SYSTEM

Now we look at the limits that we might have wanted to place on our vision and that we have been placing on ourselves or on a relationship. Since we all create our own reality, we have a set of beliefs in place that supports it.

We are what we imagine. Our very existence consists in our imagination of ourselves. The greatest tragedy that can befall us is to go unimagined.

— N. Scott Momaday

Some are often obvious and others, like many of the assumptions we make, are subtler and hidden.

Write down all the reasons that your vision would never work: "My brother is inflexible," "I always start crying when faced with conflict, I am too emotional," "I am not good at conflict," "I don't know how to explain how I feel," and so on. Eventually, we often land at "I am afraid I will be hurt," or "People who are _____ are _____" (fill in the blanks).

For example, I was raised in Minnesota. Just as in any location, we Midwesterners share a set of collective beliefs, some of which can be quite limiting. For example, "emotional people are irrational or not to be trusted" might be one of them. So if I want to approach another person with a full and open heart, I first need to recognize and remove a belief or assumption that limits my ability to create what I want.

Everything is possible; we, and the person with whom we battle, are capable of every trait or action under the sun. Some things might appear to be impossible, for example, having a meaningful relationship with someone who has serious emotional issues. Your initial position of how this meaningful relationship might look might not come to pass, but if you are clear about your underlying hopes and wishes and let go of any stumbling blocks, a new solution can begin to take form. When creating a new vision, affirming what is found underneath our iceberg, or the *essence* of what will satisfy our longing, opens up all types of possible solutions instead of just one. The power of expectations and vision cannot be overrated.

Now take each belief or assumption that destroys your vision and turn it around. Both versions could be equally true. It is your choice. For example:

- "My brother is inflexible" might change to "My brother and I are flexible as we create new, innovative solutions."

- "I am not good at conflict" might become "I have great abilities when working with conflict."

- "I am too emotional" could become "I express my emotions and wishes clearly and effectively."

We are what we pretend to be, so we must be careful about what we pretend to be.

— Kurt Vonnegut

- "I'm afraid I will be hurt" could be "When I speak with my brother, I am supported and safe."

We will now combine our vision with these assumptions to develop a new way of being.

STEP THREE: DEVELOP THE PERFECT PHRASE

When I look at my hypothetical brother in the garden vision, I see that I want to have a nurturing, open, and supportive relationship with him. I have set up some limiting beliefs about our abilities and how I might be perceived if I present this hope.

Now I need to create a phrase that holds my new vision within it. To make the phrase most effective, Gershon and Straub offer the following tips:

1. *Use the present tense.* "I will be healthy" puts this reality into the future. "I am healthy" or "I have a nurturing relationship with my brother" affirms that this is a present reality. As the philosophy goes, believe it, and it will be true.

2. *Choose positive words.* We are more open and receptive to positive images and words. Instead of saying "I won't hurt my brother," try "I nurture and support my brother."

3. *I can only control myself.* Our declarations must be about our relationships and us. An affirmation that says, "My brother is a patient and doting friend" not only doesn't work but it also isn't very empowering. To say instead, "I have a strong and nurturing relationship with my brother" allows your sibling to be just who he is in his own surprising and unique way.

STEP FOUR: PROVIDE A PICTURE TO GO WITH IT

Since humans have a great affinity for symbol, add a picture to ground the phrase. If you want great abundance, see money falling from the sky all around you. If your affirmation includes confidence and peace in conflict, see yourself centered and joyful working in a dispute. You may wish to gather symbols from your garden to include in your mental picture.

Vision without action is a daydream. Action without vision is a nightmare.

— Japanese proverb

STEP FIVE: SAY IT UNTIL YOU SEE IT

Simply repeating your phrase while visualizing your picture ten times a day can yield amazing results. You may have one to eight different affirmations that you repeat at a time. You are teaching yourself a new story. In the morning, as you awake, and at night, as you are going to sleep, are powerful times to affect your belief system. Say the affirmation until it becomes true. Shakti Gawain, in *Creative Visualization*, explains, "Rather than saying affirmations by rote, try to get the feeling that you really have the power to create that reality (which in fact you do!). This will make a big difference in how effective they are." Gawain also offers a beautiful phrase to seal this work that leaves you open to even greater possibilities. After repeating the affirmation she adds, *"This, or something better, now manifests for me in totally satisfying and harmonious ways, for the highest good of all concerned."*

STEP SIX: FEEL IT IN YOUR BODY

The use of body movement or positioning can further commit a new viewpoint or discipline to reality. *Body prayer*, the reciting of scripture or chanting praise taught by many spiritual traditions, brings us this precept from antiquity. We find body prayer arriving in many new and fun forms such as Gabrielle Roth's Wave Dance, Ananda yoga, and Phoenix Rising yoga therapy.

In Ananda yoga, for example, practitioners do many of the traditional yoga postures with accompanying affirmations. In Tree pose, one stands in the posture breathing and repeats, "I am calm, I am poised." In Cobra pose, one is asked to repeat, "I rise joyfully to meet each new opportunity." One way to integrate your new stories or affirmations is to connect them with a body movement. If you are hoping to be more flexible in conflict, bending forward gently to touch your toes might be a great place from which to say your affirmation. If you are working to find more peace and relaxation, perhaps being in a quiet seated position might help your mind and body to remember this truth. Saying your affirmations as you exercise can be another way to remember and connect to your new beliefs.

A man, to carry on a successful business, must have imagination. He must see things as in a vision, a dream of the whole thing.

— Charles M. Schwab

TEACHING YOUR WAY INTO A NEW HABIT

An alternate approach to integrating a new skill and shifting our mental attitudes is to teach it to another. Maria Montessori based her revolutionary teaching philosophy on this notion. She found that when younger children were placed in the classroom with older ones who were expected to teach learned activities, the older children integrated and mastered skills as they introduced the activities to the younger children.

I invite you to teach a practice or activity from this book to another. *Please ask her permission first!* The roles of teacher and student should be voluntary; otherwise, we make assumptions about our position and power in a relationship that might be disrespectful. When we are asked if we want to learn something new or if we want to practice a new skill together, it is rare that we refuse. It is when we perceive that someone believes we are deficient that we back away.

Essentially, as the old adage has it, *we learn best what we teach.* I have found that a student's tough questions are rallying points to dig deeper into, clarify, and personally integrate what I teach. To be a successful teacher, I must continue to practice and experiment. *We also teach best that which we have truly learned.* This belief supports our mental game; when we can effectively teach a skill, our confidence increases and affirms positive expectations about our future success using that skill.

FIFTY TO ONE HUNDRED DAYS OF PRACTICE MAKE PERFECT

When I have wished to learn a new habit, teachers have counseled me to practice it for at least six weeks. For example, if you wish to add meditation to your daily routine, schedule it on your calendar for the prescribed period. I find if I pick a distinct time each day and see it as something I deem as important, as, say, a conference call with my boss (which this is, isn't it?), it gets done.

Ritual can help in this practice. Spiritual leaders have long used rites and rituals to create habits to support their followers. For example, to teach detachment or letting go, the Catholic Church has created a practice

No bubble is so iridescent or floats longer than that blown by the successful teacher.

— Sir William Osler

213

of weekly confession prior to communion. The Sabbath meal in Judaism serves as a similar weekly reminder. Fasting, a practice found particularly in many Eastern religious traditions, is yet another ritual that teaches detachment.

You can easily create a ritual to help a practice find its way into your day. One friend wears a rubber band around her wrist to remind herself to breathe! When I enter a room to mediate a dispute, I touch one hand to my head and then to my heart to remind myself that I must listen for both words and emotions as intently as possible. After years of doing this ritual, my hand moves almost without my thinking, I relax, and my mind and body adjust.

When in conflict, I want to stop before yelling at my children! So moving from theory to practice, I created a small ritual to remind myself to slow down. When I feel my anger rising, by contracting the back of my throat, I make a sound much like waves on the sand or like Darth Vader, depending on your perspective! It is a basic centering tool in yoga called "sounding breath" that one begins to do instinctively when faced with a difficult posture, or asana. This breathing has become a habit when anger appears, and without thinking, I now inhale and exhale in this loud manner. It has become a reminder as I hear myself that I need to stop and reflect. It also tells my children that I have reached my limit and need a minute to pull myself together.

Throughout human history we have created and redefined our habits. This is evolution. Be kind to yourself as you attack your old belief systems. We all have the ability to change our attitudes about conflict today.

In theory there is no difference between theory and practice. In practice there is.

— Yogi Berra

Playing the Game: An Invitation

*Only through the experience of trial and suffering
can the soul be strengthened, vision cleared, ambition inspired,
and success achieved.*

— Helen Keller

No matter how well you apply the concepts found in this book, conflict will still be messy. I have always wanted to gracefully dance through disputes without stumbling. As a child I loved TV sitcoms like *The Brady Bunch* and *The Partridge Family,* in which any conflict could be wrapped up neatly within a half-hour and the protagonists looked lovely throughout. However, conflict births new insights and solutions, and in my experience, birth is always messy. There are unsightly fluids and scary moments. There is pain. No matter how much you plan and try to control the process, it is never what you expected.

I rarely get through a personal conflict without looking back and cringing a bit. I often winced as I wrote about my own disputes in these pages. I saw, upon reflection, consistent untidiness. I was never quite as poised as I would have liked. There were loose ends still to be tied up. Some of these disputes continue to press on, asking me to grow and evolve a bit more.

The evolutionary process of conflict is tough to thwart. As with young plants whose seeds were planted at the side of a rock, growth may take some strange twists, yet progress occurs despite the obstacles we might put in our paths. I am happier and stronger because I use these principles and skills, even if not always perfectly. The quality of my life has improved, and I have far less fear, since I am better equipped to engage in difficult situations.

I recently met with a friend who lost her mother to cancer more than thirty years ago. She described how she had tried to ignore this experience, choosing instead to grow up quickly and "keep it light." A few months ago, she decided that it was time to return to this trauma and work it through to completion. She described it as a conflict between herself, her mother, and the power of grief and motherhood. As she jumped back onto the spiral path of this battle, she explained that the grief felt as fresh and real as it had thirty years before. She found that she had returned exactly to the spot where she had chosen to jump off of conflict's wheel so long ago. Firmly in the Water phase of this conflict, she is focused on relaxing into the grief and is using meditation and counseling to guide herself through.

Her courage in tackling this issue is paying off. I've never seen her stronger or happier. She would tell you that it is never too late and that the conflict is never too big. As poet and philosopher Rainer Maria Rilke once said, "Perhaps all of the dragons of our lives are princesses who are only waiting to see us act, just once, beautiful and brave. Perhaps everything that frightens us is, in its deepest being something that wants our love."

I hope that this work will bring you more joy and expansion. May it inspire us all to co-create innovative solutions to the polemic issues of our times. In conclusion, I invite you to integrate the material contained in this book by selecting a conflict and working through the following steps:

1. Refer to part 1, "The Participants," and ask yourself:

    •   Who are my opponents?

    •   What is my conflict style?

    •   What is my opponent's style?

    •   What transforming gifts can I give, and which ones do I need to receive?

You will not grow if you sit in a beautiful flower garden, but you will grow if you are sick, if you are in pain, if you experience losses, and if you do not put your head in the sand, but take the pain and learn to accept it, not as a curse or punishment but as a gift to you with a very, very specific purpose.

— Elisabeth Kübler-Ross

By your stumbling, the world is perfected.

— Sri Aurobindo

2. Referring back to part 2, "The Rules," develop a picture for your current conflict:

- When did this conflict begin?

- Have I fought this battle before?

- In what phase (Earth, Water, Fire, or Air) do I currently reside?

- Am I stuck? If so, what practices might I employ to support resolution?

The most instructive experiences are those of everyday life.

— Friedrich Nietzsche

WAY OF CONFLICT MANDALA

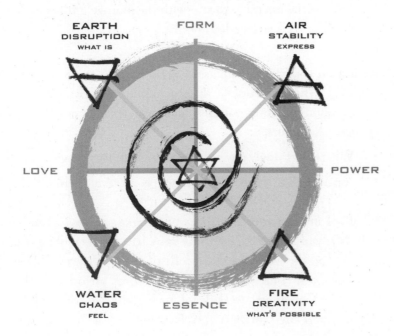

3. Turn to the appropriate phase in part 3, "The Elemental Playbook":

- Practice recognizing the attributes of each phase. Each phase feels different, and as you integrate this information it becomes easier to identify a current stage.

- Employ the corresponding elemental principle.

But what is your duty?
The demands of every day.

— Johann Wolfgang von
Goethe

- In every conflict, regardless of location, hold these tenets:

  1. *Appreciate* all involved.

  2. *Separate* from your story.

  3. *Contemplate*, listening carefully.

  4. *Communicate* truthfully.

- Notice your growing edges. How far are you able to go today? See yourself in a laboratory and objectively observe the effect of your efforts.

- Make the commitment to stick with the conflict. Simply holding the intention to stay with the journey until completion can have tremendous results.

Come, come, whoever you are,
Wanderer, worshiper, lover of
leaving — it doesn't matter,
Ours is not a caravan of
despair.
Come, even if you have broken
your vow a hundred times.
Come, come again, come.

— Jelaluddin Rumi

4. Reflect on your "mind talk" surrounding this dispute and your abilities. Return to part 4, "Improve Your Conditioning," to turn around negating patterns and give yourself a "fighting chance." Ask yourself:

- Where do I doubt my abilities to resolve this issue?

- Am I stuck in the belief that there is no resolution?

Finally, I invite you to remember two things. Please be gentle with yourself. Many of the practices in this book have been taught as rules of conduct around the world for thousands of years. They are "life skills" and thus take a lifetime to master. I don't think anyone becomes the Dalai Lama or Gandhi in a week, let alone Buddha, Muhammad, Moses, or Christ. And, I beg you, have fun! Remember that life is simply one great glorious game that we are asked to play. And play we should.

The following is a comparison of the four paths of Creation Spirituality and the Four-Fold Way and how they relate to the Way of Conflict. These systems formed the initial inspiration for this book and hold a wealth of information about the world's mystical and indigenous traditions.

CREATION SPIRITUALITY

Matthew Fox is an author and Episcopal priest who has studied the medieval Christian mystics extensively, with special emphasis on the philosophies of Thomas Aquinas and Meister Eckhart. Through these studies, Fox identifies four clear themes, which he calls the four paths of Creation Spirituality:

- Via Positiva, or Positive Path: The experience of seeing and celebrating the earth. On this path we experience awe and delight as we enjoy the diversity of the universe. We fall in love with the world.

- Via Negativa, or Negative Path: This path exposes us to the dark or unknown. Here we may experience loss and suffering as we are asked to let go and let be. We work with the shadow or the other side of the reality that delighted or amazed us on the first path. It is here that we recognize that all forms are impermanent.

- Via Creativa, or Creative Path: Here we co-create with the Divine, channeling new ideas and forms. This path is equated with rebirth, just as the Negative Path would be equated with death.

- Via Transformativa, or Transformative Path: Here we implement the ideas birthed on the Via Creativa. We fight for justice and seek balance or homeostasis within our communities and within ourselves. This is a time of action and compassion.

The paths of Creation Spirituality form the framework of many of Fox's extensive writings. His seminal book on the topic is *Original Blessing.* I would also refer you to *Breakthrough: Meister Eckhart's Creation Spirituality in New Translation; Creation Spirituality: Liberating Gifts for the Peoples of the Earth; The Coming of the Cosmic Christ;* and *A Spirituality Named Compassion* for more extensive discussions of this philosophy. In these texts, Fox treats each theme in great detail and provides insight on how to conduct oneself on each path.

These paths flow as a linked journey that one follows as he experiences reality or personal growth. One might find this journey occurring over an hour, a week, or many years as he expands his awareness. To help you better conceive of this journey, let me use the model of a romantic relationship:

- Positive Path: We fall in love.

- Negative Path: We learn more about the relationship and our lover, with his or her potential to break our hearts. This causes suffering and pain.

- Creative Path: By the strength of love we forge ahead. Together we give birth to new people or ideas.

- Transformative Path: We then nurture and grow these new beings.

Matthew Fox's work is taught through the University of Creation Spirituality, Oakland, California, www.creationspirituality.org.

THE FOUR-FOLD WAY

Through an extensive cross-cultural research of indigenous traditions, author Angeles Arrien arrived at four major human archetypes. A description of these archetypes and how to develop them within can be found in her book *The Four-Fold Way* as well as in her many audiotapes and CDs on this topic. A reference list can be found on her website, www.angelesarrien.com. Each archetype represents one of four roles that a human being should develop to be balanced and holistically healthy.

Each archetype has an underlying principle that, if followed, supports its development. By living a principle, one works to embody the archetype and to mature. The four archetypes and their principles are:

- The Warrior: Show up, or choose to be present.

- The Teacher: Be open, not attached, to the outcome.

- The Healer: Pay attention to what has heart and meaning.

- The Visionary: Tell the truth without blame or judgment.

Each person has natural gifts and talents and thus will more easily embody a particular archetype. However, we are urged to move to homeostasis or balance by developing all four within us. In the above example of romantic love, the Four-Fold Way would guide us in deepening our relationship by using its principles and embodying its archetypes. To strengthen our relationship we must:

- Be a Warrior: Be present physically, mentally, and emotionally to our lover.

- Be a Teacher: Allow our lover to be and to become without trying to control.

- Be a Healer: Listen carefully to what holds meaning and inspiration in our lover's and in our own heart.

- Be a Visionary: Take responsibility for our actions and always be honest.

THE WAY OF CONFLICT

Both Fox and Arrien provide sound advice on how to work with the phases and energy of conflict. *The Way of Conflict* relates to the four paths of Creation Spirituality and the archetypes of the Four-Fold Way in the following manner:

1. EARTH: We identify a conflict and gather information on the situation.

   - Principle: Appreciate the conflict, your opponent, and yourself.

   - Fox: *Positive Path* — Celebrate and be grateful for what is.

   - Arrien: *Way of the Warrior* — Show up or choose to be present.

2. WATER: We realize that a solution cannot be found in the world as it is ordered today.

   - Principle: Separate — let go and flow.

   - Fox: *Negative Path* — Let go and let be. Empty yourself.

   - Arrien: *Way of the Teacher* — Be open to the outcome, not attached to the outcome.

3. FIRE: We arrive at creative new ways to resolve the situation at hand.

   - Principle: Contemplate — creatively listen.

   - Fox: *Creative Path* — Co-create with the Divine.

   - Arrien: *Way of the Healer* — Pay attention to what has heart and meaning.

4. AIR: We work to implement our new ideas, spiraling back to the Earth phase if these ideas do not completely resolve the conflict.

- Principle: Communicate.

- Fox: *Transformative Path* — Fight for justice with compassion.

- Arrien: *Way of the Visionary* — Tell the truth without blame or judgment.

The Way of Conflict acknowledges and incorporates both the spiritual journey described in the four paths of Creation Spirituality and the development of the four archetypes of *The Four-Fold Way*. These systems correlate to the wisdom found not only in the spiritual traditions they encompass but also to Eastern mystical teachings of Buddhism, Taoism, Sufism, Judaism, and Hinduism to name a few. This philosophy is also present in ancient military and martial arts in the tradition of China's three-thousand-year-old Sun Tzu lineage and the more recent practice of Aikido. It is also being proven in the New Science, as described by physicists Fritjof Capra, David Bohm, Brian Swimme, and Rupert Sheldrake. I am indebted to all these teachers and too others to numerous to list who have so generously shared their insight and research.

ACKNOWLEDGMENTS

Many amazing friends, family, students, and business associates have influenced the contents of these pages. I hope I have fully articulated my appreciation to everyone, whether here or in person. I want to especially thank:

Jason Gardner at New World Library for his abundant support and expertise, Patricia Hass for showing me some of the ropes of publishing, Sue MacGrath for making that possible, and Mimi Kusch for great attention to editing details and for wonderful additions.

Paul Mahon for being a great publishing attorney and friend.

Maribeth Goodman, wise teacher and friend, for birthing this project with me and exposing the extraordinary power of the *mandorla*.

Diana and Marcus Stevens, whose literary and creative sustenance were invaluable.

Rosemary Partridge for her willingness to see more, and to all the students at the University of Creation Spirituality/Naropa.

The team of reviewers who each added their valuable mark to this work, including Angeles Arrien, Megan Ault, Dan Baker, F. Craig and Deborah Barber, David Baum, Julie Causey, Ana Perez Chisti, Bruce

Combs, Matthew Fox, Marilynn Hall, Mary Klages, Carmen McSpadden, Annie Mahon, Craig Neal, Lynne Olsen, Ginger Combs Ramirez, and Tom Stenzell.

Rob Rath for his top-notch artistic talents and illustrations.

Finally, I am deeply, deeply grateful for Bruce, Cameron, Cody, and Senya. I appreciate your patience as I wrote (and wrote and wrote) and also as I tested out my theories! I am thankful for your powerful assistance both in forming the book and in shouldering some of my responsibilities. I feel blessed to be part of each of your lives and to have you in mine.

NOTES

INTRODUCTION: CONFLICT AS CONTEST

xx *to kill one person is to kill all mankind...*
    On that account: We ordained
    For the Children of Israel
    That if anyone slew
    A person — unless it be
    For murder or for spreading
    Mischief in the land —
    It would be as if
    He slew the whole people:
    And if anyone saved a life,
    It would be as if he saved
    The life of the whole people. (Koran 5:32)

xx *The basic oneness of the universe...*Fritjof Capra, *The Tao of Physics: An Exploration of the Parallels between Modern Physics and Eastern Mysticism* (Shambhala: Boston, 1999), 131.

xxi *main characteristic of these successful organizations...*James Collins and Jerry Porras, *Built to Last: Successful Habits of Visionary Companies* (New York: HarperCollins, 1994), 43–45.

xxiii *mutually assured benefit...*Quoted in William Ury, *Third Side: Why We Fight and How We Can Stop* (New York: Penguin, 2000), 81.

xxiv *Know the other...*Sun Tzu, *The Art of War: A New Translation*, trans., essay, and comm. by the Demna Translation Group (Boston: Shambhala, 2001), 44.

xxv *The most intense conflicts*...Quoted on www.brainyquotes.com. From C.G. Jung, "The Structure and Dynamics of the Psyche," *Collected Works*, volume 8.

CHAPTER 1: DISCOVERING YOUR ELEMENTAL NATURE

3 *Man...has the self*...Quoted in Bede Griffiths, *Universal Wisdom: A Journey Through the Sacred Wisdom of the World* (San Francisco: HarperCollins, 1994), 113.

8 *Know the other*...Sun Tzu, *The Art of War: A New Translation*, trans., essay, and comm. by the Demna Translation Group (Boston: Shambhala, 2001), 44.

8 *You are an Air or Water person*...Deepak Chopra, *Perfect Health: The Complete Mind/Body Guide* (New York: Harmony, 1991), 24.

8 *Buddhist and Hindu initiates*...Huston Smith, *The World's Religions* (San Francisco: HarperCollins, 1991), 28; and Irini Rockwell, "Understanding Who We Are Through the Five Buddha Families," *Shambhala Sun* (November 2002): 74.

8 *Taoism assigns*...R. L. Wing, *The I Ching Workbook* (New York: Doubleday, 1979), 15.

9 *I shall not*...Maya Angelou, *I Shall Not Be Moved: Poems* (New York: Random House, 1997), 33.

9 *that's the way I am — fiery*...Mike Allen, *Washington Post*, 16 November 2002, A01.

10 *the healthy person nurtures*...Sobonfu Somé, *The Spirit of Intimacy: Ancient Teachings in the Ways of Relationships* (Berkeley: Berkeley Hills, 1997), 69.

10 *And so the general*...Sun Tzu, *Art of War*, 8.

12 *You cannot step twice*...Malcolm Godwin, *Who Are You? 101 Ways of Seeing Yourself* (New York: Penguin, 2000), chap. 98.

12 *The finest quality*...Quoted in Jason Gardner, ed., *Sacred Earth: Writers on Nature and Earth* (Novato, Calif.: New World Library, 1998), 43.

13 *First we need to roam*...Quoted in Gardner, *Sacred Earth*, 103.

14 *Thus, pictures which wildfire creates*...Norman Mclean, *Young Men and Fire* (University of Chicago Press, 1992), 294.

15 *I loved the prairie*...Quoted in William Kitteridge and Annick Smith, eds., *The Last Best Place* (Seattle: University of Washington Press, 1988), 533.

CHAPTER 2: IDENTIFYING THE TEAM'S PERSONALITY

18 *These founders were deeply concerned*..."The American Soul: An Interview with Jacob Needleman, Ph.D.," *Science of Mind* (July 2002): 29.

19 *When working to form metal*...M.C. Richards, *Centering, In Pottery, Poetry and the Person* (Hanover: Wesleyan, 1989), 38.

22 *The earth does not withhold*..."Carol of Words" from Walt Whitman, *The Walt Whitman Reader: Selections from Leaves of Grass* (New York: Courage Press), 210.

22 *No, no, we are not satisfied*...*A Testament of Hope: The Essential Writings of Martin Luther King, Jr.* (San Francisco: HarperCollins, 1986), 219.

24 *Twenty years from now*…Quoted in Eric Harr, *The Portable Personal Trainer: 100 Ways to Energize Your Workouts and Bring Out the Athlete in You* (New York: Broadway, 2001), 11.

CHAPTER 3:
UNCOVERING THE ELEMENTS OF A BALANCED TEAM

26 *Through my eyes flow the tears*…Monica McGoldrich, *You Can Go Home Again* (New York: Norton, 1995), 131.

30 *Love the earth*…Quoted in Mary Pipher, *The Shelter of Each Other: Rebuilding Our Families* (New York: Putnam, 1996), 250.

31 *The moment one definitely*…Quoted in Sy Safransky, *Sunbeams: A Book of Quotations* (Berkeley: North Atlantic Books, 1990), 29.

CHAPTER 4: PLAYING WELL WITH OTHERS

34 *Asking questions*…Quoted in Lillian Eichler Watson, *Light from Many Lamps* (New York: Simon & Schuster, 1988), 162; quoted in Huston Smith, *The World's Religions* (San Francisco: HarperCollins, 1991), 211; and quoted in Maggie Oman Shannon, *One God, Shared Hope: Twenty Threads Shared by Judaism, Christianity and Islam* (Boston: Red Wheel, 2003), 63, 103, 131.

35 *Be patient toward all*…Rainer Maria Rilke, *Letters to a Young Poet* (New York: Vintage, 1986), 34.

36 *I believe that the first test*…Quoted in Sy Safransky, *Sunbeams: A Book of Quotations* (Berkeley: North Atlantic Books, 1990), 120.

37 *Evolved Individuals*…R. L. Wing, *The I Ching Workbook* (New York: Doubleday, 1979), 40.

37 *Too often we underestimate*…Leo Buscaglia, *Born for Love: Reflections on Loving* (New York: Ballantine, 1994), 232.

38 *Quantum physicists tell us*…Margaret J. Wheatley, *Leadership and the New Science* (San Francisco: Berret-Koehler, 1992), 63; and Ariah Zohar and I. N. Marshall, *The Quantum Self: Human Nature and Consciousness Defined by the New Physics* (New York: William Morrow, 1990), 41.

39 *your acknowledgement is sincere*…William Ury, *Getting Past No: Negotiating with Difficult People* (New York: Bantam, 1991), 42.

39 *Johnson administration's*…M. Scott Peck, M.D., *People of the Lie: The Hope for Healing Human Evil* (New York: Touchstone, 1983), 242.

CHAPTER 5: THE OBJECT OF THE GAME

45 *When a quarrel heats up*…Quoted in David Augsburger, *Conflict Mediation across Cultures, Pathways, and Patterns* (Louisville, Ky.: W. Westminster/John Knox Press, 1992), 150.

47 *This story, a parable imparted*...Versions of the parable of the Blind Men and the Elephant are found in the writings of Sufi poet Rumi, Sufi theologian Muhammad al-Ghazzali (1058–1128 C.E.), Aziz ibn-Muhammad-I Nasafi (thirteenth century C.E) and in Pali Buddhist Udana 68, 69 (second century B.C.E.).

50 *Tribal cultures build*...Angeles Arrien, *Signs of Life: The Five Universal Shapes and How to Use Them* (New York: Putnam, 1998), 31.

50 *Systems constantly emit*...Ariah Zohar and I. N. Marshall, *The Quantum Society: Mind, Physics, and a New Social Vision* (New York: William Morrow, 1994), 148; and Margaret J. Wheatley, *Leadership and the New Science* (San Francisco: Berret-Koehler, 1992), 82–87.

51 *systems constantly dance between chaos*...Wheatley, *Leadership*, 13.

54 *something larger than any side*...Sun Tzu, *The Art of War: A New Translation*, trans., essay, and comm. by the Demna Translation Group (Boston: Shambhala, 2001), xvii.

54 *No man is an island*...*The Columbia World of Quotations* (New York: Columbia University Press, 1996), number 16915, www.bartelby.com.

55 *the mandorla adorns*...Robert Johnson, *Owning Your Own Shadow: Understanding the Dark Side of the Psyche* (San Francisco: HarperCollins, 1991), 97–100.

56 *The object of all conflict*...Sun Tzu, *Art of War*, xvi.

57 *intersects a white and a black circle*...Johnson, *Owning Your Own Shadow*, 118.

57 *Sobonfu Somé says*...Lecture attended by the author, University of Creation Spirituality, Oakland, CA, August 13, 2001.

CHAPTER 6: INTRODUCING CONFLICT'S FOUR QUARTERS

60 *Chaos is necessary*...Margaret J. Wheatley, *Leadership and the New Science* (San Francisco: Berret-Koehler, 1992), 13.

61 *Galaxies are also fractal spirals*...Wheatley, *Leadership*, 81.

63 *cross-culturally, the spiral is*...Angeles Arrien, *Signs of Life: The Five Universal Shapes and How to Use Them* (New York: Putnam, 1998), 47.

63 *classic symbol of death and rebirth*...Matthew Fox, *A Spirituality Named Compassion and the Healing of the Global Village: Humpty Dumpty and Us* (San Francisco: HarperCollins, 1990), 116.

63 *The only important thing is to follow nature*...Quoted in Sy Safransky, *Sunbeams: A Book of Quotations* (Berkeley: North Atlantic Books, 1990), 56.

65 *The science of alchemy I like*...Quoted in John Hedley Brooke, *Science and Religion: Some Historical Perspectives* (Cambridge: Cambridge University Press, 1991), 67.

CHAPTER 7: TIME ON THE SIDELINES

70 *The growing edge is the point*...David Gershon and Gail Straub, *Empowerment: The Art of Creating Your Life as You Want It* (New York: Delta, 1989), 13; my emphasis.

70 *Stress exposure*...James Loehr, *Stress for Success* (New York: Random House, 1997), 4.

70 *neocortex is the largest portion*...Joseph Chilton Pearce, *The Biology of Transcendence: A Blueprint for the Human Spirit* (Rochester, Vt.: Park Street Press, 2002), 24–30.

70   *our reptilian, survival-focused brain*...Dan Baker, M.D., *What Happy People Know: How the New Science of Happiness Can Change Your Life for the Better* (New York: Rodale, 2003), 28–29.

72   *When a man finds that it is his destiny*...Quoted in Sy Safransky, *Sunbeams: A Book of Quotations* (Berkeley: North Atlantic Books, 1990), 27.

72   *One ever feels his twoness*...W. E. B. DuBois, *The Souls of Black Folk* (New York: Bantam, 1989), 3.

73   *center of the equidistant cross*...Angeles Arrien, *Signs of Life: The Five Universal Shapes and How to Use Them* (New York: Putnam, 1998), 42.

CHAPTER 8: HOME BASE

75   *All life is interrelated*...Quoted in James W. Washington, ed., *A Testament of Hope: The Essential Writings of Martin Luther King, Jr.* (San Francisco: HarperCollins, 1986), 254.

77   *Protester carried signs*...Cornell Christion, Originally published Feb. 28, 1993, "The Memphis Sanitation Strike: Blood and strife brought dignity for city workers," *The Commercial Appeal*, Memphis, TN www.gomemphis.com.

77   *royal personhood*...Matthew Fox, *Coming of the Cosmic Christ*, 139.

78   *Centering is a real psychophysiological*...Tom Crum, *The Magic of Conflict: Turning a Life of Work into a Work of Art* (New York: Simon & Schuster, 1987), 53; my emphasis.

78   *athletes give optimal performances*...James Loehr, *Stress for Success* (Random House, 1997), 59.

79   *Love is understanding*...Thich Nhat Hanh, *Peace Is Every Step: The Path of Mindfulness in Everyday Life* (New York: Bantam, 1991), 79.

81   *Nothing is more revealing than movement*...quoted in *Forbes Magazine*, May 14, 2001, Volume 167, Number 11, New York, NY, 280.

81   *dance is the same word for breath*...Matthew Fox, *One River, Many Wells: Wisdom Springing from Global Faiths* (New York: Putnam, 2000), 233.

81   *We move in [the Mystery]*...Kathy Juline, "Movement as Spiritual Practice: An Interview with Gabrielle Roth." In *Science of Mind: Change Your Thinking, Change Your Life* 71, no. 2 (February 1998): 45.

82   *You must understand the whole of life*...Quoted in Sy Safransky, *Sunbeams: A Book of Quotations* (Berkeley: North Atlantic Books, 1990), 19.

83   *your tantien, or original chi*...Kaleo Ching and Elise Dirlam-Ching, *Tao of Creativity: The Inner Journey of Chi Gung, Meditation, Visualization, Writing and Art* (Berkeley, Calif.: self-published, 1999), 75; and Diane Stein, *Essential Reiki: A Complete Guide to an Ancient Healing Art* (Freedom, Calif.: Crossing Press, 1995), 33.

83   *Martial art Aikido masters*...Terry Dobson, *Aikido in Everyday Life: Giving in to Get Your Way* (Berkeley: North Atlantic, 1993), 78; and Crum, *Magic*, 55.

85   *Sanskrit term for meditation*...Fritjof Capra, *The Tao of Physics: An Exploration of the Parallels between Modern Physics and Eastern Mysticism* (Shambhala: Boston, 1999), 131.

85   *discipline of bringing in*...M. C. Richards, *Centering, In Pottery, Poetry and the Person* (Hanover: Wesleyan, 1989), xviii.

CHAPTER 9: THE OLDEST GAME IN THE BOOK

88 *Every being that thrives*...Brian Swimme and Thomas Berry, *The Universe Story: From the Primordial Flaring Forth to the Ecozoic Era: A Celebration of the Unfolding of the Cosmos* (San Francisco: HarperCollins, 1992), 54.

88 *A conflict is first and foremost*...Robert A. Baruch Bush and Joseph P. Folger, *The Promise of Mediation: Responding to Conflict Through Empowerment and Recognition* (San Francisco: Jossey-Bass, 1994), 81–82.

88 *Just as Socrates*...Quoted in James W. Washington, ed., *A Testament of Hope: The Essential Writings of Martin Luther King, Jr.* (San Francisco: HarperCollins, 1986), 291.

89 *Tibetan Buddhist initiates*...Robert Johnson, *Owning Your Own Shadow: Understanding the Dark Side of the Psyche* (San Francisco: HarperCollins, 1991), 102.

89 *see mandals in science*...Ruediger Dahlke, *Mandalas for Meditation* (New York: Sterling, 2001), 34.

CHAPTER 10: PHASE 1

95 *This is a story about King Arthur*...The original tale of Lady Ragnell appeared as a fifteenth-century English romance. There are many derivations of this tale, which include the black knight as a giant, Arthur personally seeking the answers, and Lady Ragnell as an old crone. One of my favorite retellings is by Angeles Arrien, which includes the three answers that Gawain finds along his journey. Regardless, every version poses the famous question and gives the same correct answer.

97 *"Nothing in life is to be feared*...Quoted in Lillian Eichler Watson, *Light from Many Lamps* (New York: Simon & Schuster, 1988), 131.

99 *high and low, broad and narrow*...Sun Tzu, *The Art of War: A New Translation*, trans., essay, and comm. by the Demna Translation Group (Boston: Shambhala, 2001), 4.

99 *Knowing the other and knowing oneself*...Sun Tzu, *Art of War*, 12.

100 *Tibetan Buddhist Shambhala warrior*...Quoted in Matthew Fox, *One River, Many Wells: Wisdom Springing from Global Faiths* (New York: Putnam, 2000), 414.

100 *cross-culturally the trained warrior*...Angeles Arrien, *The Four-Fold Way: Walking the Paths of the Warrior, Teacher, Healer and Visionary* (San Francisco: HarperCollins, 1993), 7.

102 *ap.prec.iate...2. to be fully conscious*...*Webster's Encyclopedic Unabridged Dictionary of the English Language* (New York: Portland House, 1989), 73.

102 *Recent neurological studies*...Dan Baker, M.D., *What Happy People Know: How the New Science of Happiness Can Change Your Life for the Better* (New York: Rodale, 2003), 81.

103 *Openness to the environment*...Margaret J. Wheatley, *Leadership and the New Science* (San Francisco: Berret-Koehler, 1992), 84.

103 *In Buddhism in general*...H.H. Dalai Lama and Howard C. Cutler, M.D., *The Art of Happiness: A Handbook for Living* (New York: Penguin, 1998), 178–79.

103 *Those that make you return*..."Checkmate," from Jelaluddin Rumi, *The Essential Rumi*, trans. Coleman Barks with John Moyne, A. J. Arberry, Reynold Nicholson (San Francisco: HarperCollins, 1995), 176.

103 *At the heart of the universe*...Brian Swimme and Thomas Berry, *The Universe Story: From*

the Primordial Flaring Forth to the Ecozoic Era: A Celebration of the Unfolding of the Cosmos (San Francisco: HarperCollins, 1992), 75.

104 yamas...and niyamas...Sri Swami Satchidananda, trans. and comm., *The Yoga Sutras of Patanjali* (Yogaville, Va.: Integral Yoga, 2001), 125–27.

105 *Much of chanoyu*...Kakuzo Okakura, *The Book of Tea* (Tokyo: Kodansha, 1989), 148.

107 *Ancient religion and modern science*...Quoted in Chet Raymo, *Natural Prayers* (St. Paul: Ruminator Books, 1999), 8.

107 *you have a shield from fear*...Baker, *What Happy People Know*, 100.

108 *Spend three to five minutes*...Baker, *What Happy People Know*, 101–2.

108 *Although the enemy is numerous*...Sun Tzu, *Art of War*, 23.

109 *Please Call Me by My True Names*...Thich Nhat Hanh, *Peace Is Every Step: The Path of Mindfulness in Everyday Life* (New York: Bantam, 1991), 123–24.

111 *If your friends tell you that you behave*...Arthur Mindell, *Sitting in the Fire: Large Group Transformation Using Conflict and Diversity* (Portland, Ore.: Lao Tse Press, 1995), 207.

112 *You can alter*...K. C. Cole, *First You Build a Cloud and Other Reflections on Physics as a Way of Life* (New York: Harcourt Brace, 1999), 65.

112 *We die to each other daily*...Quoted in Sy Safransky, *Sunbeams: A Book of Quotations* (Berkeley: North Atlantic Books, 1990), 75.

113 *An art object*...Quoted in Angeles Arrien, *Change, Conflict and Resolution from a Cross-Cultural Perspective*, 1991 by Angeles Arrien. Audiocassette.

113 *Great Spirit...grant*...Quoted in Ariah Zohar and I. N. Marshall, *The Quantum Society: Mind, Physics, and a New Social Vision* (New York: William Morrow, 1994), 196.

114 *you are evil, and I am good*...Matthew Fox, *Sins of the Spirit, Blessings of the Flesh: Lessons for Transforming Evil in Soul and Society* (New York: Harmony, 1999), 89.

114 *It is not me, it is someone*...Quoted on "All Things Considered," *National Public Radio*, January 29, 2000.

114 *If the DNA in our bodies'*...Fox, *Sins of the Spirit*, 72.

114 *Once upon a time a man*...Quoted in Safransky, *Sunbeams*, 39.

115 *Now will you tell me*...Norton Juster, *The Phantom Tollbooth* (New York: Random House, 1961), 168.

115 *If even one of those assumptions*...Cole, *First You Build*, 64.

115 *suspend or unearth assumptions*...Peter Senge, *Strategies and Tools for Building a Learning Organization* (New York: Doubleday, 1994), 361.

115 *[f]aced with chaos or conflict*...Sun Tzu, *Art of War*, 92.

119 *"Do not worry..."* Quoted in Michael Pollard, *Maria Montessori* (Harrisburg, Pa.: Morehouse, 1990), 12.

120 *I have come to appreciate*...Maria Montessori, *The Discovery of the Child* (New York: Ballantine, 1967), 126.

120 *To pay attention*...Quoted in Raymo, *Natural Prayers*, 3.

120 *When a child is given a little leeway*...Montessori, *Discovery*, 198.

121 *During this time,*...Quoted in Michael Pollard, *Maria Montessori* (Harrisburg, Pa.: Morehouse, 1990), 25.

121 *We must be humble and root out*...Montessori, *Discovery*, 153.

CHAPTER 11: PHASE 2

123 *This is a story from long ago*...I have found some form of this tale used by an interesting variety of moralists and by Buddhist and Hindu teachers. In some forms, the oak is uprooted by wind, in others a hurricane or a flood. Regardless, it is the weed's humility and flexibility that win the day. See Sri Swami Satchidananda, trans. and comm., *The Yoga Sutras of Patanjali* (Yogaville, Va: Integral Yoga, 1999), 152, for the tale's application to steady, consistent spiritual practice.

126 *Our lives will be changed*...Quoted in Sy Safransky, *Sunbeams: A Book of Quotations* (Berkeley: North Atlantic Books, 1990), 10.

127 *If an organization*...Quoted in James Collins and Jerry Porras, *Built to Last: Successful Habits of Visionary Companies* (New York: HarperCollins, 1994), 81.

128 *defines a conflict as a "war"*...Arthur Mindell, *Sitting in the Fire: Large Group Transformation Using Conflict and Diversity* (Portland, Ore.: Lao Tse Press, 1995), 214.

129 *Your grief for*...Jelaluddin Rumi, *The Essential Rumi*, trans. Coleman Barks with John Moyne, A. J. Arberry, Reynold Nicholson (San Francisco: HarperCollins, 1995), 174.

129 *stand apart or to detach*...Angeles Arrien, *The Four-Fold Way: Walking the Paths of the Warrior, Teacher, Healer and Visionary* (San Francisco: HarperCollins, 1993), 112; and Matthew Fox, *A Spirituality Named Compassion* (San Francisco: HarperCollins, 1990), 90.

130 *Faced with a reality*...Fritjof Capra, *The Tao of Physics: An Exploration of the Parallels between Modern Physics and Eastern Mysticism* (Shambhala: Boston, 1999), 155.

130 *visionary and lasting companies*...Collins and Porras, *Built to Last*, 82.

130 *You guessed it — the jellyfish*...Quoted in Chet Raymo, *Natural Prayers* (St. Paul: Ruminator Books, 1999), 145.

130 *fighting against this phase*...Ana Perez Chisti, "Core Readings: Creation Spirituality and Liberation." Oakland: University of Creation Spirituality, June 14–18, 1999. Lecture.

132 *Something we cannot see, touch*...Margaret J. Wheatley, *Leadership and the New Science* (San Francisco: Berret-Koehler, 1992), 94.

132 *We do not go out searching*...James Carse, *Finite and Infinite Games* (New York: Free Press, 1986), 140–41.

133 *there can be many points of view*...Ariah Zohar and I. N. Marshall, *The Quantum Self: Human Nature and Consciousness Defined by the New Physics* (New York: William Morrow, 1990), 153.

133 *No finitely describable system*...Quoted in Zohar, *Quantum Society*, 137.

134 *[L]ife is a matter of telling ourselves stories*...Walter Truett Anderson, *Reality Isn't What It Used to Be: Theatrical Politics, Ready-to-Wear Religion, Global Myths, Primitive Chic, and Other Wonders of the Postmodern World* (San Francisco: HarperCollins, 1990), 102.

134 *Clinging is never kept within bounds*...D. T. Suzuki and William Barrett, ed., *Zen Buddhism: Selected Writings of D. T. Suzuki* (New York: Doubleday, 1996), 79.

134 *If I cannot tease you*...workshop attended by author, Paulden, AZ, October 23–November 3, 2000.

135 *human being as more of a river*...Deepak Chopra, *Perfect Health: The Complete Mind/Body Guide* (New York: Harmony, 1991), 11–12.

136   On a personal level, the principle of harmony... Kakuzo Okakura, *The Book of Tea* (Tokyo: Kodansha, 1989), 148.

137   easiest way to get rid of a Minus is to change it to a Plus... Benjamin Hoff, *The Tao of Pooh* (New York: HarperCollins, 1983), 61.

137   be tough on the problem... Roger Fisher and William Ury with Bruce Patton, ed., *Getting to Yes: Negotiating Agreement without Giving In* (Houghton Mifflin: New York, 1991), 26.

138   From a hidden place... Neil Douglas Klotz, *Prayers of the Cosmos: Meditations on the Aramaic Words of Jesus* (San Francisco: HarperCollins, 1990), 84.

138   her great aversion to racism... Debbie Ford, *The Dark Side of the Light Chasers: Reclaiming your Power, Creativity, Brilliance and Dreams* (New York: Riverhead, 1998), 40–42.

138   tong len... Pema Chödrön, *Awakening Loving-Kindness* (Boston: Shambhala, 1996), 138–139.

139   forgiveness can happen in degrees... workshop attended by author, St. Paul, MN, October, 1990.

140   we let go and create space... Sun Tzu, *Art of War*, 100.

140   "Open Space Technology"... Harrison Owen, *Open Space Technology: A User's Guide* (San Francisco: Berrett-Koehler, 1998), 72–73.

142   if we can be at ease... Matthew Fox, *Original Blessing* (Santa Fe: Bear & Company, 1983), 160.

142   Enter into your own ground... Quoted in Matthew Fox, *Breakthrough: Meister Eckhart's Creation Spirituality in New Translation* (New York: Doubleday, 1991), 465.

142   At one Montana meeting... Lecture attended by the author, University of Creation Spirituality, Oakland, California, January 11–15, 1999.

143   What is happening right now?... Quoted in Peter Senge, *Fifth Discipline Fieldbook: Strategies and Tools for Building a Learning Organization* (New York: Doubleday, 1994), 26.

145   He championed many causes... Keshavan Nair, *A Higher Standard of Leadership: Lessons from the Life of Gandhi* (San Francisco: Berret-Koehler, 1997), 143.

145   But, I hope I have no policy... Mahatma Gandhi, *All Men are Brothers: Autobiographical Reflections* (New York: Continuum, 1994), 66.

145   This ahimsa is the basis... Gandhi, *All Men*, 23.

146   My imperfections and failures... Gandhi, *All Men*, 46.

146   Truth is not to be found... Gandhi, *All Men*, 65.

146   If I had no sense of humor... Gandhi, *All Men*, 156.

146   A votary... Gandhi, *All Men*, 32.

146   God demands nothing less... Gandhi, *All Men*, 62.

147   I am a Christian... quoted in Hesselbein ed., *The Drucker Foundation : The Community of the Future* (Hoboken: Jossey-Bass, 1997), 88.

CHAPTER 12: PHASE 3

149   Once upon a time, in Russia... This Russian folktale is often called "Vasilisa the Wise" or "Vasilisa the Fair." It is considered one of the derivations of *Cinderella*, which appears throughout the world and has its earliest appearances in India (fifth century

B.C.E.) and China (ninth century B.C.E). A version of this story with a detailed deconstruction of this folktale as it relates to modern psychology can be found in Clarissa Pinkola Estés, *Women Who Run with the Wolves* (New York: Ballantine, 1992), 75–114.

152   *It takes a golden ear*…M. C. Richards, *Centering, In Pottery, Poetry and the Person* (Hanover: Wesleyan, 1989), 58.

156   *Because Thou lovest*…Quoted in Huston Smith, *The World's Religions* (San Francisco: HarperCollins, 1991), 72.

157   *the root of the word* contemplate…Webster's Dictionary, 315.

157   *All mysticism is characterized*…Ursula King, *Christian Mystics: The Spiritual Heart of the Christian Tradition* (New York: Simon & Schuster, 1998), 15–16.

157   *[c]reativity is nothing else*…Erich Jantsch, *The Self-Organizing Universe: Scientific and Human Implications of the Emerging Paradigm of Evolution* (New York: Pergamon, 1980), 296.

158   *Passion burns down*…Quoted by Andrew Harvey, "Rumi and Eckhart Lectures," at the University of Creation Spirituality, January 2001.

159   *an abundance of novelties*…Brian Swimme, *The Universe Is a Green Dragon: A Cosmic Creation Story* (Santa Fe: Bear & Company, 1984), 114.

159   *power called shih*…Sun Tzu, *The Art of War: A New Translation*, trans., essay, and comm. by the Demna Translation Group (Boston: Shambhala, 2001), 71.

159   *Elegant solutions act like epidemics*…Malcolm Gladwell, *The Tipping Point: How Little Things Make a Big Difference* (Boston: Little Brown, 2000), 7–9.

160   *These same three stages*…Thelma Hall, *Too Deep for Words: Rediscovering Lectio Divina with 500 Scripture Texts for Prayer* (New York: Paulist Press, 1988), 28, 44.

161   *Stand still*…David Wagoner, "Lost," from *Traveling Light: Collected and New Poems* (Champaign, Ill.: University of Illinois Press, 1999).

161   *You have to stare the world*…Mahatma Gandhi, *All Men are Brothers: Autobiographical Reflections* (New York: Continuum, 1994), 49.

162   *You can only hope to find a lasting solution*…Quoted in Sy Safransky, *Sunbeams: A Book of Quotations* (Berkeley: North Atlantic Books, 1990), 22.

162   *field emitted from the heart region*…G. Schwartz and L. Russek, "Heart-Focused Attention and Heart-Brain Synchronization: Energetic and Physiological Mechanisms," *Alternative Therapies in Health and Medicine* 4, no. 5 (1998): 44.

163   *neural receptors in our hearts*…Robert K. Cooper, "How Are You Applying the Latest Neuroscience Discoveries on What Motivates the Human Heart and Mind?" *Lessons in Leadership* Series 4 (1999): 59.

163   *The friend who can be silent*…Henri Nouwen, *Out of Solitude: Three Meditations on the Christian Life* (Notre Dame: Ave Maria Press, 1984), 34.

163   *Creativity comes from*…Quoted in Jill Rosenfield, "Here's an Idea!" *Fast Company* 33 (April 2000): 97.

164   *The greatest thing*…Quoted in Chet Raymo, *Natural Prayers* (St. Paul: Ruminator Books, 1999), 8.

165   *Dreams are regarded as a valuable*…Kelly Bulkeley, *Spiritual Dreaming: A Cross-cultural and Historical Journey* (New York: Paulist Press, 1995), 2.

166   *Some dreams are classified as*…Bulkeley, *Spiritual Dreaming*, 175–77.

166   *If it were my dream*...Lecture attended by the author, University of Creation Spirituality, Oakland, California, October 26–30, 1998.

167   *Medieval priest St. John*...Hall, *Too Deep for Words*, 28.

167   *The psychological mechanism*...Quoted in Angeles Arrien, *The Tarot Handbook: Practical Applications of Ancient Visual Symbols* (London: Diamond Books, 1995), 12.

168   *According to the Kabbalah*...Rachel Naomi Remen, M.D., *My Grandfather's Blessings, Stories of Refuge, Strength, and Belonging* (New York: Riverhead, 2000), 2–3.

170   *Trust thyself*...Quoted in Lillian Eichler Watson, *Light from Many Lamps* (New York: Simon & Schuster, 1988), 176.

170   *Find two partners to participate*...Quoted in Peter Senge, *Fifth Discipline Fieldbook: Strategies and Tools for Building a Learning Organization* (New York: Doubleday, 1994), 377.

172   *What would the "best*...Some questions were adapted from Angeles Arrien's audiocassette, "Change and Conflict from a Cross-cultural Perspective," 1991.

174   *"What is true for you*...Joanna Macy, *Coming Back to Life: Practices to Reconnect Our Lives, Our World* (British Columbia: New Society, 1998), 127.

175   *Isn't this what poetry is*...Richards, *Centering*, 58.

176   *When power leads man towards arrogance*...Theodore Sorensen, *Let the Word Go Forth: The Speeches, Statements, and Writings of John F. Kennedy 1947 to 1963* (New York: Laurel, 1991), 209.

176   *Perception if it is true*...Richards, *Centering*, 58.

177   *Wisdom resides*...Quoted in Matthew Fox, *Illuminations of Hildegard of Bingen* (Santa Fe: Bear & Company, 1985), 49.

177   *Wisdom resides in all*...Fox, *Illuminations*, 109.

177   *Once I did this*...Fox, *Illuminations*, 27.

177   *God has arranged*...Fox, *Illuminations*, 36.

178   *Truly, the Holy Spirit*...Gabrielle Uhlein, *Meditations with Hildegard of Bingen* (Santa Fe: Bear & Company, 1983), 46, 38.

CHAPTER 13: PHASE 4

181   *Before now, in a small village in China*...This Chinese folktale is sometimes told without the two elder brothers and called either "The Magic Brocade" or "The Chuang Brocade." This version was adapted from "The Magic Brocade," as included in Joanna Cole's *Best-Loved Folktales of the World* (New York: Doubleday, 1982), 540–44.

184   *It is not knowing that is difficult, but the doing*...Quoted in B. W. Huntsman, ed., *Wisdom Is One* (Rutland, Vt.: Tuttle, 1985), 108.

186   *Sincere words are not embellished*...Quoted in R. L. Wing, *The Tao of Power* (New York: Doubleday, 1986), 179.

188   *True art takes note*...Mahatma Gandhi, *All Men are Brothers: Autobiographical Reflections* (New York: Continuum, 1994), 163.

188   *Learn from Ali*...Jelaluddin Rumi, *The Essential Rumi*, trans. Coleman Barks with John Moyne, A. J. Arberry, Reynold Nicholson (San Francisco: HarperCollins, 1995), 223–24.

190   *Don't judge*...Rumi, *Essential Rumi*, 223.

190 *We can't run from the body* ... Kathy Juline, "Movement as Spiritual Practice: An Interview with Gabrielle Roth." *Science of Mind: Change Your Thinking, Change Your Life* 71, no. 2 (February 1998): 47.

193 *Work without a why* ... Quoted in Matthew Fox, *Original Blessing: A Primer in Creation Spirituality Presented in Four Paths, Twenty-Six Themes, and Two Questions* (Sante Fe: Bear & Co., 1983), 239.

194 *It is good for the spirits* ... Quoted in Kakuzo Okakura, *The Book of Tea* (Tokyo: Kodansha, 1989), 150.

194 *The two forces* ... Margaret J. Wheatley, *Leadership and the New Science* (San Francisco: Berret-Koehler, 1992), 87.

195 *bringing in ... rather than* ... M.C. Richards, *Centering: In Pottery, Poetry and the Person* (Hanover, N.H.: Wesleyan, 1989), xviii.

195 *"content" conversations* ... Douglas Stone, Bruce Patton, and Sheila Heen, *Difficult Conversations: How to Discuss What Matters Most* (New York: Penguin, 1999), 7–8.

196 *The harder the conflict, the more glorious the triumph* ... Thomas Paine, *The Thomas Paine Reader* (New York: Penguin, 1987), 116.

196 *We have great difficulty* ... K. C. Cole, *First You Build a Cloud and Other Reflections on Physics as a Way of Life* (New York: Harcourt Brace, 1999), 21.

197 *The word* network ... conversation with the author, Washington, D.C., October 16, 2001.

197 *And so knowing victory is* ... Sun Tzu, *The Art of War: A New Translation*, trans., essay, and comm. by the Demna Translation Group (Boston: Shambhala, 2001), 11.

198 *Prayer tends to follow* ... Larry Dossey, M.D., *Healing Words: The Power of Prayer and the Practice of Medicine* (San Francisco: HarperCollins, 1993), 24.

198 *Discovery is a place* ... Tom Crum, *The Magic of Conflict: Turning a Life of Work into a Work of Art* (New York: Simon & Schuster, 1987), 129.

199 *Hold on to what* ... Quoted in Maggie Oman Shannon, *Prayers for Healing: 365 Blessings, Poems, and Meditations from Around the World* (Berkeley: Conari Press, 2000), 179.

199 *All shall be well* ... Quoted in Shannon, *Prayers for Healing*, 150.

199 *I have a dream* ... Quoted in James W. Washington, ed., *A Testament of Hope: The Essential Writings of Martin Luther King, Jr.* (San Francisco: HarperCollins, 1986), 219.

201 *And who among us* ... Quoted in Washington, *Testament of Hope*, x.

201 *After discovering* ... From the sermon, "The Three Dimensions of a Complete Life," by Martin Luther King Jr. This sermon was delivered in various forms at churches and schools from 1952 to 1967.

201 *[The] means must be* ... Quoted in Washington, *Testament of Hope*, 45, 253.

202 *So the nonviolent* ... Quoted in Washington, *Testament of Hope*, 39.

CHAPTER 14: THE MENTAL GAME

207 *Half this game* ... quoted in Lowell Streiker, *Nelson's Big Book of Laughter Thousands of Smiles From A to Z* (Nashville: Nelson Reference, 2000), 452.

207 *nature as governed* ... Matthew Fox and Rupert Sheldrake, *Natural Grace: Dialogues on Creation, Darkness, and the Soul in Spirituality and Science* (New York: Doubleday, 1997), 25.

208 *no attains their goal*…"Do thou thy allotted task; for action is superior to inaction. With inaction even life's normal course is not possible." Chapter 3, verse 8. John Strohmeier ed. *The Bhagavad Gita According to Gandhi* (Berkeley: Berkeley Hills, 2000), 62.

208 *Studies show that if athletes*…Sharon Begley, "Expectations May Alter Outcomes Far More than We Realize," *Wall Street Journal*, 7 November 2003, B1.

209 *to create a new reality*…David Gershon and Gail Straub, *Empowerment: The Art of Creating Your Life as You Want It* (New York: Delta 1989), 50.

211 *Use the present tense*…David Gershon and Gail Straub, *Empowerment: The Art of Creating Your Life as You Want It* (New York: Delta, 1989), 27–29.

212 *Rather than saying*…Shakti Gawain, *Creative Visualization: Use the Power of Your Imagination to Create What You Want in Your Life* (Novato, Calif.: New World Library, 1978), 40.

212 This, or something better…Gawain, *Creative Visualization*, 33.

CONCLUSION

216 *You will not grow*…Quoted in Sy Safransky, *Sunbeams: A Book of Quotations* (Berkeley: North Atlantic Books, 1990), 91.

216 *Perhaps all of the dragons*…Rainer Maria Rilke, *Letters to a Young Poet* (New York: Vintage, 1986), 92.

218 *Come, come, whoever you are*…Quoted in Safransky, *Sunbeams*, 67.

APPENDIX

219 *Via Positiva, or Positive Path*…Matthew Fox, *Creation Spirituality: Liberating Gifts for the Peoples of the Earth* (San Francisco: HarperCollins, 1991), 17–22.

221 *The Warrior*…Angeles Arrien, *The Four-Fold Way: Walking the Paths of the Warrior, Teacher, Healer, and Visionary* (San Francisco: HarperCollins, 1993), 7.

BIBLIOGRAPHY

Anderson, Walter Truett. *Reality Isn't What It Used to Be: Theatrical Politics, Ready-to-Wear Religion, Global Myths, Primitive Chic, and Other Wonders of the Postmodern World.* San Francisco: HarperCollins, 1990.

Angelou, Maya. *I Shall Not Be Moved: Poems.* New York: Random House, 1997.

Arrien, Angeles. *Change, Conflict and Resolution from a Cross-Cultural Perspective.* 1991 by Angeles Arrien. Audiocassette.

———. *The Four-Fold Way: Walking the Paths of the Warrior, Teacher, Healer, and Visionary.* San Francisco: HarperCollins, 1993.

———. *The Nine Muses: A Mythological Path to Creativity.* New York: Putnam, 2000.

———. *Signs of Life: The Five Universal Shapes and How to Use Them.* New York: Putnam, 1998.

———. *The Tarot Handbook: Practical Applications of Ancient Visual Symbols.* London: Diamond Books, 1995.

Association for Conflict Resolution (ACR), www.acresolution.org.

Augsburger, David. *Conflict Mediation across Cultures, Pathways and Patterns.* Louisville, Ky.: W. Westminster/John Knox Press, 1992.

Aureli, Filippo, and Frans B. M. Waal, eds. *Natural Conflict Resolution.* Berkeley and Los Angeles: University of California Press, 2000.

Baker, Dan, M.D. *What Happy People Know: How the New Science of Happiness Can Change Your Life for the Better.* New York: Rodale, 2003.

Begley, Sharon. "Expectations May Alter Outcomes Far More Than We Realize." *Wall Street Journal,* 7 November 2003.

Bulkeley, Kelly. *Spiritual Dreaming: A Cross-cultural and Historical Journey*. New York: Paulist Press, 1995.

Buscaglia, Leo. *Born for Love: Reflections on Loving*. New York: Ballantine, 1994.

Bush, Robert A. Baruch, and Joseph P. Folger. *The Promise of Mediation: Responding to Conflict Through Empowerment and Recognition*. San Francisco: Jossey-Bass, 1994.

Capra, Fritoj. *The Tao of Physics: An Exploration of the Parallels between Modern Physics and Eastern Mysticism*. Boston: Shambhala, 1999.

Carse, James. *Finite and Infinite Games*. New York: Free Press, 1986.

Ching, Kaleo, and Elise Dirlam-Ching. *Tao of Creativity: The Inner Journey of Chi Gung, Meditation, Visualization, Writing and Art*. Berkeley, Calif.: self-published, 1999.

Chopra, Deepak. *Perfect Health: The Complete Mind/Body Guide*. New York: Harmony, 1991.

Cole, Joanna. *Best-Loved Folktales of the World*. New York: Doubleday, 1982.

Cole, K. C. *First You Build a Cloud and Other Reflections on Physics as a Way of Life*. New York: Harcourt Brace, 1999.

Collins, James C., and Jerry I. Porras. *Built to Last: Successful Habits of Visionary Companies*. New York: HarperCollins, 1994.

Cooper, Robert K. "How Are You Applying the Latest Neuroscience Discoveries on What Motivates the Human Heart and Mind?" *Lessons in Leadership* 4 (1999): 2–5.

Covey, Stephen R. *The 7 Habits of Highly Effective People, Powerful Lessons in Personal Change*. New York: Simon & Schuster, 1989.

Crum, Thomas. *The Magic of Conflict: Turning a Life of Work into a Work of Art*. New York: Simon & Schuster, 1987.

Dahlke, Ruediger. *Mandalas for Meditation*. New York: Sterling, 2001.

Dalai Lama, H.H., and Howard C. Cutler, M.D. *The Art of Happiness: A Handbook for Living*. New York: Penguin, 1998.

Dobson, Terry. *Aikido in Everyday Life: Giving in to Get Your Way*. Berkeley, Calif.: North Atlantic, 1993.

Dossey, Larry, M.D. *Healing Words: The Power of Prayer and the Practice of Medicine*. San Francisco: HarperCollins, 1993.

DuBois, W. E. B. *The Souls of Black Folk*. New York: Bantam, 1989.

Estés, Clarissa Pinkola. *Women Who Run with the Wolves: Myths and Stories of the Wild Woman Archetype*. New York: Ballantine, 1992.

Fisher, Roger, and William Ury, with Bruce Patton, ed. *Getting to Yes: Negotiating Agreement without Giving In*. New York: Houghton Mifflin, 1991.

Ford, Debbie. *The Dark Side of the Light Chasers: Reclaiming Your Power, Creativity, Brilliance, and Dreams*. New York: Riverhead, 1998.

Fox, Matthew. *Breakthrough: Meister Eckhart's Creation Spirituality in New Translation*. New York: Doubleday, 1991.

———. *Creation Spirituality: Liberating Gifts for the Peoples of the Earth*. San Francisco: HarperCollins, 1991.

———. *Illuminations of Hildegard of Bingen*. Santa Fe, N. Mex.: Bear & Company, 1985.

———. *One River, Many Wells: Wisdom Springing from Global Faiths*. New York: Putnam, 2000.

———. *Original Blessing.* Santa Fe, N. Mex.: Bear & Company, 1983.

———. *Sins of the Spirit, Blessings of the Flesh: Lessons for Transforming Evil in Soul and Society.* New York: Harmony, 1999.

———. *A Spirituality Named Compassion and the Healing of the Global Village: Humpty Dumpty and Us.* San Francisco: HarperCollins, 1990.

Fox, Matthew, and Margaret Wheatley. "Leadership in Crazed Times." 2000 by the University of Creation Spirituality. Audiocassette.

Fox, Matthew, and Rupert Sheldrake. *Natural Grace: Dialogues on Creation, Darkness, and the Soul in Spirituality and Science.* New York: Doubleday, 1997.

Gandhi, Mahatma. *All Men are Brothers: Autobiographical Reflections.* New York: Continuum, 1994.

Gardner, Jason, ed. *Sacred Earth: Writers on Nature and Spirit.* Novato, Calif.: New World Library, 1998.

Gawain, Shakti. *Creative Visualization: Use the Power of Your Imagination to Create What You Want in Your Life.* Novato, Calif.: New World Library, 1978.

Gershon, David, and Gail Straub. *Empowerment: The Art of Creating Your Life as You Want It.* New York: Delta, 1989.

Gladwell, Malcolm. *The Tipping Point: How Little Things Make a Big Difference.* Boston: Little Brown, 2000.

Godwin, Malcolm. *Who Are You? 101 Ways of Seeing Yourself.* New York: Penguin, 2000.

Golden, Arthur. *Memoirs of a Geisha.* New York: Vintage, 1997.

Griffiths, Bede. *Universal Wisdom: A Journey Through the Sacred Wisdom of the World.* San Francisco: HarperCollins, 1994.

Hall, Thelma. *Too Deep for Words: Rediscovering Lectio Divina with 500 Scripture Texts for Prayer.* New York: Paulist Press, 1988.

Hanh, Thich Nhat. *Peace Is Every Step: The Path of Mindfulness in Everyday Life.* New York: Bantam, 1991.

Harvey, Andrew, and Matthew Fox. "Rumi and Eckhart: Love and Knowledge on the Mystic Path, January 18–22, 2000." 2000 by the University of Creation Spirituality. Audiocassette.

Hildegard of Bingen. Comm. by Matthew Fox. *Illuminations of Hildegard of Bingen.* Santa Fe, N. Mex.: Bear & Company, 1985.

Hoff, Benjamin. *The Tao of Pooh.* New York: HarperCollins, 1983.

Huntsman, B. W., ed. *Wisdom Is One.* Rutland, Vt.: Tuttle, 1985.

Jantsch, Robert. *The Self-Organizing Universe: Scientific and Human Implications of the Emerging Paradigm of Evolution.* New York: Pergamon, 1980.

Johnson, Erich A. *Owning Your Own Shadow: Understanding the Dark Side of the Psyche.* San Francisco: HarperCollins, 1991.

Juline, Kathy. "Movement as Spiritual Practice: An Interview with Gabrielle Roth." *Science of Mind: Change Your Thinking, Change Your Life* 71, no. 2 (February 1998): 47–50.

Juster, Norton. *The Phantom Tollbooth.* New York: Random House, 1961.

King, Ursula. *Christian Mystics: The Spiritual Heart of the Christian Tradition.* New York: Simon & Schuster, 1998.

Kitteridge, William, and Annick Smith, eds. *The Last Best Place.* Seattle: University of Washington Press, 1988.

Klotz, Neil Douglas. *Prayers of the Cosmos: Meditations on the Aramaic Words of Jesus.* San Francisco: HarperCollins, 1990.

Loehr, James E. *Stress for Success.* New York: Random House, 1997.

Maclean, Norman. *Young Men and Fire: A True Story of the Mann Gulch Fire.* Chicago: University of Chicago Press, 1992.

Macy, Joanna. *Coming Back to Life: Practices to Reconnect Our Lives, Our World.* Gabriola Island, B.C.: New Society, 1998.

McGoldrich, Monica. *You Can Go Home Again.* New York: Norton, 1995.

Mindell, Arnold. *Sitting in the Fire: Large Group Transformation Using Conflict and Diversity.* Portland, Ore.: Lao Tse Press, 1995.

Montessori, Maria. *The Discovery of the Child.* New York: Ballantine, 1967.

Moses, Jeffrey. *Oneness: Great Principle Shared by All Religions.* New York: Ballantine, 1989.

Muldoon, Brian. *The Heart of Conflict.* New York: Putnam, 1996.

Nair, Keshavan. *A Higher Standard of Leadership: Lessons from the Life of Gandhi.* San Francisco: Berret-Koehler, 1997.

Nasar, Sylvia. *A Beautiful Mind: The Life of Mathematical Genius and Nobel Laureate John Nash.* New York: Touchstone, 2001.

The New Jerusalem Bible, Standard Edition. New York: Doubleday, 1989.

Nouwen, Henri. *Out of Solitude: Three Meditations on the Christian Life.* Notre Dame, Ind.: Ave Maria Press, 1984.

Okakura, Kakuzo. *The Book of Tea.* Tokyo: Kodansha, 1989.

Oman, Maggie. *Prayers for Healing: 365 Blessings, Poems, and Meditations from Around the World.* Berkeley, Calif.: Conari Press, 2000.

Oman Shannon, Maggie. *One God, Shared Hope: Twenty Threads Shared by Judaism, Christianity, and Islam.* Boston: Red Wheel Weiser, 2003.

Owen, Harrison. *Open Space Technology: A User's Guide.* San Francisco: Berrett-Koehler, 1998.

Paine, Thomas. *The Thomas Paine Reader.* New York: Penguin, 1987.

Pearce, Joseph Chilton. *The Biology of Transcendence: A Blueprint for the Human Spirit.* Rochester, Vt.: Park Street Press, 2002.

Pearsall, David. "The Heart's Code." 1998 by Audio Renaissance. Audiocassette.

Perez Chisti, Ana. "Core Readings: Creation Spirituality and Liberation." Oakland: University of Creation Spirituality, June 14–18, 1999. Lecture.

———. "Hildegard and Rumi." Oakland: University of Creation Spirituality, June 21–25, 1999. Lecture.

Pipher, Mary. *The Shelter of Each Other: Rebuilding Our Families.* New York: Putnam, 1996.

Pollard, Michael. *Maria Montessori.* Harrisburg, Pa.: Morehouse, 1990.

Raymo, Chet. *Natural Prayers.* St. Paul, Minn.: Ruminator Books, 1999.

Remen, Rachel Naomi, M.D. *My Grandfather's Blessings: Stories of Strength, Refuge, and Belonging.* New York: Riverhead, 2000.

Richards, M. C. *Centering, In Pottery, Poetry, and the Person.* Hanover, N.H.: Wesleyan, 1989.

Rilke, Rainer Maria. *Letters to a Young Poet.* New York: Vintage, 1986.

Rumi, Jelaluddin. *The Essential Rumi.* Trans. Coleman Barks, with John Moyne, A. J. Arberry, Reynold Nicholson. San Francisco: HarperCollins, 1995.

Safransky, Sy. *Sunbeams: A Book of Quotations.* Berkeley, Calif.: North Atlantic Books, 1990.

Satchidananda, Sri Swami. Trans. and comm. *The Yoga Sutras of Patanjali.* Yogaville, Va.: Integral Yoga, 1999.

Schwartz, G., and L. Russek. "Heart-Focused Attention and Heart-Brain Synchronization: Energetic and Physiological Mechanisms." *Alternative Therapies in Health and Medicine* 4, no. 5 (1998): 44–62.

Senge, Peter. *Fifth Discipline Fieldbook: Strategies and Tools for Building a Learning Organization.* New York: Doubleday, 1994.

Smith, Huston. *The World's Religions.* San Francisco: HarperCollins, 1991.

Smith, Steve, ed. *Ways of Wisdom.* Lanham, Md.: University Press of America, 1983.

Somé, Sobonfu. *The Spirit of Intimacy: Ancient Teachings in the Ways of Relationships.* Berkeley, Calif.: Berkeley Hills, 1997.

Sorensen, Theodore. *Let the Word Go Forth: The Speeches, Statements, and Writings of John F. Kennedy 1947 to 1963.* New York: Laurel, 1991.

Stein, Diane. *Essential Reiki: A Complete Guide to an Ancient Healing Art.* Freedom, Calif.: Crossing Press, 1995.

Stone, Douglas, Bruce Patton, and Sheila Heen. *Difficult Conversations: How to Discuss What Matters Most.* New York: Penguin, 1999.

Sun Tzu. *The Art of War: A New Translation.* Trans., essay, and comm. by the Demna Translation Group. Boston: Shambhala, 2001.

Suzuki, D. T., and William Barrett, ed. *Zen Buddhism: Selected Writings of D. T. Suzuki.* New York: Doubleday, 1996.

Swimme, Brian. *The Universe Is a Green Dragon: A Cosmic Creation Story.* Santa Fe, N. Mex.: Bear & Company, 1984.

Swimme, Brian, and Thomas Berry. *The Universe Story: From the Primordial Flaring Forth to the Ecozoic Era: A Celebration of the Unfolding of the Cosmos.* San Francisco: HarperCollins, 1992.

Uhlein, Gabrielle. *Meditations with Hildegard of Bingen.* Santa Fe, N. Mex.: Bear & Company, 1983.

Ury, William. *Getting Past No: Negotiating with Difficult People.* New York: Bantam, 1991.

———. *The Third Side: Why We Fight and How We Can Stop.* New York: Penguin, 2000.

Washington, James W., ed. A *Testament of Hope: The Essential Writings of Martin Luther King Jr.* San Francisco: HarperCollins, 1986.

Watson, Lillian Eichler. *Light from Many Lamps.* New York: Simon & Schuster, 1988.

Webster's Encyclopedic Unabridged Dictionary of the English Language. New York: Portland House, 1989.

Wheatley, Margaret J. *Leadership and the New Science.* San Francisco: Berret-Koehler, 1992.

Whyte, David. *The Heart Aroused: Poetry and Preservation of the Soul in Corporate America.* New York: Doubleday, 1994.

Wing, R. L. *The I Ching Workbook.* New York: Doubleday, 1979.

———. *The Tao of Power.* New York: Doubleday, 1986.

Zohar, Ariah, and I. N. Marshall. *The Quantum Self: Human Nature and Consciousness Defined by the New Physics.* New York: William Morrow, 1990.

———. *The Quantum Society: Mind, Physics, and a New Social Vision.* New York: William Morrow, 1994.

A credentialed mediator and facilitator, Dr. Deidre Combs is the founder of Combs & Company, a consulting firm that provides conflict skills training, coaching, and strategic planning services. She is a faculty member of the University of Creation Spirituality and Naropa University, as well as an interfaith minister. Combs was employed for over fifteen years by the corporate sector in project management and marketing leadership roles. Combs & Company's diverse clients include many corporate, nonprofit, and educational organizations, such as IBM and the U.S. Forest Service. Combs holds a B.A. in mathematics and Spanish from the University of Wisconsin at Madison, a Master's from George Washington University, and a Doctorate of Ministry from the University of Creation Spirituality. She lives in Bozeman, Montana, with her husband and three children. Her websites are www.wayofconflict.com and www.combsandcompany.com.

New World Library is dedicated to
publishing books and audio products
that inspire and challenge us to improve
the quality of our lives and our world.

Our products are available
in bookstores everywhere.
For our catalog, please contact:

New World Library
14 Pamaron Way
Novato, California 94949

Phone: (415) 884-2100 or (800) 972-6657
Catalog requests: Ext. 50
Orders: Ext. 52
Fax: (415) 884-2199

Email: escort@newworldlibrary.com
Website: www.newworldlibrary.com